The March of the Rainbowed Angel

From Judgement at Sinai to God's King set on His Holy Hill of Zion

Richard B. Mellowes

Meli Publications
Caerphilly
First published 2013

ISBN 978-0-9550991-6-8

Printed and bound by
IMPRESS
Fosse Road, off Pike Road,
Oakley Hay Industrial Estate,
CORBY, Northamptonshire, NN18 9QA
Tel: 01536 46288
www.impress-print.co.uk

Contents

Chapter no.	Chapter title	Page

List of tables

Preface

The subject matter of this study is far from trivial. It focuses on a series of prophetic visions that present to the perceptive disciple the exalted role they will undertake following acceptance at the judgment seat. This role will be done in tandem with the Lord Jesus Christ as King of kings, as he establishes Israel at the centre of a commonwealth of nations, and fills the earth with the glory and righteousness of God.

In presenting this study we have sought to pull together a wide range of Scriptural passages into a coherent whole. This has not been a short work. Rather, it is the end result of reading, meditation, study, and prayer, over many years. It is the result also of listening to many addresses, and gradually forming what the author sincerely hopes are justifiable conclusions, based on the accompanying exposition.

The subject material presented here is too often ignored or treated superficially by those called to honour and glory in God's kingdom. There are perhaps various reasons for this. Maybe it is because it is perceived as too difficult. Maybe it is because we have lost our focus on the kingdom and the glory that is set before us. Or maybe there is a more sinister reason. Perhaps too many brethren and sisters are being unduly influenced by humanist thought that pervades western society. The notion of the saints undertaking a role in carrying out the judgments written on the enemies of God's people is seen as unpalatable, or even politically incorrect!

But in fact, the work of the Rainbowed Angel presents us with a glorious picture of the manner in which Yahweh's way of righteousness and truth, kept and preserved from Eden onwards (see Gen. 3:24), will be brought to bear on all nations, bringing untold blessings after sin has been purged from the earth.

The core of the study was originally compiled for a series of Bible School studies more than 10 years ago. Since then, this material has been reviewed, revised, and expanded. It is now offered to the brotherhood with the prayer that it will enthuse, encourage, and strengthen a faithful remnant in these last, dark days of the kingdom of men.

My text has been read by Bro. Trevor and Sis. Tricia Vine, Bro. Geoff and Sis. Ruth Cave, and Bro. Paul Danks. My thanks are due to them for the corrections they have made, and for the enormously helpful suggestions regarding the content, most if which I have adopted. As authors always quite properly acknowledge at this point, any errors which remain are solely my responsibility.

Richard Mellowes
Caerphilly
March 2013.

Conventions

The phrase "the Rainbowed Angel" is used throughout as a shorthand convention to denote the multitudinous body of Christ and the immortalised saints. It is based on the vision of the "mighty angel" who has a "rainbow... upon his head" as depicted in Revelation 10:1.

Quotations from the Bible are all from the Authorised, or King James Version, unless stated otherwise. However, in the quotations from the Old Testament, "LORD", which translates Yahweh, has been given as Yahweh. The meaning of this Divine, memorial Name ('He (who) will be') is closely related to the theme of the book, and therefore the use of this original Hebrew name seems entirely appropriate. The only other change from the standard wording in the text of quotations is that "church" is usually given as "ecclesia". In addition, all pronouns relating to God are printed with an initial capital letter.

KJV spelling has been retained in quotations throughout. In some instances therefore the spelling of a word will vary between the text and a quotation from the KJV. Where this is the case, the difference is deliberate.

Transliterations of Hebrew and Greek words are taken (generally) from the lexicon of the Online Bible, and are shown in italics.

Bible translations that are referred to are abbreviated as follows:-
    ERV = (English) Revised Version (of 1881)
    KJV = King James Version (i.e. Authorised Version) of 1611
    NEB = New English Bible
    OLB = Online Bible
    Rotherham = Rotherham, J.B. 1903. The Emphasized New Testament. A new translation designed to set forth the exact meaning, the proper terminology, and the graphic style of the sacred original... . London: H.R. Allenson.
    RSV = Revised Standard Version
    TRC = Tyndale Rogers Coverdale Bible (the "Matthew Bible" of 1537); a combination of the work of Tyndale and Coverdale.

Other works are cited in the text and listed in the Bibliography use the "Harvard" referencing style.

Chapter 1 – Introduction

The saints need constant encouragement during their mortal pilgrimage by reminders of the glory that is in store for them. To that end, this study will focus on the role of the redeemed and glorified saints acting as a unified body along with their Master, the Lord Jesus Christ, immediately following their approval at the judgment seat.

In the course of this study we shall discover that the body of saints in their future glory is portrayed in the inspired Word using a variety of symbols. One such symbol, is that of the "mighty angel... clothed with a cloud", who has a "rainbow... upon his head". This angel is presented to us in Revelation 10:1, and will be examined in detail in the next chapter. Based on this vision we have selected the symbol of the Rainbowed Angel as our title, and will use this as a Scripture-based shorthand to refer to the company of the redeemed saints at the time of the establishment of the Kingdom of God on earth.

A key aspect of this study will be to demonstrate beyond reasonable doubt, from Scripture, that the judgment seat before which we must all appear will be in Sinai. It is from that region that the saints will appear to the world to begin the process, along with the King of Kings, of bringing all nations under the righteous rule of Yahweh.

Another key aspect will be to show that Scripture presents the future body of glorified saints, often referred to by Christadelphians as 'the multitudinous Christ', by a variety of symbols. Examples include the cherubim(s), the four living creatures, the one like unto the Son of Man, a certain man, Yahweh of hosts, and the four and twenty elders, among others. In each case there is the concept of a multitude of immortal people, acting in complete harmony and fellowship under the direction of their leader and master, the Lord Jesus Christ. The unity and harmony is so complete that the symbolism sometimes uses the concept of a single man, but with a multitudinous aspect incorporated within the symbol. One example of this principle is the "one *like* unto the Son of Man" (Rev. 1:13), whose "voice (is) as the sound of many waters" (verse 14). Since seas and waters are used in Scripture as a symbol of peoples and nations, it is clear that the explanation of the symbol is that the man represents a multitude, albeit a multitude that will have adopted the Name of the one who is their leader, so that they are all incorporated in him. They will be energised by his immortal power, derived from his Father, the Creator of all things, and they perform his will and work to perfection.

These visions are revealed that we may understand God's purpose. They open up a whole series of intertwined Scriptures in both Old and New Testaments, providing convincing evidence of the unity of the Word of God, and the consistency of His purpose. They also constitute an exciting vision for the saints during the days of their probation. They are indeed things that should motivate us, and stir us up in the Lord's work. With such visions set before us may we be encouraged to prepare diligently for that day when the Son of God will be revealed in power and great glory, to manifest God's judgments in the earth, and to fill it with Yahweh's glory.

Chapter 2 – The mighty angel with the rainbow upon his head

Revelation 10 in context

Before expounding the vision of the Rainbowed Angel from Revelation 10 it is necessary to put this chapter into context in the Apocalypse as a whole. The book of Revelation is carefully structured. The prophetic visions are presented in groups of seven; the seals, trumpets, and vials. They are also preceded by a separate group of seven; the letters to the seven ecclesias. Each group of seven is itself introduced by a vision of the Kingdom. The visions are for the benefit and encouragement of the saints of all ages, but each one had particular relevance for the mortal saints at the specific epoch which had been reached by the continuous historic prophecies. Thus, visions of the kingdom intervene at intervals during the opening out of the prophetic scheme from the book or scroll that the Lamb of God was worthy to open (see Rev. 5:1-10).

Revelation 10 comprises one of these intervening visions. It thus relates to events still future, and is part of the encouragement given to mortal saints. It also includes another element of the structured sevens; the seven thunders. We shall comment briefly on these later. Suffice it to say that they represent judgments of the Almighty that are still in the future, and that will follow the return of Christ. No further detail relating to them was revealed to the apostle John. The point we need to note is that this chapter concerns the kingdom of God that is still to come.

The mighty Rainbowed Angel as Jesus Christ himself

Much of our study will be concerned with the fact that the Rainbowed Angel is a figure or symbol for the 'multitudinous Christ'; that is Jesus Christ along with the complete body of redeemed saints, the manifestation of the sons of God, who are the future kings that will rule all nations. However it is also necessary to appreciate that Jesus Christ, personally and individually, is the one key element of this great body. The heart and head of this multitudinous body is "the man of (Yahweh's) right hand... the son of man whom Thou madest strong for Thyself" (Psa. 80:17). Thus Christ, personally, is indicated by some of the symbols, and we need to note this, before moving on to consider the multitudinous aspects of the symbols.

Of this mighty angel it is written that "his face *was* as it were the sun" (Rev. 10:1). This statement is parallel with a previous personal experience of the Master.

> "(He) was transfigured before them: and his face did shine as the sun, and his raiment was white as the light" (Matt. 17:2).

At that time Jesus experienced the glory that was promised to him in order to strengthen him for the ordeals of the crucifixion that lay ahead. John, in his vision, sees Jesus experiencing the fullness of that glory at the time when he comes again to rule the world in righteousness. John is seeing Jesus as the "Sun of righteousness" (Mal. 4:2).

His voice is described as being loud, "as *when* a lion roareth" (Rev. 10:3). This is no surprise, for the Lord Jesus Christ is the lion of the tribe of Judah. So in this aspect also the symbol indicates the Lord Jesus Christ personally.

There is a connection here back to Joel's prophecy where it is stated that "Yahweh also shall roar out of Zion" (3:16). This refers, chronologically, to the period after the march of the Rainbowed Angel to Jerusalem is ended, and Christ, along with the saints, is enthroned in Jerusalem. However, it shows that the concept of 'roaring' in judgment applies throughout the career of the Rainbowed Angel. This is also confirmed by the same figure in Jeremiah in a prophecy relating to Yahweh's judgments on "all the kingdoms of the world" (Jer. 25:26). God then commands Jeremiah to prophesy these words.

> "Yahweh shall roar from on high, and utter His voice from His holy habitation; He shall mightily roar upon His habitation; He shall give a shout, as they that tread *the grapes*, against all the inhabitants of the earth" (Jer. 25:30).

The loud voice like a lion roaring is linked in Revelation 10 to the voice of the seven thunders.

> The angel "cried with a loud voice, as *when* a lion roareth: and when he had cried, seven thunders uttered their voices" (Rev. 10:3).

Chapter 2 – The mighty angel with the rainbow upon his head

Thunder in Scripture is used, appropriately, to represent God's judgments. It first occurs in Exodus 9 in connection with the plague of hail which came on the Egyptians, which was clearly one of a series of judgments on this idolatrous and cruel people. In that passage thunder is mentioned no less than five times. In an allusion to these events the Psalmist makes clear their effect on those who were subject to these thunder judgments.

> "The voice of Thy thunder *was* in the heaven: the lightnings lightened the world: the earth trembled and shook" (Psa. 77:18).

The meaning of the symbol is made even clearer by Isaiah when he warns the inhabitants of Jerusalem about the consequences of their false worship. In the following passage note that the word "visited" has the sense of visiting punishment and judgment upon those who are guilty.

> "Thou shalt be visited of the LORD of hosts with thunder, and with earthquake, and great noise, with storm and tempest, and the flame of devouring fire" (Isa. 29:6).

These symbols of 'roaring' and 'thunder' thus become significant in Revelation 10 in relation to Christ personally, when we remember that God has committed all judgment unto His Son.

> "For the Father judgeth no man, but hath committed all judgment unto the Son… and hath given him authority to execute judgment also, because he is the Son of man" (Jno. 5:22,27).

So the lion voice, followed by the voice of seven thunders, indicates judgments to be wrought by Christ. However, these judgments are still in the future, beyond the return of Christ and the judgment seat, for they are not detailed in Revelation. It may be that John (and we) have been spared the details because, in our mortal state, they are too terrible to contemplate. Certainly when John ate the little book given to him by the angel, on which presumably the details of the seven thunders were written, they made his belly bitter (Rev.10:10). Hence the command not to write the details of the seven thunders.

> "[The angel] cried with a loud voice, as *when* a lion roareth: and when he had cried, seven thunders uttered their voices. And when the seven thunders had uttered their voices, I was about to write:

and I heard a voice from heaven saying unto me, Seal up those things which the seven thunders uttered, and write them not" (Rev. 10:3-4).

It may well be that the "seven thunders" cover the "time of trouble, such as never was" mentioned by Daniel (12:1). So we conclude that this mighty angel represents the Lord Jesus Christ at the time when he will manifest himself vested with all his Father's power and glory to embark on that process which will end with triumphant voices in heaven proclaiming...

> "The kingdoms of this world are become *the kingdoms* of our Lord, and of his Christ; and he shall reign for ever and ever" (Rev. 11:15).

From heaven

The next element of the opening verse of Revelation 10 that now commands our attention is the place from which the angel comes to commence his work.

> "I saw another mighty angel come down from heaven, clothed with a cloud: and a rainbow *was* upon his head, and his face *was* as it were the sun, and his feet as pillars of fire" (Rev. 10:1).

Given that, in part at least, the angel represents Christ, there is no problem in grasping the statement that he comes "from heaven" at the time when he commences the process of establishing the kingdom of God on earth. However, the notion of the angel coming "from heaven" becomes a little more complex when we understand that the angel also represents the multitudinous body of redeemed saints in their future glory. In that context, what is meant by "heaven"? We suggest that the key to the answer lies in the way the apostle Paul describes, in Ephesians, the exalted and privileged status of the saints in Christ in the days of their mortality. In understanding this facet of "from heaven" we shall in fact begin to open up the fact that this angel does indeed represent the redeemed saints.

In Ephesians the saints in Christ are described as being "in heavenly *places* in Christ" (Eph. 1:3; see also 1:10 (mg.); 2:6; 3:10,15; 6:12 (mg.)). This figure is derived from Genesis 1 where the waters in heaven are divided from those under the heaven, which themselves are then separated from the land. The result is that there are three areas;

heavens, earth, and seas. In contrast to the saints who are symbolically in the heavens, the wicked nations of the earth are represented by the seas; those who live in ignorance of the Word and ways of the Almighty.

> "But the wicked *are* like the troubled sea, when it cannot rest, whose waters cast up mire and dirt. *There is* no peace, saith my God, to the wicked" (Isa. 57:20-21).

The third area between the heaven and the seas, that is, the earth, seems to represent those people who have a knowledge of the Truth, and who either reject it, or who accept it and then fall away, but who are nevertheless responsible to judgment. Thus the Psalmist seems to refer to the call of all the 'responsible' to the judgment seat in the following passage; both "the heavens" and "the earth" are summoned. Since the true and faithful saints are represented by "the heavens", it is ultimately only the heavens that display the righteousness of God.

> "He shall call to the heavens from above, and to the earth, that He may judge His people. Gather My saints together unto Me; those that have made a covenant with Me by sacrifice. And the heavens shall declare His righteousness: for God *is* judge Himself." (Psa. 50:4-6).

As an aside, it is interesting to note that the preceding verses in this Psalm seem to relate to the arrival of the Rainbowed Angel at Jerusalem.

> "The mighty God, *even* Yahweh, hath spoken, and called the earth from the rising of the sun unto the going down thereof. Out of Zion, the perfection of beauty, God hath shined. Our God shall come, and shall not keep silence: a fire shall devour before Him, and it shall be very tempestuous round about Him" (Psa. 50:1-3).

This of course is the fulfilment of the purpose of the Almighty, and is the outcome of the justification of the saints by their faith at the judgment seat. As so often is the case in Scripture, the end of the matter or purpose of God is expressed first, followed by the way to achieving that end.

Heaven in Scriptural symbolism, as employed in Revelation, thus represents the position and status of the saints; and in the visions of the future, describes their status in the kingdom. It is employed in this way in one of the previous visions.

> "After this I looked, and, behold, a door *was* opened in heaven: and the first voice which I heard *was* as it were of a trumpet talking with me; which said, Come up hither, and I will shew thee things which must be hereafter. And immediately I was in the spirit: and, behold, a throne was set in heaven, and *one* sat on the throne" (Rev. 4:1-2).

John is allowed to see, as it were through a door, into the culmination of God's purpose with the saints. It is as if he is allowed to see into the holy of holies in the tabernacle or temple. There, above the ark and under the mercy seat is a throne, where dwells the glory of Yahweh. Note that on the ark in the tabernacle there was to be a "crown of gold" (Exo. 25:11). The same theme is picked up in the promise to those who would overcome from Laodicea in the immediately preceding verses.

> "To him that overcometh will I grant to sit with me in my throne, even as I also overcame, and am set down with my Father in his throne" (Rev. 3:21).

This is Christ's throne, which is the throne of David, a throne which is in "heavenly places" and has full Divine authority; a throne which is to be shared by the redeemed saints. It is of course a literal throne, vested with the full Divine authority of God Himself. It is the throne of David on which the Lord Jesus Christ will sit.

> "The LORD hath sworn *in* truth unto David; He will not turn from it; Of the fruit of thy body will I set upon thy throne" (Psa. 132:11).

> "Thou shalt conceive in thy womb, and bring forth a son, and shalt call his name JESUS. He shall be great, and shall be called the Son of the Highest: and the Lord God shall give unto him the throne of his father David" (Lk. 1:31-32).

The collective promise of these passages is therefore clear. The redeemed saints will share the Divine kingly authority of their Master when they rule with him in his kingdom.

But what are we to make of the fact that John saw a "mighty angel come down from heaven"? And how does this fit with our suggested interpretation of "heaven" or "in heavenly places" in relation to the saints in the kingdom? The angels are God's messengers, as signified by both the Hebrew and Greek words used in the Biblical text. The Psalmist explains that as God's ministers, the angels of heaven, by definition, inevitably and faithfully perform God's will.

> "Bless the LORD, ye His angels, that excel in strength, that do His commandments, hearkening unto the voice of His word. Bless ye the LORD, all *ye* His hosts; *ye* ministers of His, that do His pleasure" (Psa. 103:20-21).

Given that in the kingdom the saints will be "as the angels of God in heaven" (Matt. 22:30), we can readily appreciate that the mighty angel that came down from heaven, and which John saw, was an apt symbol for the saints in the kingdom. This was a vision of Christ and the saints being manifested as Divinely ordained kings and priests to rule the earth and bring it in subjection to Yahweh's authority and righteousness.

The realm of the angel

Concerning this angel, John wrote that…

> "…he set his right foot upon the sea, and *his* left *foot* on the earth" (Rev. 10:2).

Given the preceding exposition of the significance of the heavens in relation to the earth and sea, this is a very precise statement concerning the extent of the dominion of the mighty angel. That angel, representing Christ with the immortal saints, rules over the earth and sea; that is over all who have not accepted the gospel and been found worthy at the judgment seat. They do not rule over the heavens, because they ARE the heavens.

It is perhaps appropriate that the dominion of the angel is expressed in this way. It has echoes of Nebuchadnezzar's image of the kingdom of men in Daniel 2. The king saw it in its final stage, when it stands erect on its feet and two legs. Then the whole image was struck on the feet by the stone, representing Christ; it was toppled over, and ground to powder like chaff, which was then blown away. This blasphemous kingdom of men will be replaced by the Kingdom of God, which, unlike Nebuchadnezzar's image, shall stand for ever.

17

It is suggested in Eureka, (Thomas 1902, pp. 157-158) that the "sea" (Rev. 13:1) represents the dominion of the ten horns of the apocalyptic beasts, and that the "earth" (Rev. 13:11) represents the dominion of the two-horned dragon power. The beast of the sea in Revelation 13:1 had ten horns. Likewise, the latter day counterpart of this beast that will go into perdition also has ten horns, and "sitteth upon many waters" (Rev. 17:1,3). That same latter day beast rules over those "that dwell on the earth... whose names were not written in the book of life" (Rev. 17:8).

Clothed with a cloud

Having established that some elements of the symbolism relating to the Rainbowed Angel indicate that it represents the Lord Jesus Christ personally, we now turn to expound more fully the fact that this angel also points to the multitudinous body of Christ and the glorified saints. Thus, considering all elements of the angel, it will present to us a vision of Christ and the saints as they prepare to work together to establish God's kingdom on earth.

The mighty angel is described as being "clothed with a cloud" (Rev. 10:1). We can readily interpret the cloud as a symbol of faithful saints from Paul's words to the Hebrews, which follow immediately after the catalogue of the faithful in chapter 11.

> "Wherefore seeing we also are compassed about with so great a cloud of witnesses, let us lay aside every weight, and the sin which doth so easily beset *us*, and let us run with patience the race that is set before us" (Heb. 12:1)[1].

---

1. There are 16 men and women of faith mentioned in Hebrews 11. To these we may add "the author and finisher of *our* faith" (Heb. 12:2), the Lord Jesus Christ. This makes a total of 17, the number that therefore represents the full cloud of witnesses. Remarkably, 17 is the sum of the numerical value of the Hebrew letters YHWH, which spell out the Divine Memorial Name of Yahweh. Thus Jesus plus the 16 representative saints comprise the multitudinous manifestation of Yahweh; the "cloud of witnesses"; the completion of Yahweh's purpose, and the fullness of His glory.

The Apocalypse itself confirms this interpretation in its opening section.

> "[Jesus Christ] hath made us kings and priests unto God and his Father; to him *be* glory and dominion for ever and ever. Amen. Behold, he cometh with clouds; and every eye shall see him, and they *also* which pierced him: and all kindreds of the earth shall wail because of him. Even so, Amen" (Rev. 1:6-7).

The "clouds" and the "kings and priests" refer to the same body of people. At this point it is worth considering how these clouds of redeemed and immortal saints are formed. Given the symbolism we have just considered, there is a remarkable passage in the Old Testament concerning Jesus, as the one "that ruleth over *men* {who} must be just" (2 Sam. 23:3). The following verse continues:-

> "And *he shall be* as the light of the morning, *when* the sun riseth, *even* a morning without clouds; *as* the tender grass *springing* out of the earth by clear shining after rain" (2 Sam. 23:4).

When he appears, it will be on a "morning **without** clouds"! How can this be reconciled with the clouds of glorified saints previously identified? We suggest that the key to the explanation lies in the "tender grass *springing* out of the earth". Mortal men and women, including those called to be saints are all described as grass that is cut down in death.

> "The grass withereth, the flower fadeth: because the spirit of Yahweh bloweth upon it: surely the people *is* grass. The grass withereth, the flower fadeth: but the Word of our God shall stand for ever" (Isa. 40:7-8).

However in the Samuel passage the grass springs out of the earth, indicating resurrection from death to life. The grass which springs up is elsewhere characterised as grass that has been cut down, or "mown grass". Thus the King's son, the Son of God…

> "… shall come down like rain upon the mown grass: as showers *that* water the earth. In his days shall the righteous flourish; and abundance of peace so long as the moon endureth" (Psa. 72:6-7).

The mown grass is watered by showers from heaven, that cause the righteous (those who have been raised and approved at the judgment seat) to flourish. This rain is the Word of God, manifest now in the

Word made flesh who has himself been exalted to spirit nature. Moses prophesied of him in these terms.

> "My doctrine shall drop as the rain, My speech shall distil as the dew, as the small rain upon the tender herb, and as the showers upon the grass" (Deut. 32:2).

The Word of God dropping on the raised, still mortal, but approved saints will command them, in words recorded by Isaiah.

> "Thy dead *men* shall live, *together with* my dead body shall they arise. Awake and sing, ye that dwell in dust: for thy dew *is as* the dew of herbs, and the earth shall cast out the dead" (Isa. 26:19).

The command to God's "dead men" to "awake, and sing" results in their transformation into immortal beings.

> "But they that wait upon the LORD shall renew (KJV mg. "change") *their* strength; they shall mount up with wings as eagles; they shall run, and not be weary; *and* they shall walk, and not faint" (Isa. 40:31).

This very process of change from mortality to immortality is picked up by the inspired apostle Paul, using Isaiah's words.

> "Behold, I shew you a mystery; we shall not all sleep, but we shall all be changed, in a moment, in the twinkling of an eye, at the last trump: for the trumpet shall sound, and the dead shall be raised incorruptible, and we shall be changed" (1 Cor. 15:51-52).

The final stage of this process relates to the dew mentioned in both Deuteronomy 32 and Isaiah 26. When the sun rises it evaporates dew into the atmosphere, and that water is converted into clouds. Similarly the raised and immortalised saints, like dew, will be raised or evaporated into clouds. So although the morning when the Son of God appears was initially a "morning without clouds", the Sun of Righteousness transforms the dew into clouds of saints, so that he is clothed with a cloud[1].

---

1. The Hebrew word translated "without" can have the sense of "before"; cf. Job 15:32 and Zeph. 2:2 where it is so translated. This confirms the sense that in the resurrection morning there will initially be no clouds, only the dew on the ground. But as the Sun of righteousness rises clouds will be formed, as the saints are transformed into immortal glory.

They will be "clothed upon with (their) house from heaven" (2 Cor. 5:2), which is immortality. At that point the saints will share power and authority with the king of kings, having been born again from the dust of the earth to undying youth and the power of an endless life, forever beyond temptation and sin. Once again it is the Psalmist who pulls together these ideas so beautifully.

> "Thy people *shall be* willing in the day of thy power, in the beauties of holiness from the womb of the morning: thou hast the dew of thy youth" (Psa. 110:3).

A rainbow upon his head

As previously indicated we intend to use the phrase 'the Rainbowed Angel' as a shorthand phrase to describe not only the angel of Revelation 10, but also to describe the other Scriptural symbols used of Christ and the saints in glory. But we must consider the Scriptural source of our title phrase. The mighty angel that John saw had "a rainbow... upon his head" (Rev. 10:1).

The rainbow is naturally associated with clouds and rain, which we have just considered. The rainbow in nature is formed when sunlight is refracted through droplets of water. So we would expect the rainbow as a symbol to be associated with the redemption of the saints, given the passages we have just considered, in which "clouds" represent faithful, redeemed believers. As the Sun of Righteousness shines on and through that dew of the resurrected saints, we would expect a bow to be formed, confirming that they are the redeemed ones. Thus in its origin the rainbow is a sign of a covenant of redemption and salvation, and of the preservation of life. Consider God's words to Noah.

> "Behold, I establish My **covenant** with you, and with your seed after you; and with every living creature that is with you... And I will establish My **covenant** with you; neither shall all flesh be cut off any more by the waters of a flood; neither shall there any more be a flood to destroy the earth... This is the token of the **covenant** which I make between Me and you and every living creature that is with you, for perpetual generations: I do set My bow in the cloud, and it shall be for a token of a **covenant** between Me and the earth. And it shall come to pass, when I bring a cloud over the earth, that the bow shall be seen in the cloud: and I will remember My **covenant**,

which is between Me and you and every living creature of all flesh; and the waters shall no more become a flood to destroy all flesh. And the bow shall be in the cloud; and I will look upon it, that I may remember the everlasting **covenant** between God and every living creature of all flesh that is upon the earth. And God said unto Noah, This is the token of the **covenant**, which I have established between Me and all flesh that is upon the earth" (Gen. 9:9-17).

We have quoted this passage at length to illustrate, as shown by the highlighted words, that the word "covenant" remarkably occurs seven times in these words from God to Noah. It was a Divinely perfect and complete covenant; thus God is quite emphatic, repeating the phrase "My covenant". It was, and is His covenant, and His rainbow. Moreover, it is an "everlasting (Heb. *olahm*) covenant". It thus pertains to that promised future age when God's glory will fill the earth, and is a very appropriate symbol to be used in the vision of Revelation 10. It speaks of those who have been redeemed and preserved alive through resurrection to inherit the kingdom. It also speaks of an assurance that although the Rainbowed Angel will bring about the terrible seven thunder judgments, the end result will not be to destroy life from the earth, but to preserve alive a righteous remnant to reflect the Creator's glory.

Note also that the bow was the "token" of the covenant. The Hebrew word for token (*oth*) has a number of significant occurrences which outline various parts of the process of redemption. Firstly, circumcision was also a token of a covenant.

"Ye shall circumcise the flesh of your foreskin; and it shall be a token of the covenant betwixt Me and you" (Gen. 17:11).

A key element in the process of salvation was, and is, the cutting off of the flesh and all its ways.

Service to God at Sinai was also to be a token to Israel that God was indeed with them. Moses was instructed about this when he communed with God at Sinai, on the occasion when the bush burned but was not consumed.

"And (God) said, Certainly I will be with thee; and this *shall be* a token unto thee, that I have sent thee: when thou hast brought forth

the people out of Egypt, ye shall serve God upon this mountain"
(Exo. 3:12).

The final outworking of this element of the rainbow token of the
covenant will be when the judgment takes place at Sinai. This will
follow the pattern set by Israel gathered there to receive the Law, prior
to possessing the promised land of their inheritance. We expound this
much more fully in chapter 5. Note that many of those who will be
gathered to Sinai will be those who have "made a covenant with (God)
by sacrifice" (Psa. 50:5). Further comments on this Psalm are included
earlier in this chapter.

Passover blood on the doorposts and lintels of the houses of the
Israelites was also a token of deliverance; the outward sign of inner
faith, so that the destroying angel passed over.

> "The blood shall be to you for a token upon the houses where ye
> *are*: and when I see the blood, I will pass over you, and the plague
> shall not be upon you to destroy *you*, when I smite the land of
> Egypt" (Exo. 12:13).

Finally in this context we note the use of the word token in the context
of the delivery of Rahab, by faith, from the destruction of Jericho. She
asked for a token of assurance from the spies that they would keep
their promise, and she was given a highly significant token.

> "Now therefore, I pray you, swear unto me by Yahweh, since I have
> shewed you kindness, that ye will also shew kindness unto my
> father's house, and give me a true token… Behold, *when* we come
> into the land, thou shalt bind this line of scarlet thread in the window
> which thou didst let us down by: and thou shalt bring thy father, and
> thy mother, and thy brethren, and all thy father's household, home
> unto thee" (Josh. 2:12, 18).

Rahab requested a true token. The spies told her to bind a line of
scarlet thread in her window, to mark out her house for deliverance.
The Hebrew word for "line" is *tiqvah*, the normal word for "hope,
expectation". Thus it was to be a mark of Rahab's hope and
expectation, of her faith and belief that she would indeed be delivered.

This all leads back to Revelation 10. The angel had a rainbow upon his
head, the token or outward sign that those represented by the angel

were indeed the redeemed ones. It is therefore remarkable that the Hebrew *oth* for "token" first occurs, translated as "signs" in Genesis 1 in relation to the creation of the heavenly bodies.

> "And God said, Let there be lights in the firmament of the heaven to divide the day from the night; and let them be for signs, and for seasons, and for days, and years… And God made two great lights; the greater light to rule the day, and the lesser light to rule the night: *He made* the stars also" (Gen. 1:14, 16).

As signs or tokens, the sun moon and stars point forward to the kingdom era when the Rainbowed Angel will appear to perform his work. The saints in that day will shine like the heavenly bodies.

> "Then shall the righteous shine forth as the sun in the kingdom of their Father. Who hath ears to hear, let him hear" (Matt. 13:43).

> "They that be wise shall shine as the brightness of the firmament; and they that turn many to righteousness as the stars for ever and ever" (Dan. 12:3).

This picture is completed when we go back to the first occurrence of the "rainbow" in Revelation, where it is associated with "four and twenty elders", representing a company of covenanted kings and priests called forth from Jew and Gentile, who are associated with a throne, and who acknowledge the supreme power of the king enthroned, in whose name they rule.

> "He that sat was to look upon like a jasper and a sardine stone: and *there was* a rainbow round about the throne, in sight like unto an emerald. And round about the throne *were* four and twenty seats: and upon the seats I saw four and twenty elders sitting, clothed in white raiment; and they had on their heads crowns of gold… The four and twenty elders fall down before him that sat on the throne, and worship him that liveth for ever and ever, and cast their crowns before the throne, saying, Thou art worthy, O Lord, to receive glory and honour and power: for thou hast created all things, and for thy pleasure they are and were created" (Rev. 4:3,4,10,11).

Chapter 3 – The Rainbowed Angel and other related symbolic visions of the redeemed saints

Why other similar symbols?

We began this study with a consideration of the mighty angel of Revelation 10 with the rainbow upon his head. However, as we noted earlier, the things symbolised by this angel are presented in a number of other Scriptures using similar, closely related, but not identical symbols. We shall now proceed to consider these, and to ponder why Divine wisdom saw fit to reveal similar things in so many different ways.

One of the reasons for starting with Revelation 10 is that in the context of this chapter, the body represented (in this case by the angel with the rainbow on his head) is shown ready and fully prepared to enact God's future judgments. The five other passages we wish now to consider, and which use related symbols, detail different stages of the career of Christ and the saints, represented by this mighty angel, in carrying out these Divine judgments. The first two passages deal with phases prior to, and actually at the judgment seat of Christ. The latter three set out specific elements of the judgment work of the Rainbowed Angel after the saints have been made immortal. In terms of a chronological sequence, as suggested in Table 1, Revelation 10 comes in the middle (3rd out of 6), and is the point at which the work of enacting Yahweh's judgments on the nations begins. It also presents a convenient summary of the body of glorified saints, the 'multitudinous Christ', now constituted as such, but not yet engaged on their specific work. Although the symbol of the rainbow itself only occurs in two of these visions, as already noted 'the Rainbowed Angel' is a convenient shorthand name for the multitudinous Christ throughout their work.

It must be acknowledged that the work of each phase of the career of the Rainbowed Angel will probably not be quite so rigidly defined as Table 1 might imply. For example, those phases dealing with Israel will also involve judgments on those surrounding nations that attack or oppose Israel.

These various visions and their significance are summarised in Table 1. A more detailed exposition of each then follows. After that we shall consider in detail the actual march of the Rainbowed Angel.

Table 1 – Visions of Christ and the redeemed saints

Chapter	Vision	Significance
Rev. 1:12-20	"*One* like unto the Son of Man"	Christ with the saints in the mortal ecclesia – preparation for future glory
Dan. 10:5-19	"a certain man"	Resurrection and immortalisation of the saints
Rev. 10:1-5	The Rainbowed Angel	Christ and saints ready to carry out God's judgments on the nations
Zech. 14:3-5	Yahweh my God… and all the saints	Yahweh and His saints defeat Gog and his allies and deliver Israel
Ezek. 1:1 – 2:3	"the likeness of four living creatures"	Christ and the saints are sent to the remnant of rebellious Israel
Dan. 7:9-14, 21-27	The Ancient of days and one like the Son of man	Christ and the saints defeat Daniel's 4th beast & the apostasy

One like unto the Son of Man – Revelation 1

A comparison of the relevant verses in Revelation 1 and 10 easily shows that although the visions are not identical, there are sufficient likenesses to demonstrate that the overall symbol represents essentially the same thing.

Table 2 – A comparison of Revelation 10 and Revelation 1

The Rainbowed Angel	One like unto the Son of Man
10:1 – "his face *was* as it were the sun"	1:16 – "his countenance *was* as the sun shineth in his strength"
10:1 – "his feet as pillars of fire"	1:15 – "his feet like unto fine brass, as if they burned in a fire"
10:3 – " (he) cried with a loud voice, as *when* a lion roareth: and when he had cried seven thunders uttered their voices"	1:15 – "his voice as the sound of many waters"
10:2 – "he had in his hand a little book open"	1:16, 20 – "he had in his right hand seven stars… The seven stars are the angels of the seven ecclesias"

The Rainbowed Angel and other related symbolic visions of the redeemed saints

The basic meaning of the symbol in Revelation 1 is the same as that already identified for the Rainbowed Angel; it is a figure for Christ and the saints. Note that it is not solely the Lord Jesus Christ personally. It is not the Son of Man, but "one like unto the Son of Man"; like him, but not precisely the same in identity. One key is that "his voice (is) as the sound of many waters" (Rev. 1:15). Waters in Scripture represent multitudes and nations of people (cf. e.g. Isa. 57:20). There is thus a multitude incorporated in this symbol. But this multitude is not wicked. They are associated with the Son of Man. God has visited the Gentiles "to take out of them a people for His name" (Acts 15:14). This multitude comprises those who have responded to this call from the Gentiles, together with a remnant of Israel who have accepted Christ ("the tabernacle of David" which is being built again – Acts 15:16), who have joined together in the ecclesia of Christ.

So the "*one* like unto the Son of Man" represents the ecclesia in the days of flesh, while the Master walks among the lightstands. This is indicated by the last line in the table above. At this stage of the development of the multitudinous Christ the Lord is still preparing the ecclesia for eternity. He holds in his hand the elders and faithful ("the seven stars") in the ecclesia, while he examines, exhorts, and rebukes them. Interestingly the same symbol is picked up in one of the Old Testament passages concerning the Rainbowed Angel that we shall consider later in our study. There, in a vision of things following on from the judgment, Moses wrote that "all His saints *are* in Thy hand" (Deut. 33:3).

The seven stars in his right hand (Rev. 1:16) should be contrasted with the Rainbowed Angel, who has in his hand "a little book open" (Rev. 10:2) which contains the details of the unwritten seven thunder judgments. Therefore although the essential identity of the symbols (the "*one* like unto the Son of man" and the Rainbowed Angel) is the same, the different things they hold in their hand indicate that they are being presented at different stages in their career. The former is at the mortal stage of the ecclesia; the latter at the point when Christ and the saints are about to pour out God's judgments on the world.

A certain man

The key verses that describe this "man" that Daniel saw are as follows.

> "Then I lifted up mine eyes, and looked, and behold a certain man (KJV mg. "one man") clothed in linen, whose loins *were* girded with fine gold of Uphaz: his body also *was* like the beryl, and his face as the appearance of lightning, and his eyes as lamps of fire, and his arms and his feet like in colour to polished brass, and the voice of his words like the voice of a multitude" (Dan 10:5-6).

We note first that there is a historical context and significance to this chapter. That is not our primary concern in this study, though it does, as we would expect, have a bearing on what the vision signifies for the future. The vision of the "certain man" is revealed to Daniel in the third year of Cyrus. This refers to his third year as ruler of Babylon; 537/536 BC. Daniel mourns for "three full weeks" (verse 2). This tallies with the twenty one days of verse 13, during which, as the "certain man" explains to Daniel, the "prince of the kingdom of Persia withstood" him, until he was assisted by Michael, one of God's chief princes. Historically, the twenty one days stand for twenty one years. This was the period of time that began when the adversaries of the Jews influenced the King of Persia to put a stop to the rebuilding of the temple in Jerusalem (see Ezra 4:23,24). The twenty one year period ended in 516 BC, when the rebuilding work was completed, amidst great celebrations, as recorded in Ezra 6:15. The completion of the temple becomes highly significant when we consider the future import of the vision of Daniel 10.

We are not left to speculate about whether or not the vision has a future significance, for this was explained to Daniel.

> "Now I am come to make thee understand what shall befall thy people in the latter days: for yet the vision *is* for *many* days" (Dan. 10:14).

The other key feature to note at this point is that the "certain man" (KJV mg. "one man") is representative of many, because "the voice of his words (was) like the voice of a multitude" (verse 6). Furthermore, when this same one (it would appear) touched Daniel's lips, he is described as "*one* like the similitude of the sons of men (Heb. *adam*)" (verse 16). It has been suggested (Thomas [no date], p. 113 et seq.) that the

The Rainbowed Angel and other related symbolic visions of the redeemed saints
phrase "a certain man", describing this symbolic man, would be better translated as "the man of the one". The essential point to grasp is that this "man" represented a multitude comprising a unified corporate body, comprising sons of Adam with whom the Almighty was dealing in a special way (raising them from the dead and granting to them the gift of immortality), because they are His saints. This is therefore the same body of people that is represented by the Rainbowed Angel of Revelation 10, though Daniel's vision relates to a slightly earlier period of time as we shall see. Firstly, it is appropriate to set out the comparisons and links between Daniel 10 and Revelation 10.

Table 3 – A comparison of the Rainbowed Angel and "a certain man"

The Rainbowed Angel - Rev. 10	A certain man - Dan. 10
v 1 – "clothed with a cloud"	v 5 – "clothed in linen" v 5 – "(his) loins were girded with fine gold"
v 1 – his face as it were the sun"	v 6 – "his body also *was* like the beryl" v 6 – "his face as the appearance of lightning" v 6 – "his eyes as lamps of fire"
v 1 – "his feet as pillars of fire"	v 6 – "his arms and his feet like in colour to polished brass"
v 3 – "a loud voice, as *when* a lion roareth: and when he had cried seven thunders uttered their voices"	v 6 – "the voice of his words like the voice of a multitude"

Table 3 presents four key elements that relate to the Rainbowed Angel for which the "certain man" has parallel attributes.

Firstly, although the colour of the cloud is not given, since it represents saints in a state of redemption, it is reasonable to assume a white or light coloured cloud, similar in colour to linen (of which more below).

Since the cloud clothing represents redeemed saints it is reasonable also to link this to clothing like "fine gold", given that such gold is a symbol of tried faith (cf. 1 Pet. 1:7).

Secondly, the face of the Rainbowed Angel being like the sun is clearly parallel to lightning, and to lamps of fire, and possibly also to the body like beryl, as beryl is yellow in colour. Next, the polished brass of the feet of the "certain man" symbolises red, Adamic flesh, polished by the experiences of mortal life to reflect the perfect character of the Lord Jesus Christ. These experiences, and the polishing and justification that follow give the "certain man" the right to execute God's judgments, indicated by the feet like pillars of fire. Lastly, the similarity in the description of the voices is self-evident, confirming that both the Rainbowed Angel and the "certain man" represent a corporate multitude.

Corruption puts on incorruption

We must now give some attention to the detail of the interactions between Daniel and the angelic "certain man" in Daniel 10. It is well established (Thomas [no date], p. 113 et seq.) that this portrays the process of resurrection, from being awakened from the sleep of death through to the transition from mortality to immortality and incorruptibility. Thus we shall simply summarise the key stages in the process. This is relevant to our study because this "certain man" (along with the Rainbowed Angel) represents the multitudinous Christ body. It is therefore highly appropriate that this vision should show the process by which this multitudinous body of saints inherits immortality. The stages are set out in the table below, remembering that Daniel stands as representative of all the saints in this vision.

The Rainbowed Angel and other related symbolic visions of the redeemed saints

Table 4 – The process of resurrection and immortalisation in Daniel 10

Process	Daniel 10 text
Asleep in death	"I was left alone… there remained no strength in me: for my comeliness was turned in me into corruption, and I retained no strength" (verse 8).
The call to the dead to awake	"Yet heard I the voice of his words: and when I heard… then was I in a deep sleep on my face, and my face toward the ground" (verse 9).
Alive again, but still mortal in nature to appear before the judgment seat	"An hand touched me, which set me upon my knees and *upon* the palms of my hands. And he said unto me… stand upright: for unto thee am I now sent. And when he had spoken this word unto me, I stood trembling… And when he had spoken such words unto me, I set my face toward the ground, and I became dumb" (verses 10, 11, 15).
Confession of unworthiness and utter dependence on the Almighty	"… then I opened my mouth, and spake, and said unto him that stood before me, O my lord, by the vision my sorrows are turned upon me, and I have retained no strength. For how can the servant of this my lord talk with this my lord? For as for me, straightway there remained no strength in me, neither is there breath left in me" (verse 16-17).
Assurance of justification – by faith	"Then there came again and touched me *one* like the appearance of a man, and he strengthened me, And said, O man greatly beloved, fear not: peace *be* unto thee, be strong, yea, be strong" (verses 18-19).
The gift of immortal strength bestowed	"And when he had spoken unto me, I was strengthened, and said, Let my lord speak; for thou hast strengthened me" (verse 19).

Given that the process of resurrection is set out in this vision, it is instructive to return to some of the details concerning the "certain man" set out in Table 3, comparing the Rainbowed Angel of Revelation 10 with Daniel 10.

Note firstly, that in the first parallel statement in Daniel 10, the "certain man" is clothed in linen. The Hebrew here for "linen" is *bad*, signifying coarse linen. This is the word used for the special linen garment that the High Priest wore on the Day of Atonement when he went into the most holy place. A completely different word is used for the "fine linen" (Hebrew *shesh*) used for the other garments of the priests, and for various parts of the tabernacle. The coarse linen represented the nature of sinful flesh borne by all, including Christ. But Christ, having offered one sacrifice for sin has entered into the holy place as our Melchisedec High Priest. He is now immortal, "made… after the power of an endless life" (Heb. 7:16). He has put off his mortal nature, an action typed once each year by the High Priest when he came out of the most holy place. "Aaron shall come into the tabernacle of the congregation, and shall put off the linen (Heb. *bad*) garments, which he put on when he went into the holy *place*, and shall leave them there" (Lev. 16:23). At the start of the process of resurrection the saint is still mortal in nature, although he has been called from the dead to eternal life. So at this stage in the process, although he is clothed in linen as he is to be accounted righteous, it is still the coarse linen of mortality. This is represented in the symbolic vision by the "certain man" appearing at the start of the vision in a coarse linen garment. The symbolism is absolutely precise and appropriate.

As already noted, he is also clothed on his loins with fine gold. Again this is appropriate in the context of the process of resurrection. This represents tried faith; faith that has been purified by trial experience. It is because of this faith that those inestimable words which we all hope to hear will be spoken to him; "O man greatly beloved, fear not: peace *be* unto thee, be strong, yea, be strong".

As the symbol progresses we learn of the eyes like lamps of fire. The Hebrew word for "lamps" is *lappid*. Scripture defines this word very precisely.

> "For Zion's sake will I not hold my peace, and for Jerusalem's sake I will not rest, until the righteousness thereof go forth as brightness, and the salvation thereof as a lamp *that* burneth" (Isa. 62:1).

The Hebrew for "lamp" is once again *lappid*. It is defined as meaning "salvation". Once again, how appropriate is the symbolism of Daniel 10, for it is the culmination of God's work of salvation with the saints that is being portrayed. This in turn leads on to the arms and feet

The Rainbowed Angel and other related symbolic visions of the redeemed saints
coloured like polished brass. The Hebrew for "polished" only occurs in one other passage, where it is translated "burnished".

> "Their feet *were* straight feet; and the sole of their feet *was* like the sole of a calf's foot: and they sparkled like the colour of burnished brass" (Ezek. 1:7).

This is a description of the feet of the four living creatures, alias the cherubim, another Scriptural symbol of the redeemed saints in their future glory. Once again we marvel how precisely consistent the inspired Word is in the way it uses words and symbols to convey God's purpose and mind! This passage actually takes us to another verse that speaks of the role of the Rainbowed Angel in the future, when as a multitude they will roar with a lion-like voice, and carry out the judgments embodied in the seven thunders. As the Rainbowed Angel ends its march at Jerusalem it will enact the Armageddon judgments against the nations gathered against the city. The angel will have these same calves' feet of polished or burnished brass to overcome the hostile nations, for they will now be empowered with Divine nature; the process of resurrection to glory will have been completed.

> "Now also many nations are gathered against thee, that say, Let her be defiled, and let our eye look upon Zion. But they know not the thoughts of the LORD, neither understand they His counsel: for He shall gather them as the sheaves into the floor. Arise and thresh, O daughter of Zion: for I will make thine horn iron, and I will make thy hoofs brass: and thou shalt beat in pieces many people: and I will consecrate their gain unto the LORD, and their substance unto the Lord of the whole earth" (Mic. 4:11-13).

This has brought us to the point at which the preparation of the Rainbowed Angel has been completed. The ecclesial pilgrimage is over; the saints have been raised from the dead, justified and made immortal. They are now ready to embark on the process of carrying out God's judgments.

Zechariah 14

The next passage in the sequence in Table 1 is Zechariah 14. The links from here to Revelation 10 are a bit more subtle, with the obvious exception of the feet.

Table 5 – The Rainbowed Angel and Zechariah 14

The Rainbowed Angel - Rev. 10	Zechariah 14
verses 1-2 – "his feet as pillars of fire… he set his right foot upon the sea, and *his* left *foot* upon the earth"	verses 3-5 – "Then shall Yahweh go forth… His feet shall stand in that day upon the mount of Olives"
verses 3-4 – "loud voice… their voices… their voices… a voice" (cf. Rev. 1:15 – "his voice as the sound of many waters" – which represents a multitude)	verse 5 – "Yahweh my Elohim shall come, *and* all the saints with thee"

In Revelation 10 the mighty Rainbowed Angel is poised ready to commence his work of judgment via the seven thunders. His dominion is now set to encompass all nations, represented by one foot on the sea and one on the earth. In Zechariah 14, that process has begun. This mighty angel is executing God's purpose at Jerusalem, by evicting and conquering those nations who have dared to threaten and enter Yahweh's chosen city, and have sought to annihilate the nation of Israel.

In addition to that obvious verbal link there are other, perhaps less immediately obvious connections between Zechariah 14 and Revelation 10. We have already noted the parallel between the feet as pillars of fire (Rev. 10:1) and the feet of the four living creatures (cherubim) like burnished brass (Ezek. 1:7). Those feet are likened to calf's feet, which, as previously observed, connects to Micah 4, where, in an Armageddon passage the daughter of Zion (i.e. the saints – born in, or children of Zion; cf. "of Zion it shall be said, This and that man was born in her" (Psa. 87:5)) treads down Zion's enemies with "hoofs of brass" (cf. the feet of the "certain man" in Dan. 10:6). This in turn links us back to Zechariah 14, which also uses Armageddon language. There Yahweh says "I will gather all nations against Jerusalem to battle" (Zech. 14:2). This is language that is picked up in Revelation 16. There, the three unclean frog spirits

> "go forth unto the kings of the earth and of the whole world, to gather them to the battle of that great day of God Almighty… And he

34

The Rainbowed Angel and other related symbolic visions of the redeemed saints

gathered them together into a place called in the Hebrew tongue Armageddon" (Rev. 16:14,16).

So, by making connections with other Scriptures, we can confirm what is in fact indicated in Zechariah 14 itself, that the feet of Yahweh that stand on the mount of Olives are in fact the feet of the Rainbowed Angel, who will be active at Armageddon.

This is further confirmed by a similar, indirect connection from the "loud voice" of the Rainbowed Angel to Zechariah 14. As previously observed this is parallel to the one like unto the Son of Man of Revelation 1, whose "voice (was) as the sound of many waters" (v 15). These waters represent a multitude of people or nations, in the context of Revelation 1, the multitude of redeemed saints. This then ties in with Zechariah 14, where, Yahweh, Whose feet stand on the mount of Olives is given a multitudinous facet. "Yahweh (shall) go forth… His feet shall stand in that day upon the mount of Olives… and Yahweh my Elohim shall come, *and* all the saints with thee" (verses 3-5). "Yahweh my Elohim" carries the sense of 'He shall be my mighty ones'. This is in fact a description of the "saints". Notice that the "*and*" is in italics and was therefore interpolated by the translators. "All the saints with thee" is in fact a description or qualification of the previous phrase, "He shall be my mighty ones". Thus, this manifestation of Yahweh as a multitude of saints at Armageddon as portrayed in Zechariah 14 is in fact equivalent to the "loud voice" of the Rainbowed Angel.

We therefore learn from Zechariah 14 that one part of the work of the Rainbowed Angel will be at Jerusalem, to overcome the nations gathered there as sheaves ripe for threshing, despite their intention to take and rule that city. More detail of this will be examined later in our study when we follow the march of the Rainbowed Angel and arrive at Jerusalem.

The four living creatures – Ezekiel 1

The next passage we wish to consider is the vision of the four living creatures in Ezekiel 1. We suggest that this follows Zechariah 14 in our chronological sequence (see Table 1) for reasons to be set out below. Firstly, consider yet again the close similarities with Revelation 10.

Table 6 – The Rainbowed Angel and Ezekiel's four living creatures

The Rainbowed Angel – Rev. 10	The likeness of four living creatures – Ezek. 1
v 1 - "mighty angel"	v 24 – "when they went... the noise... as the voice of the Almighty"
v 1 – "come down from heaven"	v 1, 4 – "the heavens were opened... a whirlwind came out of the north"
v 1 – "clothed with a cloud"	v 4 – "a great cloud"
v 1 – "a rainbow *was* upon his head"	v 26, 28 – "above the firmament that was over their heads... as the appearance of a bow that is in the cloud in the day of rain"
v 1 – "his face *was* as it were the sun"	v 27, 28 – " I saw as it were the appearance of fire, and it had brightness round about... so *was* the appearance of the brightness"
v1 – "his feet as pillars of fire"	v 7 – "their feet... sparkled like the colour of burnished brass" v 13, 14 – "the living creatures, their appearance *was* like burning coals of fire... and out of the fire went forth lightning... a flash of lightning"
v 2 – "he set his right foot upon the sea, and *his* left *foot* upon the earth" (i.e. dominion)	v 26 – "the likeness of a throne" (i.e. dominion)
v 3 – "a loud voice, as *when* a lion roareth"	v 10 – "face of a lion" v 24 – "the noise of great waters, as... the voice of speech, as the noise of an host"

The similarities in the symbols employed in connection with the four living creatures and the Rainbowed Angel are self-evident. In both cases the symbol of the rainbow is used; both have the figure of the

The Rainbowed Angel and other related symbolic visions of the redeemed saints
cloud; and both present the idea of a multitude of people using the linked symbols of the noise, voice and great waters. They both speak to us of the cloud of witnesses redeemed by God's covenant and mercy. That cloud of witnesses is represented respectively, in these passages, by the four living creatures and by the mighty angel with the rainbow upon his head.

Lest we be in any doubt that these are indeed symbols of the redeemed saints in their future glory, we can link Ezekiel 1 with the Apocalypse and get a very precise definition. The "four living creatures" of Ezekiel 1 are clearly the cherubim, since they have the same four faces as the cherubim; those of a lion, an ox, a man, and an eagle. Similarly there are "four beasts" in Revelation 4 and 5. "Beasts" here translates the Greek word *zoon*, which simply means 'a living creature'. (A totally different Greek word is used to describe the grotesque, wild beasts with many heads and horns in later chapters in Revelation.) The Apocalyptic living creatures have the same four faces (Rev. 4:7). They also sing a new song, the words of which identify them unambiguously.

> "Thou art worthy to take the book, and to open the seals thereof: for thou wast slain, and hast **redeemed us** to God by thy blood out of every kindred, and tongue, and people, and nation; and hast made us unto our God kings and priests: and we shall reign on the earth" (Rev. 5:9-10).

The living creatures or cherubim represent the redeemed saints in immortal glory. In a sense, that is the most concise summary of the meaning of Ezekiel 1. Given that this is so, and noting in connection with it the exposition we have already given of the resurrection process in Daniel 10, the next words that follow in Ezekiel are very significant to our theme. In a parable of resurrection when lying on the ground, Daniel was commanded to stand up, and was strengthened. The next chapter in Ezekiel opens with a similar scene.

> "When I saw *it* (i.e. the vision of the four living creatures in all its detail), I fell upon my face, and I heard a voice of one that spake. And he said unto me, Son of man, stand upon thy feet, and I will speak unto thee. And the spirit entered into me when he spake unto me, and set me upon my feet, that I heard him that spake unto me. And he said unto me, Son of man, I send thee to the children of Israel, to a rebellious nation that hath rebelled against me: they and

their fathers have transgressed against me, *even* unto this very day" (Ezek. 1:28 - 2:3).

Like Daniel, Ezekiel experiences a symbolic resurrection. Now it is clear that on one level these words fit clearly in to the historic context of Ezekiel's day. He was being sent to prophesy to rebellious Israel and Judah at the time of the Babylonian invasion. However, given that this opening to chapter 2 immediately follows the vision of chapter 1, and indeed is directly linked to the prophet's reaction to that vision, it would seem that maybe there is a deeper lesson. We suggest that we are being told that one of the roles of the Rainbowed Angel is to go to "the children of Israel… a rebellious nation".

In our suggested chronological sequence in Table 1 we have placed the Ezekiel 1 element of the role of the Rainbowed Angel after Zechariah 14. There, Israel is delivered from the Gentile invaders, by "Yahweh my Elohim… and all the saints". This deliverance is paralleled in Zechariah 12, where God seeks "to destroy all the nations that come against Jerusalem" (verse 9). This is followed by national repentance in Israel as they recognise Jesus of Nazareth, whom their forefathers rejected and crucified, as their Deliverer.

> "I will pour upon the house of David, and upon the inhabitants of Jerusalem, the spirit of grace and of supplications: and they shall look upon me whom they have pierced, and they shall mourn for him, as one mourneth for *his* only *son*, and shall be in bitterness for him, as one that is in bitterness for *his* firstborn" (Zech. 12:10).

In Ezekiel's day the nation was in a similar position. They had already succumbed to the Babylonians, at least to the first phase of the Babylonian captivity, for when Ezekiel saw the vision of the four living creatures he was "among the captives by the river of Chebar" (1:1). The prophet's role was to seek to induce repentance in the nation, and to recognise in Yahweh their only possible Deliverer. Thus also, when Ezekiel's opening vision is seen in its latter day context, it seems to speak of the Rainbowed Angel playing a role in inducing that repentance outlined by Zechariah, as they acknowledge who it is that has delivered them from Gog. Once that part of their work is accomplished, they then move on to conquer and destroy the apostasy. This is the work that is set out in the next section.

The Rainbowed Angel and other related symbolic visions of the redeemed saints
The ancient of days and one like the Son of Man – Daniel 7

We now come to the final phase of the career of the Rainbowed Angel as identified in the links with other Scriptures as set out in Table 1. This is the removal of the dominion of Daniel's fourth beast power, along with its little horn. The Papal apostasy and the political systems associated with it are to be consumed and destroyed. We are familiar with the identity of the fourth beast of Daniel's vision in chapter 7 of his prophecy as Rome. From Rome arises a "little horn… in this horn were eyes like the eyes of a man, and a mouth speaking great things" (Dan. 7:8). It is not the place in this study to demonstrate by a detailed exposition that this fourth beast is indeed Rome, and that the little horn is the Papacy. It is sufficient to note that the fourth beast is parallel with the legs of iron in the image of Nebuchadnezzar's dream and that the fourth beast has "great iron teeth" (v 7), in order to identify it with Rome. Similarly, since the little horn that emerges from this fourth beast is arrogant, and persecutes the saints for a time (verses 21, 22), we have more than adequate grounds for identifying the little horn as the Papacy.

Our earlier considerations have identified the Rainbowed Angel with the "*one* like unto the Son of Man" of Revelation 1:13. It is therefore clear that when we encounter "*one* like the Son of Man" in Daniel 7:13, we are looking at the same symbol, and probably with the same meaning. This same vision in Daniel 7 also presents "the Ancient of days" (verse 9), before whom the "*one* like the Son of Man" is brought. The Ancient of days is the Lord Jesus Christ in person, and in his glory; the one "whose goings forth *have been* from of old, from everlasting" (Mic. 5:2). These two elements of the vision therefore need to be considered together. The "Ancient of days" and the "*one* like the Son of Man" represent respectively, Christ, and the body of glorified saints. They are collectively represented by the Rainbowed Angel. Thus, when considering links between Revelation 10 and Daniel 7 we need to consider both the "Ancient of days" and the "*one* like the Son of man" in Daniel to get a full picture.

Table 7 – The Rainbowed Angel and Daniel 7

The mighty angel with a rainbow on his head (Rev. 10)	Daniel 7
v 1 – "clothed with a cloud"	v 9 – "the Ancient of days… whose garment *was* white as snow"
v 1 – "his feet as pillars of fire"	v 9 – "the Ancient of days… his wheels as burning fire"
v 1 – "(came) down from heaven clothed with a cloud"	v 13 – "*one* like the Son of Man of man came with the clouds of heaven"
v 2 – "he set his right foot upon the sea, and *his* left *foot* on the earth"	v 14, 27 - "There was given him dominion, and glory, and a kingdom, that all people, nations, and languages, should serve him: his dominion *is* an everlasting dominion, which shall not pass away, and his kingdom *that* which shall not be destroyed… the kingdom and dominion, and the greatness of the kingdom under the whole heaven, shall be given to the people of the saints of the most High, whose kingdom *is* an everlasting kingdom, and all dominions shall serve and obey him."

Having therefore established that the Rainbowed Angel is indicated in Daniel 7 by the symbols used there, we can now learn more from this chapter about his work. Firstly we see an innumerable multitude appear before the Ancient of days at the judgment seat.

> "A fiery stream issued and came forth from before him: thousand thousands ministered unto him, and ten thousand times ten thousand stood before him: the judgment was set, and the books were opened" (Dan. 7:10).

From this process of judgment emerges the body of redeemed saints ("*one* like the Son of man"). They are now presented to Christ, and as a body are invested with power and authority over the nations. The relevant verses are worth quoting again in full to establish this point.

The Rainbowed Angel and other related symbolic visions of the redeemed saints

> "I saw in the night visions, and, behold, *one* like the Son of man came with the clouds of heaven, and came to the Ancient of days, and they brought him near before him. And there was given him dominion, and glory, and a kingdom, that all people, nations, and languages, should serve him: his dominion *is* an everlasting dominion, which shall not pass away, and his kingdom *that* which shall not be destroyed" (Dan. 7:13-14).

May we emphasize that we believe that the "him" in these verses, which refers to the "*one* like the Son of man" is the Rainbowed Angel. Daniel is then given quite a detailed explanation of the vision to relieve his mind that was grieved and troubled at what he had seen. This explanation shows that what is actually the Rainbowed Angel removes and destroys the fourth beast and little horn, and becomes the single dominant power in the earth as the Kingdom of God is established. It is interesting that the focus of this phase of judgment carried out by the Rainbowed Angel will be on overcoming the little horn power of the apostasy.

> "I beheld, and the same (i.e. little) horn made war with the saints, and prevailed against them; until the Ancient of days came, and judgment was given to the saints of the most High; and the time came that the saints possessed the kingdom... But the judgment shall sit, and they shall take away his (i.e. the little horn's) dominion, to consume and to destroy *it* unto the end. And the kingdom and dominion, and the greatness of the kingdom under the whole heaven, shall be given to the people of the saints of the most High, whose kingdom *is* an everlasting kingdom, and all dominions shall serve and obey Him" (Dan. 7:21, 22, 26, 27).

This is a powerful vision that provides encouragement and motivation to the saints during their mortal probation, to the end that by God's grace, even we, who now sojourn as in a strange land, might attain to that future blessing and glory.

Consistent symbols

Thus far in this chapter we have compared the vision of the mighty Rainbowed Angel of Revelation 10 with a number of parallel visions in other parts of Scripture, showing how they present successive phases of the work of the multitudinous Christ. In drawing this section to a conclusion it is worth considering how, in considerable detail, the same

ideas and figures are threaded through each of the passages that we
have identified as being parallel to Revelation 10.

Table 8 – Daniel – Ezekiel – Revelation links

Ezekiel 1	Revelation 1	Daniel 10	Daniel 7
v 13, 14, 27 – "burning coals of fire… lamps… lightning"	v 14 – "eyes… as a flame of fire"	v 6 – "face as the appearance of lightning… eyes as lamps of fire"	v 9 – "fiery flame… wheels… burning fire"
v 15, 16 "wheels… beryl"		v 6 – "body… like the beryl"	v 9 – "wheels"
v 7 – "feet… colour of burnished brass"	v 15 – "feet like unto fine brass… burned in a furnace"	v 6 – "arms… feet like in colour to polished brass"	
v 28 – "bow… in the cloud"			v 13 – "clouds of heaven"
v 24 – "noise of great waters… voice of speech… noise of an host"	v 15 – "voice as the sound of many waters"		
v 26 – "throne"			v 9 – "throne"
	v 13 – "clothed with a garment down to the foot"	v 5 – "clothed in linen, *whose* loins were girded"	v 9 – "garment *was* white as snow"
	v 13 – "girt… golden girdle"	v 5 – "girded with fine gold"	
2:1,2 – [resurrection symbolized]	v 17 – 18 [resurrection symbolized]	v 10, 11, 15 – 19 – [resurrection symbolized]	
v 5 – "likeness of a man" v 26 – "appearance of a man"	v 13 – "*one* like unto the Son of man"	v 5 – "a certain man"	v 9 – "Ancient of days" v 13 – "*one* like the Son of man"

42

The Rainbowed Angel and other related symbolic visions of the redeemed saints

The consistency of the symbols is both remarkable and instructive. It is one of those confirmations of the Divine inspiration of Scripture that the Bible student repeatedly finds. But most importantly for our study, each vision is focussed on a symbolic man who represents a multitude, the company of redeemed saints. This symbolic man is parallel with the "mighty angel (who comes) down from heaven,,, (and who has) a rainbow… upon his head" (Rev. 10:1). The way in which the same symbols appear in all these passages leads us to an inevitable conclusion; that each vision is giving us a perspective on that same cloud of witnesses.

But one question remains. If each vision does indeed represent essentially the same thing, why has the Father revealed it repeatedly, and with such variety? We believe that this variety is not an indication of inconsistency or uncertainty. The repetition, along with the variety, is the Almighty's way of helping feeble mortal minds to grasp something of the depth and wisdom of the Divine mind, which cannot be portrayed in just a few words or a handful of metaphors. Furthermore, as we have seen, these different visions, although applying essentially to the same thing, reveal it to us from a variety of different perspectives. They show, as we have argued, the different, and to some extent, successive phases of the work of the Rainbowed Angel following its investiture with Divine power at the judgment seat.

> "For My thoughts *are* not your thoughts, neither *are* your ways My ways, saith the LORD. For *as* the heavens are higher than the earth, so are My ways higher than your ways, and My thoughts than your thoughts" (Isa. 55:8-9).

> "O the depth of the riches both of the wisdom and knowledge of God! How unsearchable *are* His judgments, and His ways past finding out!" (Rom. 11:33).

Chapter 4 – Thou didst march through the land in indignation

Introduction

In our study so far we have considered the vision of Revelation 10, and identified the Rainbowed Angel there as a symbol of the resurrected and immortalised saints. We have then seen how this same body of glorified saints is represented in other related visions in Scripture. These each share similar detailed symbols, indicating that the one who is the substance of the vision is this same glorified throng. We have also noted that the other visions are not identical in every respect. This we have suggested points to slightly different chronological phases of the career of the Rainbowed Angel. However, despite these different perspectives, there is no doubt that each vision deals with the glorified multitude of the saints, along with the King of kings, the Lord Jesus Christ, as "Lord of lords, and King of kings" (Rev. 17:14).

How do we know the Rainbowed Angel marches through the land?

We now change our focus to begin the consideration of the "march" of the Rainbowed Angel; that is to say the progressive stages of his Divinely ordained work. There are indeed various progressive stages to this march. We shall endeavour to place them in a logical and coherent sequence, based on Scriptural evidence. It must however be acknowledged that it is not always possible to decide conclusively on the chronological order of the relevant passages of Scripture, though we are sure that the overall concept is sound. As Bro. Thomas commented; "different prophets in vision have seen him (i.e. the Rainbowed Angel) approaching Jerusalem at different stages of his work" (Thomas 1909, p. 544-545).

Next, it is perhaps fair to ask if this concept of a "march" is indeed Scriptural. The question needs to be asked not least because of the military connotations to the idea of a "march", as of an army.

The starting point for the answer to this question is in Habakkuk 3. Some details of Habakkuk 3 are discussed later in this chapter, and again in chapter 7. Collectively the evidence is quite clear. Habakkuk 3 concerns the work of the Rainbowed Angel.

44

Thou didst march through the land in indignation

For the moment we wish simply to demonstrate, starting with this chapter, that the concept of a "march" is Scriptural and valid. The prophet states explicitly:-

"Thou didst march through the land in indignation, thou didst thresh the heathen in anger" (Hab. 3:12).

"Thou" refers both to "God" (Heb. *Eloah*) from verse 3, and "LORD" (Heb. *Yahweh*) from verse 8. It is clear from the context that both these terms refer to the same being. Verses 3-7 describe the work of judgment that *Eloah* is engaged upon. Then, in verse 8, the prophet enquires whether "Yahweh" was displeased to cause Him to carry out the judgments written. Thus *Eloah* and *Yahweh* here are identical with each other. *Yahweh*, meaning 'He (who) shall be", and *Eloah,* meaning 'the Mighty One' (an emphatic form of *Ail*) refer to the Lord Jesus Christ. He was the personal fulfilment of the prophecy embodied in the *Yahweh* Name, and was **the particular** Mighty One, hence the title *Eloah*. This seems to be confirmed by the next phrase which further qualifies "God" in verse 3 as "the Holy One".

The Holy One, the Lord Jesus Christ, is the "Word… made flesh" (Jno. 1:14). But this personal manifestation of the Father in His Son was not the completion of His purpose to manifest Himself. The completion will be manifestation in a multitude, signified by Yahweh Elohim; 'He (Who) shall be mighty ones'. This is one of the great themes of Scripture. Picking up the language of Habakkuk regarding the "Holy One", we can trace this theme through just one sample passage.

"For the LORD *is* our defence; and the Holy One of Israel *is* our king. Then Thou spakest in vision to Thy holy one, and saidst, I have laid help upon *one that is* mighty; I have exalted *one* chosen out of the people. I have found David My servant; with My holy oil have I anointed him: with whom My hand shall be established: Mine arm also shall strengthen him… Also I will make him *My* firstborn, higher than the kings of the earth… His seed also will I make *to endure* for ever, and his throne as the days of heaven… Once have I sworn by My holiness that I will not lie unto David. His seed shall endure for ever, and his throne as the sun before Me." (Psa. 89:18-21,27,29,35-36).

The process is clear. Yahweh chooses, anoints, and strengthens His Holy One, who himself has an everlasting seed. That multitudinous seed is the Rainbowed Angel, and is here in Habakkuk 3.

Eloah may be identified as the leader of this host in Habakkuk 3. This is not stated explicitly, but is implied by the statement "Thou didst march through the land"; a statement more naturally applicable to an army rather than an individual. The fact that he does in fact lead an army "from Teman, and… from mount Paran" (verse 3) will become clear below when we examine the links between this passage and Deuteronomy 33.

First, note the fact that it is clear from Habakkuk 3 that this is a military style expedition as the Almighty executes His righteous judgments on the nations. Verse 12 already quoted uses Armageddon language, as the heathen are threshed (Armageddon meaning, in the Hebrew tongue, 'a heap of sheaves in a valley for judgment', with the implication that the judgment figuratively involves threshing). In addition, the succession of following verbs reinforces the concept that this is an army on the march.

"Thou wentest forth…Thou woundest… Thou didst strike through… they (i.e. the enemy) came out as a whirlwind to scatter me… (but) Thou didst walk through the sea…" verses 13-15).

The question may be posed as to whether it is appropriate or correct to view this "march" in this way, if it involves the Rainbowed Angel; that is Christ and the immortal saints. Given our understanding of the commands of Christ that as his disciples we should not involve ourselves in military service, is it really plausible that the saints in the future will have this kind of role? We believe that it is not only plausible, but that it is what the Scriptures reveal. Whilst the law of God for his people has always been that they should not kill, driven by personal animosity and hatred, there have been times in the past when the servants of God have specifically been required to kill God's enemies. Saul's example is perhaps sufficient to illustrate this. He was rebuked and condemned by God through Samuel for not slaying Agag, king of the Amalekites. God had told Saul, "Go and utterly destroy the sinners the Amalekites" (1 Sam. 15:18), but "Saul and the people spared Agag" (verse 9). At the present time, Christ's disciples are unambiguously commanded not to kill, for he himself instructed that "all they that take the sword shall perish with the sword" (Matt. 26:52). But it is also clear

46

Thou didst march through the land in indignation

from Scripture that there is a time coming when the immortal saints with Christ will be required to carry out righteous judgment in order to "destroy the sinners" (Isa. 13:9) out of the earth. The crucial point here is that it will be **righteous** judgment, which can only be enacted by the saints once they are made immortal. Only by this means will righteousness prevail, and will God's glory fill the earth.

The words of the Psalmist are relevant at this point.

> "Let the saints be joyful in glory: let them sing aloud upon their beds. *Let* the high *praises* of God *be* in their mouth, and a two-edged sword in their hand; to execute vengeance upon the heathen, *and* punishments upon the people; to bind their kings with chains, and their nobles with fetters of iron; to execute upon them the judgment written: this honour have all his saints. Praise ye Yah" (Psa. 149:5-9).

The words are self-explanatory, even though those with pacifist inclinations may work at putting another meaning on them. It is significant that this passage occurs in one of the last five Psalms, all of which have a kingdom theme and setting, and all of which begin and end with the words "Praise ye Yah*"*, that is, 'Hallelujah'. This work of the Rainbowed Angel is one vital part of enabling the earth to be filled with the glory of Yahweh.

A mighty warrior with a mission

The Rainbowed Angel has been described (Thomas 1909, p. 537; but see whole section pp. 533-570) as "a strong and mighty warrior prepared for combat". In addition to the exposition above there are other passages that confirm this concept. Yahweh Himself is described as a "man of war" (Exo. 15:3) by Moses in relation to the exodus from Egypt. The Lord Jesus Christ is of course the personal manifestation of Yahweh. He is the bridegroom from heaven, and is presented elsewhere in the Psalms in a military aspect.

> "In them hath he set a tabernacle for the sun, Which *is* as a bridegroom coming out of his chamber, *and* rejoiceth as a strong man to run a race" (Psa. 19:4,5).

The Hebrew for "strong man" here is *gibbor*, which has the sense of a "'mighty warrior'. The link to the "bridegroom" here points to Christ, and this is confirmed by the use of this word elsewhere in relation to God manifest in Christ ("the mighty God" – Heb. *Ail gibbor*; Isa. 9:6). The context of Psalm 19 suggests that in prophetic terms it relates to the preaching of the "everlasting gospel" (that is, the gospel preached in the Millennial age) demanding submission of the nations to the righteous rule of Christ (cf. Rev. 14:6,7).

> "His (the bridegroom's) going forth *is* from the end of the heaven, and his circuit unto the ends of it: and there is nothing hid from the heat thereof. The law of Yahweh *is* perfect, converting the soul: the testimony of Yahweh *is* sure, making wise the simple" (Psa. 19:6,7).

The "strong man" is therefore probably the Rainbowed Angel, the multitudinous Christ man. Although described here as a "bridegroom", the earlier verses of the Psalm state that there is a multitudinous aspect. "The heavens (plural) declare the glory of God... their (plural) line is gone out through all the earth (that is, the everlasting gospel)" (Psa. 19:1,4).

It is worth pausing here to consider the word "bridegroom" and its associations. The Hebrew word for the "chamber" in Psalm 19:5 is *chuppah*, defined by the OLB lexicon as "canopy, chamber, closet, Divine protection". Joel also uses it in a context that gives Scriptural support to this definition by using it alongside another Hebrew word (*cheder*) that refers specifically to the bridegroom's chamber.

> "Gather the people, sanctify the congregation, assemble the elders, gather the children, and those that suck the breasts: let the bridegroom go forth of his chamber (*cheder*), and the bride out of her closet (*chuppah*)" (Joel 2:16).

So when Psalm 19 refers to the bridegroom going forth out of the bride's chamber (*chuppah*) the marriage has clearly taken place. So here is the multitudinous Christ-man, the bridegroom from heaven, united to his ecclesial bride, going forth as the Rainbowed Angel. The Hebrew word *chuppah* is only used on one other occasion, where it is translated as "defence".

> "It shall come to pass, *that he that is* left in Zion, and *he that* remaineth in Jerusalem, shall be called holy, *even* every one that is written among the living in Jerusalem: when the Lord shall have washed away the filth of the daughters of Zion, and shall have

Thou didst march through the land in indignation

> purged the blood of Jerusalem from the midst thereof by the spirit of
> judgment, and by the spirit of burning. And Yahweh will create upon
> every dwelling place of mount Zion, and upon her assemblies, a
> cloud and smoke by day, and the shining of a flaming fire by night:
> for upon all the glory *shall be* a defence" (Isa. 4:3-5).

This seems to relate to the time when the Rainbowed Angel has
completed his work to deliver the remnant of natural Israel from the
invader and occupier of their land. Jerusalem is now cleansed, and
defended by the presence of the Rainbowed Angel, like a bride
protected in her closet or under her canopy, ready for her marriage. It
is as if this remnant is being prepared ultimately to become part of
Christ's bride. Interestingly the chapter begins by referring to "seven
women" in Zion taking hold of "one man", which is presumably the
multitudinous Christ-man. The fact that the following verses refer to the
"branch of Yahweh (being) beautiful and glorious" (Isa. 4:1-2) seems to
confirm this interpretation.

It is also worth commenting at this point on the fact that the Rainbowed
Angel is described as just that, an "angel"; that is, a messenger, sent
with a Divine mission. That mission is to preach the everlasting gospel,
and to bring the nations into submission before the King of kings. This
will be the work and destiny of the saints working with Christ following
the completion of the Judgment.

> "The saints of the most High shall take the kingdom, and possess
> the kingdom for ever, even for ever and ever... And the kingdom
> and dominion, and the greatness of the kingdom under the whole
> heaven, shall be given to the people of the saints of the most High,
> whose kingdom *is* an everlasting kingdom, and all dominions shall
> serve and obey him" (Dan. 7:18,27).

> "And the seventh angel sounded; and there were great voices in
> heaven, saying, The kingdoms of this world are become *the
> kingdoms* of our Lord, and of his Christ; and he shall reign for ever
> and ever" (Rev. 11:15).

A multitude of saints will be on this march

This fact may be established by linking Habakkuk 3 with Deuteronomy
33. The first key point is the fact that both passages deal with the same
geographical area. Note also that Habakkuk states that at the start of

His march, "God (*Eloah*) came from **Teman**, and the Holy One from mount **Paran**" (verse 3). We must also remind ourselves, as discussed earlier, that God or Eloah is also described as Yahweh later in Habakkuk 3. Thus the link with Deuteronomy 33 becomes clear.

> "The LORD (*Yahweh)* came from **Sinai**, and rose up from **Seir** unto them; He shined forth from mount **Paran**, and He came with ten thousands of saints: from His right hand *went* a fiery law for them" (Deut. 33:2).

Teman, Paran, and Seir are all in the north eastern part of the Sinai peninsula, to the south and south-west of the Dead Sea (see map on page 91). So both passages are speaking of Yahweh with His saints coming from the same geographical area towards the land of Israel, from which "He shall thrust out the enemy" (verse 27). This passage also confirms what we deduced from Habakkuk; that Yahweh will appear from Sinai in multitudinous manifestation, with "ten thousands of saints". "He will be" not just Eloah, the Mighty One, and the Holy One, that is the Lord Jesus Christ, but also a host of saints, His mighty ones or Elohim.

We shall return to Deuteronomy 33 in more detail later in this study. For now it is sufficient to note, and to reiterate, that this "march" of the Rainbowed Angel involves both the Lord Jesus Christ and the multitude of his glorified saints. As a unified body they will emerge from the judgment at Sinai to establish the throne of the Lord in Zion.

March of Rainbowed Angel typed at the Exodus

This leads us neatly, for the first time, to Psalm 68, where once again in a similar context, we find a multitude on a march.

> "O God, when Thou wentest forth before Thy people, when Thou didst march through the wilderness" (Psa. 68:7).

Clearly, Habakkuk 3 is echoing these words when the prophet says

> "Thou wentest forth for the salvation of Thy people" (verse 13).

In Psalm 68:7, "God" translates the Hebrew "*Elohim*", a plural word meaning "mighty ones". This in turn connects with Deuteronomy 33.

Thou didst march through the land in indignation

There Yahweh appears as a multitude, with "ten thousands of saints", who may be identified with the Elohim of the Psalm.

Having established therefore the identity of context between Habakkuk 3, Deuteronomy 33 and Psalm 68, we will now examine the links between Psalm 68 and the exodus. These show that the exodus from Egypt to Canaan was in fact a type of the 'exodus' of the saints from mortality at Sinai, to inherit the things promised to Abraham, as immortal beings.

The key to understanding this type is the fact that the opening words of Psalm 68 are a quotation from the words of Moses concerning the setting forward and the resting of the ark. The Psalm begins:

> "Let God arise, let his enemies be scattered: let them also that hate Him flee before Him" (Psa. 68:1).

These are originally recorded as words of Moses.

> "It came to pass, when the ark set forward, that Moses said, Rise up, LORD, and let Thine enemies be scattered; and let them that hate Thee flee before Thee. And when it rested, he said, Return, O LORD, unto the many thousands of Israel" (Num. 10:35-36).

Though there is no record of God instructing Moses to utter these words when the ark moved or rested, it is difficult to imagine that they were not commanded by God. The context in which they were initially spoken is given by earlier words in Numbers 10.

> "It came to pass on the twentieth *day* of the second month, in the second year, that the cloud was taken up from off the tabernacle of the testimony. And the children of Israel took their journeys out of the wilderness of Sinai; and the cloud rested in the wilderness of Paran... And they departed from the mount of the LORD three days' journey: and the ark of the covenant of the LORD went before them in the three days' journey, to search out a resting place for them. And the cloud of the LORD *was* upon them by day, when they went out of the camp" (verses 11,12,33,34).

This was the first time that the host of Israel had moved from Sinai since they initially arrived there shortly after departure from Egypt. They had been there since the third month of the first year; that is from about six to eight weeks after leaving Egypt (cf. Exo.19:1). During that period of almost a year at Sinai they had received the Law from Yahweh through Moses; they had constructed the tabernacle; they had been constituted "a peculiar treasure unto (Yahweh) above all people… a kingdom of priests, and an holy nation" (Exo. 19:5, 6), and the visible glory of God had begun to dwell among them (cf. Exo. 40:34, 38). It was now time for them to break camp and to march to their promised inheritance, the land of Canaan, which was only a relatively short journey.

"(*There are* eleven days' *journey* from Horeb by the way of mount Seir unto Kadeshbarnea.)" (Deut. 1:2).

But sadly, due to the lack of faith in the ten spies and the nation who heard their report, the nation was condemned to wander in the wilderness until that faithless generation perished. What should have been an eleven day journey took thirty eight years!

The important point to emphasize here is that by quoting from Numbers 10 in this way, the inspired writer of Psalm 68 is using the wilderness march of the children of Israel as a type of the march of a host that is still future. We believe that this future application concerns the march of the Rainbowed Angel, the host of saints as they appear in the earth after approval at the judgment seat.

It is worth at this point re-visiting the logic by which we have connected Habakkuk 3 with the Rainbowed Angel. The march to war in Habakkuk 3 is led by Eloah, the Mighty One. This leader is also called Yahweh in the chapter, a Name prophetic of a future manifestation of the Deity. The language of Habakkuk 3 implies that the Mighty One is leading an army. Whilst not stated explicitly within the chapter, the fact that this is so is confirmed by the close connection with Deuteronomy 33. Both chapters mention some of the same geographical locations, and also mention others in the same area. Since Deuteronomy 33 does explicitly mention a multitude, "ten thousands of saints", we are able safely to conclude that Habakkuk 3 is indeed speaking of the Rainbowed Angel; the redeemed saints led by Christ. Psalm 68 also has similar language about the march of a multitude, so we are also able to conclude that the Psalm is speaking of the Rainbowed Angel. This in turn leads us to understanding the wilderness journey of Israel from Sinai to Canaan as a type of the march of the Rainbowed Angel, due to the way in which Psalm 68 quotes from Numbers 10.

Thou didst march through the land in indignation

We shall examine the detailed outworking of the prophetic type in Psalm 68 in the next chapter. We will conclude this chapter by noting some spiritual, prophetic allusions back in Numbers 10. The relevant verses have already been quoted but bear repetition.

> "It came to pass, when the ark set forward, that Moses said, Rise up, Yahweh, and let Thine enemies be scattered; and let them that hate Thee flee before Thee. And when it rested, he said, Return, O Yahweh, unto the many thousands of Israel" (Num. 10:35-36).

The "ark" represents the Lord Jesus Christ. It contained the two tables of stone with the ten commandments (the word made flesh), a pot of hidden manna that did not corrupt (the bread of eternal life), and Aaron's rod that budded (representing resurrection). Over it was the Mercy Seat (Christ is our mercy seat), over which, between the cherubim, dwelt the glory of God (Christ was the personal dwelling place of the glory of God – "He that hath seen me hath seen the Father" (Jno. 14:9)).

When the ark set forward, Moses was to say "rise up, Yahweh". The Hebrew for "rise up" is a common word (koom). However it is used prophetically of resurrection in a Messianic context, as for example, in the promises to David; "I will raise up thy seed after thee" (1 Chron. 17:11). This word has various shades of meaning, even in a prophetic context. In the 2 Samuel 7 record of the promise to David it is also translated "set up" (verse 12) concerning David's seed, and "establish" (verse 25) concerning his house. It is probably not unreasonable to see a Messianic connection in Numbers 10, and therefore also in Psalm 68:1, where it is translated "arise".

Back in Numbers 10:35, Moses's words are addressed to God; "rise up, Yahweh". Interestingly, when these words are quoted in the Psalm, Yahweh becomes Elohim; "Let God arise" (verse 1). This is yet another confirmation that in its prophetic sense the words of Psalm 68 refer to a multitude; the multitudinous manifestation of Yahweh in His Mighty Ones, the redeemed saints.

Finally in this context, is the word "return" used by Moses when the ark rested.

> "Return, O Yahweh, unto the many thousands of Israel" (Num. 10:36).

Once again, this is a common word, but may possibly have a connotation of the second coming of Christ. However this is less certain, since these words are not quoted in Psalm 68.

Conclusion

In summary we believe that the reference in Psalm 68 to a "march" refers to the march of the Rainbowed Angel. Further, because the Psalm opens with a quotation from Numbers 10 regarding the marching of Israel in the wilderness, we also believe that the Psalm is telling us that those events concerning Israel in the wilderness are a type of the creation of the Rainbowed Angel.

Based on Psalm 68 we shall now go on to consider the very clear indications that the judgment seat will take place at Sinai.

Chapter 5 - The judgment seat at Sinai

Introduction

We have learned from the foregoing exposition that:-

- Deuteronomy 33, Habakkuk 3, and Psalm 68 all refer to the Rainbowed Angel
- As Deuteronomy 33 and Habakkuk 3 both refer to Sinai along with other places between Sinai and the southern border of Israel, they both refer to the emergence of the Rainbowed Angel from Sinai
- Psalm 68 also refers to Sinai, both explicitly (as we shall see below), and implicitly in that it opens with a quotation from Numbers 10 concerning Israel's departure from Sinai.

We therefore conclude that it appears that the Scriptures are teaching us that the judgment of the saints will be at Sinai, from where those who will be justified and immortalised will emerge, along with the Lord Jesus Christ. Together they will constitute the Rainbowed Angel, to be revealed to the world initially for judgment, as the seven thunders of Revelation 10 sound forth. We also conclude that the wilderness journey of the children of Israel from Sinai to Canaan is presented as a type of the march of the Rainbowed Angel. In this chapter we shall present a range of further evidence from Psalm 68, to demonstrate that these conclusions are indeed well founded.

Psalm 68 based on a type

Apart from the obvious evidence of a type provided by the quotation from Numbers 10 in Psalm 68, there are other clear links between the Psalm and the record of the exodus from Egypt. Consider the following record of Israel at Sinai.

"It came to pass on the third day in the morning, that there were thunders and lightnings, and a thick cloud upon the mount, and the voice of the trumpet exceeding loud; so that all the people that *was* in the camp trembled... And mount Sinai was altogether on a smoke, because Yahweh descended upon it in fire: and the smoke thereof ascended as the smoke of a furnace, and the whole mount quaked greatly. And when the voice of the trumpet sounded long, and waxed louder and louder, Moses spake, and God answered him by a voice. And the LORD came down upon mount Sinai, on the top of the mount: and the LORD called Moses *up* to the top of the mount; and Moses went up" (Exo. 19:16, 18-20).

With the nation encamped at Sinai, the fearful presence of their God was revealed to Israel, as the mountain quaked and burned, and as the voice of Yahweh sounded forth like a trumpet. He called Moses up the mount, and Moses obediently ascended.

It is striking how precisely Psalm 68 picks up all these points in allusions to Exodus 19 that cannot be mistaken.

"The earth shook, the heavens also dropped at the presence of God: *even* Sinai itself *was moved* at the presence of God, the God of Israel… Why leap ye, ye high hills? *this is* the hill *which* God desireth to dwell in; yea, Yahweh will dwell *in it* for ever. The chariots of God *are* twenty thousand, *even* thousands of angels: the Lord *is* among them, *as in* Sinai, in the holy *place*. Thou hast ascended on high, thou hast led captivity captive: thou hast received gifts for men; yea, *for* the rebellious also, that Yah Elohim might dwell *among them*" (Psa. 68:8,16-18).

The earthquake, the fearful presence of God Himself, the multitude that were present to witness these things, and the ascent of Moses up the mount are all picked up by the Psalmist. It is also fascinating to note that the Psalmist also picks up obliquely the four-square encampment of Israel, the order of which was established at Sinai, as recorded in Numbers 2.

"There *is* little Benjamin *with* their ruler, the princes of Judah *and* their council, the princes of Zebulun, *and* the princes of Naphtali. Thy God hath commanded thy strength: strengthen, O God, that which thou hast wrought for us" (Psa. 68:27-28).

Judah was the leading tribe in the eastern camp, which also included Zebulun. Benjamin was part of the western camp, headed by Ephraim. Likewise Naphtali was part of the northern camp headed by Dan. None of the members of the southern camp, Reuben, Simeon, and Gad, are named. However, there does seem to be a definite allusion to Reuben, to complete the picture. In Jacob's blessing on Reuben, he stated;

> "Reuben, thou *art* my firstborn, my might, and the beginning of my strength, the excellency of dignity, and the excellency of power" (Gen. 49:3).

The Hebrew for "power" is almost identical to that for "strength" in Psalm 68:28. The word in the Psalm is also repeated three times at the end of the Psalm.

> "Ascribe ye **strength** unto God: His excellency *is* over Israel, and His **strength** *is* in the clouds. O God, T*hou art* terrible out of Thy holy places: the God of Israel *is* He that giveth **strength** and power unto *His* people. Blessed *be* God" (Psa. 68:34-35).

The evidence is thus compelling that in Psalm 68 we have a picture of Israel at Sinai.

Psalm 68 as a prophecy

The evidence for Psalm 68 as a prophecy will steadily accumulate as we proceed with our exposition, and indeed is implied anyway by the fact that it is based on the type of the exodus. But it is worth bringing out some of the prophetic elements at this point in order to establish the principle.

The link between Exodus 19 and Psalm 68 has already been noted. Twice in the quotation made from Exodus 19 there is a reference to the sound of the trumpet. This is referred to in the New Testament as the sound that will call all those who are responsible, alive or dead, to the judgment (even though it may be a sound inaudible to the world at large).

> "For the Lord himself shall descend from heaven with a shout, with the voice of the archangel, and with the trump of God: and the dead in Christ shall rise first" (1 Thess. 4:16).

Given the Exodus 19 – Psalm 68 link it can therefore be concluded on this basis also that Psalm 68 has to do with the judgment seat of Christ.

Further, some verses of Psalm 68 can only be completely fulfilled in relation to the redeemed and glorified saints.

"But let the righteous be glad; let them rejoice before God: yea, let them exceedingly rejoice... The chariots of God *are* twenty thousand, *even* thousands of angels: the Lord *is* among them, *as in* Sinai, in the holy *place*... He that is our God *is* the God of salvation; and unto GOD the Lord *belong* the issues from death... They have seen Thy goings, O God; *even* the goings of my God, my King, in the sanctuary" (Psa. 68:3, 17, 20, 24).

The "issues from death" will only be resolved at the judgment seat. Only then will those who receive the gift of immortality be able truly to rejoice, and to see the King dwelling in the sanctuary. There are strong hints in these words that the judgment will take place at Sinai, for in verse 17, in a prophetic (rather than historic) context, there is a picture of many thousands of "Elohim". This word can apply to angels in the sense of those immortal Divine messengers who minister even now to the saints. But it can equally refer to the redeemed saints as "mighty ones", which we believe is the sense here. The word rendered "angels" in the KJV is *shinan*, which only occurs here. The Online Bible defines it thus; "repetitions, twice-told repetition, twice ten thousands, thousands of repetitions, twice-told thousands, myriads (in effect)." This is consistent with the concordance definition (Strong 1939). The sense is therefore of an innumerable myriad of mighty ones or redeemed saints; an awe-inspiring picture!

Furthermore, some of the other words of the Psalm can only apply to the time when the kingdom has been established.

"Because of thy temple at Jerusalem shall kings bring presents unto thee... Princes shall come out of Egypt; Ethiopia shall soon stretch out her hands unto God. Sing unto God, ye kingdoms of the earth; O sing praises unto the Lord" (Psa. 68:29, 31-32).

It is also worthy of note that verses 27 and 28 of the Psalm, which we quoted earlier, and which refer to the foursquare encampment of Israel, are equally a prophecy of the judgment seat. Those verses follow on from the point when the "issues from death" (verse 20) have been resolved. Thus the foursquare encampment represents the true, spiritual Israel of God, glorified and immortal, and now being prepared for war, to subdue the earth. Viewed in this light, there is clearly a connection with another prophetic passage in one of Balaam's utterances.

"How goodly are thy tents, O Jacob, *and* thy tabernacles, O Israel! As the valleys are they spread forth, as gardens by the river's side, as the trees of lign aloes which Yahweh hath planted, *and* as cedar trees beside the waters. He shall pour the water out of his buckets, and his seed *shall be* in many waters, and his king shall be higher than Agag, and his kingdom shall be exalted. God brought him forth out of Egypt; he hath as it were the strength of an unicorn: he shall eat up the nations his enemies, and shall break their bones, and pierce *them* through with his arrows" (Num. 24:5-8).

Balaam was looking at Israel camped in the wilderness, on the borders of Canaan, shortly before they crossed Jordan to conquer the land promised to them. But the terms of this, and indeed of all his prophecies looked beyond the time then present, to a greater future for the nation of Israel. Agag in later times was king of the Amalekites, who were the very embodiment of sin, and were in determined opposition to God's people. Prophetically they probably stand for Gog, and indeed the Septuagint renders Agag as "Gog". So here is the true Israel, the Rainbowed Angel, prepared for war, ready to "eat up" Israel's enemies and to exalt the kingdom of their leader, the King of kings, the Lord Jesus Christ.

So we conclude with absolute certainty that Psalm 68 is a prophecy, and that it is based on an earlier Old Testament type.

The judgment seat in Psalm 68

Based on the all the expository evidence so far accumulated, we believe we can safely conclude that Psalm 68 does indeed refer to the time and process of judgment of those responsible to Christ, and that this will take place at Sinai. Having arrived at that conclusion based on exposition of Scripture, it is remarkable just how many clear statements there are in the Psalm that relate to that time; the judgment seat and its aftermath. These are set out in the table below.

Table 9 – Psalm 68 and the judgment seat

Psalm 68 quotation	Comment
"But let the righteous be glad; let them rejoice before God: yea, let them exceedingly rejoice" (verse 3).	The rejoicing of the glorified saints after approval at the judgment seat.
"Why leap ye, ye high hills? *this is* the hill *which* God desireth to dwell in; yea, the LORD will dwell *in it* for ever" (verse 16).	The place where God will dwell is with His people, those who are redeemed. This process begins at Sinai. "Behold, the tabernacle of God *is* with men, and He will dwell with them, and they shall be His people, and God Himself shall be with them, *and be* their God" (Rev. 21:3).
"The chariots of God *are* twenty thousand, *even* thousands of angels: the Lord *is* among them, *as in* Sinai, in the holy *place*" (verse 17).	The myriad of redeemed saints at Sinai, with Yahweh dwelling among them. Figuratively they have entered the holy place of His temple or tabernacle.
"*He that is* our God *is* the God of salvation; and unto GOD the Lord *belong* the issues from death" (verse 20).	The issues of life and death are resolved at the judgment seat. For those found faithful and accounted righteous there is the gift of life for evermore.
"Bless ye God in the congregations, *even* the Lord, from the fountain of Israel. There *is* little Benjamin *with* their ruler, the princes of Judah *and* their council, the princes of Zebulun, *and* the princes of Naphtali. Thy God hath commanded thy strength: strengthen, O God, that which thou hast wrought for us" (verses 26-28).	The redeemed saints are now finally constituted as the spiritual Israel, and so are portrayed as encamped after the pattern of Israel in the wilderness. The judgment is past, so the northern camp is not now represented by Dan ("judge"), but by Naphtali. In blessing him Jacob said "he giveth goodly words" (Gen. 49:21). The saints have indeed heard goodly words – "Well done, *thou* good and faithful servant" (Matt. 25:21). The eastern camp is represented by Judah and Zebulun, and the

[*Table 9 continued*]	western camp by Benjamin. The southern camp of Reuben is only mentioned implicitly. Jacob describes Reuben in Gen. 49:3 as the "excellency of power". The Hebrew for "power" (*az*) is derived from the verb for "strengthen" (*azaz*) in Psa. 68:28. Thus the complete camp of Israel (natural and spiritual) is portrayed in Psalm 68.
"Because of Thy temple at Jerusalem shall kings bring presents unto Thee" (verse 29).	The kings of the earth bring presents to the King of kings. "The kings of Tarshish and of the isles shall bring presents: the kings of Sheba and Seba shall offer gifts" (Psa. 72:10).
"Princes shall come out of Egypt; Ethiopia shall soon stretch out her hands unto God" (verse 31).	Again the parallel is in Psalm 72. "Yea, all kings shall fall down before him: all nations shall serve him" (verse 11).
"Sing unto God, ye kingdoms of the earth; O sing praises unto the Lord… To Him that rideth upon the heavens of heavens, *which were* of old; lo, He doth send out His voice, *and that* a mighty voice. Ascribe ye strength unto God: His excellency *is* over Israel, and His strength *is* in the clouds" (verses 32-34).	Only once God's kingdom is established will the nations sing praise to Yahweh God of Israel. At that time they will witness His glory and strength manifested in clouds of saints, the Rainbowed Angel.

The gift of eternal life

There is a short section in the middle of Psalm 68 that now merits detailed attention, as it is crucial in our understanding of this Psalm as a picture of the judgment seat. Detailed exposition will show that not only is it rooted in the exodus with Moses, but is also used in the New Testament.

"The chariots of God *are* twenty thousand, *even* thousands of angels: the Lord *is* among them, *as in* Sinai, in the holy *place*. Thou hast ascended on high, thou hast led captivity captive: thou hast received gifts for men; yea, *for* the rebellious also, that the LORD God might dwell *among them*. Blessed *be* the Lord, *Who* daily loadeth us *with benefits, even* the God of our salvation. *He that is* our God *is* the God of salvation; and unto GOD the Lord *belong* the issues from death" (Psa. 68:17-20).

We suggest that this is a picture of the judgment seat. God and a multitude of angels are present to witness the gift of immortality being given to faithful saints. This gift has been won by the one who conquered sin and death, and who thus led captivity (the bondage to death in which sin holds us) captive. Having won that victory Jesus ascended to his Father's right hand to await the appointed day to return to earth to establish the long-promised kingdom. The exposition will take us back to a type in the days of Moses, and forward into the New Testament, where Paul provides us with an inspired insight into the meaning of this passage.

The type is clearly that period in Israel's history when they were at Sinai, having just been delivered from slavery in Egypt. The nation encamped at Sinai for almost exactly a year, during which time Moses ascended into the mount Sinai on at least eight occasions to commune with Yahweh. By this means he was instructed in the Law, the construction of the tabernacle, and the manufacture of the priestly garments, among other things. One of these ascents, the sixth, is recorded in Exodus 24.

"The LORD said unto Moses, Come up to Me into the mount, and be there: and I will give thee tables of stone, and a law, and commandments which I have written; that thou mayest teach them. And Moses rose up, and his minister Joshua: and Moses went up into the mount of God" (verses 12-13).

The following verses record that at God's command, Moses then ascended further on his own, until he was hidden by the cloud on the mount. This was one occasion, though not the only one, when Moses remained on Sinai for forty days and nights.

"Moses went up into the mount, and a cloud covered the mount. And the glory of Yahweh abode upon mount Sinai, and the cloud covered it six days: and the seventh day He called unto Moses out of the midst of the cloud. And the sight of the glory of Yahweh *was* like devouring fire on the top of the mount in the eyes of the children of Israel. And Moses went into the midst of the cloud, and gat him up into the mount: and Moses was in the mount forty days and forty nights" (Exo. 24:15-18).

Moses does not descend on this occasion until we reach chapter 32.

"Moses turned, and went down from the mount, and the two tables of the testimony *were* in his hand: the tables *were* written on both their sides; on the one side and on the other *were* they written" (Exo. 32:15).

Sadly, when he came down, he and Joshua found that Israel had taken to worshipping the golden calf.

One of the things that Moses was told while in the mount on this occasion was that God had selected two men who would receive the gift and power of the spirit of God that would enable them to work skilfully with other spirit-gifted Israelites to construct the tabernacle in the precise way, and according to the specific design that God required.

"Yahweh spake unto Moses, saying, See, I have called by name Bezaleel the son of Uri, the son of Hur, of the tribe of Judah: and I have filled him with the spirit of God, in wisdom, and in understanding, and in knowledge, and in all manner of workmanship, to devise cunning works, to work in gold, and in silver, and in brass, and in cutting of stones, to set *them*, and in carving of timber, to work in all manner of workmanship. And I, behold, I have given with him Aholiab, the son of Ahisamach, of the tribe of Dan: and in the hearts of all that are wise hearted I have put wisdom, that they may make all that I have commanded thee" (Exo. 31:1-6).

David, through the Spirit, is referring back to these events when he says in Psalm 68 "Thou hast ascended on high… thou has received gifts for men" (verse 18). "Thou" here, historically, refers to Moses, but in the fulfilment of the type it refers to the Lord Jesus Christ.

In essence the gift (probably should be singular – see comments below Eph. 2:5,8) here is that of eternal life, which is granted to those who are accounted righteous at the judgment on the basis of their faith. This is truly the grace or unmerited favour of God, for none of us can earn salvation.

> "Therefore being **justified** by **faith**, we have peace with God through our Lord Jesus Christ: by whom also we have access by **faith** into this **grace** wherein we stand, and rejoice in hope of the glory of God... For if by one man's offence death reigned by one; much more they which receive abundance of **grace** and of the **gift** of **righteousness** shall reign in **life** by one, Jesus Christ... For the wages of sin *is* death; but the **gift** of God *is* **eternal life** through Jesus Christ our Lord" (Rom. 5:1,2,17; 6:23).

Thus the "issues from death" (Psa. 68:20) will be resolved at the judgment seat.

This is all consistent with the fact that the tabernacle itself was intended as a type of the new covenant, which embodied the forgiveness of sins, and thereby the justification of saints.

> "Moses was admonished of God when he was about to make the tabernacle: for, See, saith He, *that* thou make all things according to the pattern shewed to thee in the mount. But now hath he (i.e. Jesus Christ) obtained a more excellent ministry, by how much also he is the mediator of a better covenant, which was established upon better promises. For if that first *covenant* had been faultless, then should no place have been sought for the second. For finding fault with them, He saith, Behold, the days come, saith the Lord, when I will make a new covenant with the house of Israel and with the house of Judah... For I will be merciful to their unrighteousness, and their sins and their iniquities will I remember no more" (Heb. 8:5-8,12).

The saints at the judgment seat, justified by faith, and with their sins forgiven, will be made immortal and incorruptible. They will be manifest in his presence as tried gold and precious stones.

> "That the trial of your faith, being much more precious than of gold that perisheth, though it be tried with fire, might be found unto praise and honour and glory at the appearing of Jesus Christ" (1 Pet. 1:7).

"They shall be Mine, saith the LORD of hosts, in that day when I
make up My jewels; and I will spare them, as a man spareth his own
son that serveth him" (Mal. 3:17).

How remarkable that these very details were foreshadowed in the
Divine instructions given to Moses when he was in the mount. Bezaleel
and Aholiab were...

"...to devise cunning works, to work in gold, and in silver, and in
brass, and in cutting of stones, to set *them*, and in carving of timber,
to work in all manner of workmanship" (Exo. 31:4-5).

So by tracing these interwoven Scriptures we can see clearly that we
have a picture in Psalm 68 of the judgment seat, when, by God's grace,
the redeemed, faithful saints will become partakers of the Divine nature,
being perfected jewels fit for His eternal purpose. It is interesting to
note that the gifts were received for "the rebellious also" (Psa. 68:18).
Historically no doubt this referred to the rebellious Israelites in the
wilderness, who benefitted from worship in the tabernacle that was
constructed. But this description is also true of all redeemed saints, in
terms of how they were before accepting the gospel.

"You *hath He quickened*, who were dead in trespasses and sins;
wherein in time past ye walked according to the course of this world,
according to the prince of the power of the air, the spirit that now
worketh in the children of disobedience" (Eph. 2:1-2).

How thankful we should be to our God, that He has redeemed us from
our rebellious nature, and by faith has "translated *us* into the kingdom
of His dear Son" (Col. 1:13)[1].

The "perfect man"

In Psalm 68:18 the writer says regarding the ascent on high, "thou hast
received gifts for men". The KJV margin suggests the alternative "in

1. The Emphatic Diaglott (as quoted in the OLB) renders this phrase "caused a
change of sides for the kingdom of the son". This is consistent with our
doctrinal belief that we are now heirs of the kingdom, but not actually in the
kingdom.

the man". Every other English translation that the author consulted (eight in all) follows the KJV text in putting "men" in the plural. Only the Greek Septuagint adopts a singular tense like the KJV margin. Yet this is almost certainly correct, since it tallies with the quotation and exposition of the passage by the apostle Paul. We now turn to this passage, quoted in full below, because it enlightens us further with regard to Psalm 68.

> "Unto every one of us is given grace according to the measure of the gift of Christ. Wherefore he saith, When he ascended up on high, he led captivity captive, and gave gifts unto men. (Now that he ascended, what is it but that he also descended first into the lower parts of the earth? He that descended is the same also that ascended up far above all heavens, that he might fill all things.) And he gave some, apostles; and some, prophets; and some, evangelists; and some, pastors and teachers; for the perfecting of the saints, for the work of the ministry, for the edifying of the body of Christ: till we all come in the unity of the faith, and of the knowledge of the Son of God, unto a perfect man, unto the measure of the stature of the fulness of Christ" (Eph. 4:7-13).

We believe that the "perfect man" that Paul refers to here is the 'ecclesial man', or the completed ecclesial body. The phrase does have a sense in which it refers to individuals, inasmuch as each saint is required to imitate Christ in their lives and so come, in measure to be like him. As the first century ecclesia matured, its members gained in knowledge, whilst in parallel, the New Testament body of writings was growing. Once they were complete, the temporary gifts of the Spirit were withdrawn, and the ecclesia was able to rely on the complete, inspired Word of God.

The ecclesia of saints in the aggregate, from all ages, when joined together in one corporate body and given the gift of eternal life will then be that "perfect man" that Paul writes of. This is the multitudinous body of Christ, which will receive the gift of life at the judgment seat, when he who has ascended on high returns to earth to bestow the gift he has been given "in the man".

Some might find difficulty with the concept of relating this Ephesians passage to future events, since it is written in the past tense; "he gave some, apostles... " (etc). However, we do not believe this is a real difficulty, for two reasons. Firstly, the inspired apostle is referring back to the Old Testament passages we have already quoted (Psalm 68, that itself refers back to Exodus 24 and 31). Psalm 68 is rooted in a future, kingdom context.

> "Let God arise, let His enemies be scattered: let them also that hate Him flee before Him. As smoke is driven away, *so* drive *them* away: as wax melteth before the fire, *so* let the wicked perish at the presence of God… Sing unto God, ye kingdoms of the earth; O sing praises unto the Lord" (Psa. 68:1, 2 32).

Thus the Psalm uses the events recorded in Exodus as a type of still future events, and so does Paul. Past events foreshadow events still future.

Secondly, while there is obviously, from the perspective of when Paul was writing, a past element in terms of the first century spirit gifts that were given at Pentecost, those gifts were given as part of a long-term process to create the complete, multitudinous body of Christ. They were the "earnest of our inheritance until the redemption of the purchased possession" (Eph. 1:14). The process will only be complete when all the saints are joined together in immortality as the ultimate fulfilment of the "perfect man".

We now turn to a systematic consideration of this passage from Ephesians 4.

The gift of life for the ecclesia

We begin at verse 7 where Paul introduces us to a "gift".

> "But unto every one of us is given grace according to the measure of the gift of Christ" (Eph. 4:7).

This does not refer to one of the miraculous gifts of the Holy Spirit that were given to some in the first century ecclesia. Indeed it cannot do so. The miraculous gifts of the Spirit were not given to all believers ("every one of us") even in the first century. Rather, this refers to the gift of righteousness, granted to those who are faithful. On the basis of faith, we may be accounted as righteous, and our sins will be forgiven. Paul has already presented this glorious truth earlier in the epistle.

"Even when we were dead in sins, [God] hath quickened us together with Christ, (by grace ye are saved;)... For by grace are ye saved through faith; and that not of yourselves: *it is* the gift of God:" (Eph 2:5, 8).

The same principle is developed at greater length in Romans. The essence of the conclusion of Paul's argument is stated at the start of chapter 5. These verses have already been quoted, but bear repetition in this context.

"Therefore being justified by faith, we have peace with God through our Lord Jesus Christ: by whom also we have access by faith into this grace wherein we stand, and rejoice in hope of the glory of God" (Rom. 5:1-2).

Paul develops this concept of the **gift** of grace, or forgiveness of sins leading to eternal life further in the same chapter.

"The free **gift** is not like the trespass. For if many died through one man's trespass, much more have the grace of God and the free **gift** in the grace of that one man Jesus Christ abounded for many. And the free **gift** is not like the effect of that one man's sin. For the judgment following one trespass brought condemnation, but the free **gift** following many trespasses brings justification. If, because of one man's trespass, death reigned through that one man, much will those who receive the abundance of grace and the free **gift** of righteousness reign in life through the one man Jesus Christ" (Rom. 5:15-17 RSV, my emphasis).

The argument is then summarised at the end of Paul's 'baptism' chapter.

"For the wages of sin *is* death; but the **gift** of God *is* eternal life through Jesus Christ our Lord" (Ro 6:23, my emphasis).

Although eternal life will be a free gift from God, it is also important to note the key point that it is the responsibility of the disciple to develop faith, which comes as a result of reading, hearing, and understanding the Word of God (cf. Rom. 10:17). This is the point that Paul makes at the end of Romans 4 as he concludes his argument concerning righteousness imputed for faith. He bases the argument on Abraham and then applies the principles to us.

> "It was not written for his [Abraham's] sake alone, that it [righteousness] was imputed to him; but for us also, to whom it shall be imputed, if we believe on him that raised up Jesus our Lord from the dead; who was delivered for our offences, and was raised again for our justification" (Rom. 4:23-25).

So the gift of grace that is given us by Christ is imputed righteousness and the forgiveness of sins, based on our faith in the promises of God and the shed blood of Christ. In its fullest sense this can only apply to the saints when approved at the judgment seat. Again, Paul has already indicated this earlier in Ephesians.

> "That in the ages to come He might shew the exceeding riches of His grace in *His* kindness toward us through Christ Jesus" (Eph. 2:7).

Peter also makes the same point.

> "Wherefore gird up the loins of your mind, be sober, and hope to the end for the grace that is to be brought unto you at the revelation of Jesus Christ" (1 Pet. 1:13).

This is the very point that Paul is leading to in his argument in Ephesians 4, as he refers back to Psalm 68; the gift of grace will only fully be granted at the judgment seat. So he continues, quoting (in verse 8) from Psalm 68:18;

> "Wherefore he saith, When he ascended up on high, he led captivity captive, and gave gifts unto men. (Now that he ascended, what is it but that he also descended first into the lower parts of the earth?)" (Eph. 4:8, 9).

The grace of God is offered to us in the sense of the forgiveness of sins, of righteousness imputed for faith, which is only available through the shed blood of Christ. Hence we see the relevance of the comment quoted from Romans 4 that we must "believe on him that raised up Jesus our Lord from the dead; who was delivered for our offences, and was raised again for our justification". That is because in his sinless sacrifice Jesus totally conquered sin, so that the grave could not hold him. Sin which holds us all in thrall had been overcome, so that for, and in Christ, the wages of sin are no longer due. That which holds us in captivity had itself been taken captive. Sin and death had both been overcome, by and in Christ. So, although Jesus died and was laid in, or descended into the grave, he rose victorious, and ascended to his Father.

In using this idea of captivity itself being led captive the Psalmist was referring back to an actual Old Testament incident which illustrated Christ's victory over sin and death. This was the slaying of Sisera the Canaanite general by Jael, thus sealing the victory by Deborah and Barak over Israel's, and God's enemies. Sisera, who embodied the principle of sin and rebellion against God, was slain by a nail or tent peg hammered through his head into the ground. In type it was a fulfilment of the principle of Genesis 3:15.

> "I will put enmity between thee and the woman, and between thy seed and her seed; it shall bruise thy head, and thou shalt bruise his heel" (Gen. 3:15).

By a fatal head wound, sin was in type, put to death. This glorious victory was celebrated in song by Deborah and Barak, who sang;

> "Awake, awake, Deborah: awake, awake, utter a song: arise, Barak, and lead thy captivity captive, thou son of Abinoam" (Jud. 5:12).

Thus Scripture tells us that language about taking captivity captive relates to the conquest of sin and death, which was completed by Christ. "By a sacrifice for sin, [Christ] condemned sin in the flesh" (Rom. 8:3). The result is triumphant dominion and authority over the nations, prefigured by the victorious exclamation of Deborah and Barak.

> "Then He made him that remaineth have dominion over the nobles among the people: Yahweh made me have dominion over the mighty" (Judg. 5:13).

Having referred to this victory, Paul then goes on to speak of the interim, albeit miraculous gifts of the Spirit given to members of the first century ecclesia. In looking at these words we must remember what Paul has stated elsewhere as quoted above, that God will show the exceeding riches of His grace in the age to come. Meanwhile, these first century gifts were an "earnest of our inheritance".

> "He gave some, apostles; and some, prophets; and some, evangelists; and some, pastors and teachers; for the perfecting of the saints, for the work of the ministry, for the edifying of the body of

Christ: till we all come in the unity of the faith, and of the knowledge of the Son of God, unto a perfect man, unto the measure of the stature of the fulness of Christ" (Eph. 4:11-13).

It is important to emphasize the two-fold application of these words, a principle which is true of so much of Scripture. The first century gifts of the Spirit were designed to aid the establishment and growth of the early ecclesial body. The miracles performed confirmed the truth of the gospel that was preached. The gift of tongues aided that preaching, alongside the gift of prophecy (speaking forth and expounding the Word of God) which edified the believers. Until the New Testament Scriptures were complete and widely available these gifts were necessary. Through them, for example, the apostles were able to "bring all things to… remembrance, whatsoever [Jesus had] said unto" them (Jno. 14:26). Once the New Testament was complete, the gifts were no longer necessary. The inspired holy Scriptures were now able to make them wise unto salvation through faith in Christ Jesus, and provide full instruction on how to conduct their lives (cf. 2 Tim. 3:15-17).

The growing maturity of the ecclesial body

So the ecclesia had now come to the point where they had the "unity of the faith", and all the necessary "knowledge of the Son of God. As a corporate body comprised of believing saints they were now the "perfect (i.e. complete, ecclesial) man". However, the process of building up the ecclesia to its eternal destiny was not yet complete. At that point, as now, it had only reached the "measure of the stature of the fullness of Christ" (Eph. 4:13). The next stage in the process will be the bestowal of the gift of immortality at the judgment seat at Sinai, as discussed above.

But we suggest that even that stage is not the end of the process. There is yet a further stage, the marriage of Christ and his bride, which is implicit in these words from Ephesians 4.

"But speaking the truth in love, may grow up into him in all things, which is the head, *even* Christ: from whom the whole body fitly joined together and compacted by that which every joint supplieth, according to the effectual working in the measure of every part, maketh increase of the body unto the edifying of itself in love" (Eph. 4:15-16).

71

Without doubt these verses have an application to the growth, development, and fellowship of the mortal ecclesia. The Greek word for "compacted" is *sumbibazo*, which means to 'join, put, or knit together'. The Online Bible gives as one definition, "to unite, or knit together; in affection". It is only used on five other occasions, two of which are in the same chapter in Colossians, where on both occasions it is translated as "knit together" It is used to describe the relationship between believers, and also between the Lord Jesus Christ and believers..

> "That their hearts might be comforted, being knit together in love, and unto all riches of the full assurance of understanding, to the acknowledgement of the mystery of God, and of the Father, and of Christ... not holding the Head, from which all the body by joints and bands having nourishment ministered, and knit together, increaseth with the increase of God" (Col. 2:2, 19).

We notice also that in these verses this word is used alongside "love" and "mystery". This provides a link back into Ephesians where Paul writes of marriage as a type of the relationship between Christ and the ecclesia, a relationship that will only be fully consummated after the judgment seat. Paul again uses the words "love" and "mystery".

> "Husbands, love your wives, even as Christ also loved the ecclesia, and gave himself for it... For this cause shall a man leave his father and mother, and shall be joined unto his wife, and they two shall be one flesh. This is a great mystery: but I speak concerning Christ and the ecclesia" (Eph. 5:25, 31-32).

So the process outlined in Ephesians 4 regarding grace which is the gift of Christ (cf. verse 7), and which is based on a quotation from Psalm 68, is just that, a multi-stage process. The process is completed by the marriage of Christ and his ecclesial bride, when they become not one flesh, but one Spirit. "Grace according to the measure of the gift of Christ" (Eph. 4:7) then becomes the fullness of grace, as described by Peter.

> "Gird up the loins of your mind, be sober, and hope to the end for the grace that is to be brought unto you at the revelation of Jesus Christ" (1 Pet. 1:13).

Chapter 5 – The judgment seat at Sinai

A short recapitulation is appropriate here to summarise what we believe is taught by these various Scriptures. Firstly, the saints are gathered to Sinai for judgment. Those accounted righteous are made immortal. This body of saints are then organised as the true Israel of God in a foursquare encampment ready to be manifested as the cherubim of the future age, the vehicle of the power and glory of Yahweh. This will not be the work of a moment, though we are not told how long it will take. But there is a pattern and type in Scripture. After their exodus from Egypt, Israel spent around a year at Sinai, being constituted a nation ready for war, building the Tabernacle, and being taught the laws of Yahweh. We believe that the body of saints, once changed in nature to become one Spirit with their immortal Redeemer, the consummation of their marriage, will likewise spend a period of time at Sinai, hidden from the world, but preparing for their revelation to the world in power and great glory.

It is intriguing to note that there may be another type in the Law of Moses for this period of time that the redeemed ecclesia will apparently spend with the Lord Jesus Christ, prior to being revealed as the Rainbowed Angel.

"When a man hath taken a new wife, he shall not go out to war, neither shall he be charged with any business: *but* he shall be free at home one year, and shall cheer up his wife which he hath taken" (Deut. 24:5).

It may be that Christ and his bride will fulfil this type at Sinai. Indeed, there is a reference in a later passage in Deuteronomy, which is considered in more detail later, that seems to reinforce this. In the context of "Yahweh (coming) from Sinai... with ten thousands of saints" we read that...

"... all his saints *are* in thy hand: and they sat down at thy feet; *every one* shall receive of thy words" (Deut. 33:3).

Moreover, there appears to be a lovely partial fulfilment of the type by the disciples between the resurrection and ascension of Jesus. Luke records that Jesus...

"... shewed himself alive after his passion by many infallible proofs, being seen of them (the disciples) forty days, and speaking of the things pertaining to the kingdom of God" (Acts 1:3).

As the Rainbowed Angel Christ and the saints will then march forth at the appointed time to undertake their Divine commission. Once arrived at Jerusalem, the destruction of both the Gogian host and then apostasy of Babylon the Great will follow. Jesus will then be fully established on David's restored throne. It is at this point that we believe the marriage supper of the Lamb will take place, for this event will surely be at Jerusalem. The initial warfare and work of establishing the kingdom having been completed, Christ and his bride can truly celebrate their marriage.

The concepts we have discussed above are brought together at the end of the Apocalypse. They have been prefigured in Exodus and Psalm 68.

> "Make Me a sanctuary; that I may dwell among them" (Exo. 25:8).

> "The Lord *is* among them, *as in* Sinai, in the holy *place*" (Psa. 68:17).

Now, the process is completed.

> "I John saw the holy city, new Jerusalem, coming down from God out of heaven, prepared as a bride adorned for her husband. And I heard a great voice out of heaven saying, Behold, the tabernacle of God *is* with men, and He will dwell with them, and they shall be His people, and God Himself shall be with them, *and be* their God. And God shall wipe away all tears from their eyes; and there shall be no more death, neither sorrow, nor crying, neither shall there be any more pain: for the former things are passed away" (Rev. 21:2-4).

The ecclesia is complete as a prepared and perfected bride, married to her heavenly redeemer and husband in perfect communion. As a result, God now dwells with His people. This statement takes us back again to Psalm 68, for the purpose of the events at Sinai described in that Psalm is, "that the Lord God might dwell *among them*" (verse 18).

No more death

The greatest hope for the saints at the judgment seat at Sinai is that in the mercy of God they (we) will be found acceptable, justified by faith and accounted righteous, and so be granted the gift of everlasting life. This will mark the end of our struggle against sin and mortality. All the later stages in the process outlined above are from this point inevitable. The justified and immortal saints from this point on embark on a work that no power in heaven or earth can stop. Our joy will be inexpressible. Psalm 68 describes the resolution of our struggle beautifully and powerfully.

> "Blessed *be* the Lord, *Who* daily loadeth us *with benefits, even* the God of our salvation. Selah. *He that is* our God *is* the God of salvation; and unto GOD the Lord *belong* the issues from death" (Psa. 68:19-20).

The resolution of the "issues from death" for the saints will come when they are granted the gift of eternal life, when corruption puts on incorruption, and mortality puts on immortality. Thus it is appropriate that this Psalm focuses on this climax of our redemptive experience as it paints a picture of the judgment seat for us. For Christ the issue has already been resolved; he already has the "keys of hell and of death" (Rev. 1:18). If we are found worthy, he will use those keys to unlock for us the gates of our captivity to the bondage of sin and death. As it is expressed in another passage from Revelation already quoted; "there shall be no more death".

The Hebrew word translated "issues" is used 23 times, and on all but two occasions relates to the "goings out" (or similar) of the borders of Israel, in Numbers, Joshua, and Ezekiel. Apart from Psalm 68:20, the only other occurrence is in Proverbs.

> "Keep thy heart with all diligence; for out of it *are* the issues of life" (4:23).

If we truly keep our hearts and minds in sincerity in the truth, the issues of life will be resolved in our favour at the judgment seat. We will 'go out of', or be changed from mortality to immortality.

Also worthy of note is the fact that the Hebrew root verb from which the word "issues" is translated occurs twice elsewhere in Psalm 68, as highlighted in the quotation below.

> "God setteth the solitary in families: **He bringeth out** those which are bound with chains: but the rebellious dwell in a dry *land*. O God, when **Thou wentest forth** before Thy people, when Thou didst march through the wilderness" (verses 6-7).

Whilst not perhaps immediately obvious, we suggest that both these phrases tie in with the resolution of the issues from death. Those "bound with chains" are prisoners. Such are defined elsewhere as those bound with the chains of mortality.

> "To hear the groaning of the prisoner; to loose those that are appointed to death" (Psa. 102:20).

Thus, when God "bringeth out those which are bound with chains", He will release from the grave, and from mortality those who are His saints. They will then be set in the greatest family of all, the redeemed ecclesia from all ages. Having then raised them from the dead and made them immortal, the redeemed will constitute the Rainbowed Angel, and as the people of God will be led forth to save Israel and conquer the nations. This is the sense of the phrase, "Thou wentest forth before Thy people". The Almighty, manifest in His Son, will lead that host on their "march through the wilderness". This process is also described in the Psalm in language that goes back to the Edenic promise of a seed, and God's purpose of redemption in Christ.

> "God shall wound the head of His enemies, *and* the hairy scalp of such an one as goeth on still in his trespasses" (Psa 68:21).

Conclusion

So the encampment of Israel in the wilderness that we have earlier seen portrayed in Psalm 68 is also a prophetic feature. It is portraying the encampment of the redeemed saints ready to go forth on their march through the wilderness as the Rainbowed Angel. Their first task will be to enter the land, drive out the northern invader, deliver the nation of Israel in their extremity, and set Yahweh's anointed king on His holy hill of Zion. In the process of accomplishing this task they will also subdue the Arab nations around Israel; those typed by Og king of Bashan, and Sihon king of the Amorites in Moses's day, and those described by Habakkuk as "Midian" and "Cushan". They will then be submissive before Israel.

> "Arise, shine; for thy light is come, and the glory of Yahweh is risen upon thee. For, behold, the darkness shall cover the earth, and gross darkness the people: but Yahweh shall arise upon thee, and his glory shall be seen upon thee. And the Gentiles shall come to

thy light, and kings to the brightness of thy rising… The multitude of camels shall cover thee, the dromedaries of Midian and Ephah; all they from Sheba shall come: they shall bring gold and incense; and they shall shew forth the praises of Yahweh. All the flocks of Kedar shall be gathered together unto thee, the rams of Nebaioth shall minister unto thee: they shall come up with acceptance on Mine altar, and I will glorify the house of My glory" (Isa. 60:1-3,6-7).

Chapter 6 – Israel's wilderness march – a type for the march of the Rainbowed Angel

Introduction

The statement in the title of this chapter has already been made clear in the previous chapter. Some of the connections between, on the one hand, Psalm 68, which portrays the start of the march of the Rainbowed Angel, and the exodus on the other hand, have already been noted. However the full depth of those connections has not yet been examined. When this is done it becomes even clearer that the events concerning Israel at the exodus from Egypt and in the wilderness are a pattern for the march of the redeemed saints.

We have set out below in tabular form a more comprehensive list of the remarkable number of links between the Psalm and the various parts of the exodus record. For the purposes of this table we have included the defeat of Sisera's army by Deborah and Barak, although this took place some years after Israel settled in Canaan under Joshua. Broadly speaking it may for this purpose be treated as an extension of the exodus as it is the only other part of Scripture before the prophets that sets out a type of the march of the Rainbowed Angel. The way in which different parts of Scripture are interleaved in order to create different levels of meaning for our understanding is a powerful testimony to the Divine inspiration of the Scripture. It also gives us a small insight into the Father's mind Whose thoughts are higher than our thoughts (Isa. 55:9). Further, it provides us with a tangible pattern for future events in the form of a historical record, which also facilitates our deeper understanding of God's future plans.

Table 10 – The Exodus – Psalm 68 connections

Psalm 68	The Exodus background
v 1 – "Let God arise, let His enemies be scattered: let them also that hate Him flee before Him"	Num. 10:35 – "Rise up, Yahweh, and let Thine enemies be scattered; and let them that hate Thee flee before Thee"
v 1 – "let His (God's) enemies be scattered"	Exo. 15:7 – "overthrown them that rose up against thee… consumed them as stubble"

Chapter 6 – Israel's wilderness march – a type for the march of the Rainbowed Angel

(cont'd) Psalm 68	The Exodus background
v 4 – "Sing unto God"	Exo. 15:1, 21 – "Then sang Moses... I will sing unto Yahweh, for He hath triumphed gloriously... Miriam answered... Sing ye to Yahweh"
v 4 – "extol Him... by His Name Yah"	Exo. 15:3 – "Yahweh *is* His Name"
v 5 – "God (*is*) in His holy habitation"	Exo. 15:2 – "Yahweh *is*... my God, and I will prepare Him an habitation"
v 6 – "He bringeth out those which are bound with chains"	Exo. 2:23 & 3:10 – "Israel sighed by reason of the bondage... and their cry came up unto God... bring forth My people the children of Israel out of Egypt"
v 7 – "Thou wentest forth before Thy people"	Exo. 40:35, 36 – "cloud... glory of Yahweh filled the tabernacle... when the cloud was taken up... Israel went onward"
v 7 – "when Thou didst march through the wilderness"	Judg. 5:4 – "Yahweh, when Thou wentest out of Seir, when Thou marchedst out of the field of Edom"
v 8 – "The earth shook... Sinai itself *was moved* at the presence of God"	Exo. 19:18 – "mount Sinai... Yahweh descended upon it... the whole mount quaked greatly" Judg. 5:4 – "the earth trembled"
v 8 – "the heavens also dropped at the presence of God"	Judg. 5:4 - "the heavens dropped, the clouds also dropped water". (Note – this in the context of celebrating a victory at Tabor in the north of the land (see Judg. 4:14,15), it seems to indicate that, in line with the type, God 'marched' from Sinai via Edom to defeat Sisera at mount Tabor.)
v 9 – "Thou O God, didst send a plentiful rain"	Exo. 17:6 – "I (Yahweh) will stand before thee there upon the rock in Horeb; and thou shalt smite the rock, and there shall come water out of it"

(cont'd) Psalm 68	The Exodus background
v 12 – "Kings of armies did flee apace"	Exo. 15:14, 15 – "The people shall hear, *and* be afraid… all the inhabitants of Canaan shall melt away" Judg. 4:15 – "Sisera… fled away on his feet"
v 12 – "she that tarried at home divided the spoil"	Judg. 5:29, 30 – "Her (Sisera's mother) wise ladies answered her… Have they not sped? Have they not divided the prey…?"
v 13 – "ye have lien among the pots"	Exo. 16:2, 3 – "Israel murmured… Would to God we had died by the hand of Yahweh in the land of Egypt, when we sat by the flesh pots"
vv 14,15 – "the Almighty scattered kings… the hill of God *is as* the hill of Bashan" v 22 – "I will bring again from Bashan"	Num. 21:33, 35 – Og king of Bashan went out against (Israel)… So they smote him… and they possessed his land"
v 16 – "hill… Yahweh will dwell *in it* for ever" v 24 – "they have seen Thy goings… my God, my King, in the sanctuary"	Exo. 15:17, 18 – "Thou shalt bring them in, and plant them in the mountain of Thine inheritance, *in* the place, O Yahweh… for Thee to dwell in… Yahweh shall reign for ever and ever" Exo. 25:8 – "make Me a sanctuary; that I may dwell among them"

(cont'd) **Psalm 68**	**The Exodus background**
v 17 – "The chariots of God *are* twenty thousand, *even* thousands of angels: the Lord is among them... *in* Sinai, in the holy *place*" Note - The KJV margin against "even thousands" in Psalm 68:17 has "even many thousands", implying a very large number. This is confirmed by the TRC version, which has "The chariots of God are many thousand times a thousand". Cf. also a similar phrase (translated from related Hebrew) in Numbers 10:36, quoted in adjacent column. The Hebrew for "angels" in this verse is not the usual, *malak*, but *shinan*, which according to the OLB means "repetitions, twice-told repetition, twice ten thousands, thousands of repetitions, twice-told thousands, myriads (in effect)". This word is derived from the Hebrew root *shana*, meaning "to change, alter, be changed". In other words these "angels" are a myriad of "changed ones", glorified saints, who have been "changed... in a moment" (1 Cor. 15:52) to immortality.	Exo. 15:4 – "Pharaoh's chariots... hath He cast into the sea" ... (whereas)... Deut. 33:2 – "Yahweh came from Sinai... with ten thousands of saints" Num. 10:36 – "When it (the ark) rested, he said, Return, O LORD, unto the many thousands of Israel"
v 18 – "Thou hast ascended on high"	Exo. 24:13 – "Moses went up into the mount of God"
v 18 – "thou hast received gifts for men"	Exo. 31:2, 3 – "Bezaleel... I have filled him with the spirit of God"
v 18 – "thou has led captivity captive"	Judg. 5:12 - "Awake, awake, Deborah: awake, awake, utter a song: arise, Barak, and lead thy captivity captive"
v 18 – "that Yah Elohim might dwell *among them*"	Exo. 25:22 – "there I will meet with thee, and I will commune with thee from above the mercy seat"
v 22 – "I will bring *My people* again from the depths of the sea"	Exo. 15:19 – "the children of Israel went on dry *land* in the midst of the sea"

(cont'd) Psalm 68	The Exodus background
v 24 – "they have seen Thy goings... in the sanctuary"	Exo. 13:21 – "Yahweh went before them by day in a pillar of cloud... and by night in a pillar of fire"
v 25 – "singers... players on instruments... damsels... timbrels"	Exo. 15:20, 21 – "Miriam... took a timbrel in her hand; and all the women went out after her with timbrels and with dances. And Miriam answered them, Sing ye to Yahweh"
v 26 – "congregations"	Num. 1:18 – "they assembled all the congregation... declared their pedigrees... according to the number of the names" Num. 10:3-5 - "when they shall blow with them (trumpets), all the assembly shall assemble themselves to thee at the door of the tabernacle of the congregation. And if they blow *but* with one *trumpet*, then the princes, *which are* heads of the thousands of Israel, shall gather themselves unto thee. When ye blow an alarm, then the camps that lie on the east parts shall go forward"
v 27,28 – tribes listed:- Benjamin, Judah, Zebulun, Naphtali, and (implicitly) Reuben (see pages 56-57).	Judg. 5:14-18 – tribes listed:- Issachar, Zebulun, Reuben, Dan, Asher, Naphtali.
v 30 – "*till every one* submit himself with pieces of silver"	Exo. 30:12, 13 – "they shall give every man a ransom for his soul... half a shekel after the shekel of the sanctuary" (These were sliver shekels; cf. Exo. 38:25.)
v 33 – "To Him that rideth upon the heaven of heavens"	Deut. 33:26 - "*There is* none like unto the God of Jeshurun, *Who* rideth upon the heaven in thy help, and in His excellency on the sky"

Chapter 6 – Israel's wilderness march – a type for the march of the Rainbowed Angel

There are so many details in the prophetic Psalm 68 that link back to the exodus experiences of Israel, that it is clear beyond doubt that the historical record of those events is also a prophecy of events still in the future. Those events concern the judgment seat, the march of the Rainbowed Angel, and the conquest of those nations that oppose God's purpose with Israel.

Since the overall focus of our study is the march of the Rainbowed Angel, it therefore follows that the journey of Israel through the wilderness may be seen as a type of the march of the Rainbowed Angel. We have already noted in an earlier chapter that the opening words of Psalm 68 are quoted from Numbers 10, and comprise the words that Moses was to utter each time the ark moved or rested. We now wish to take the parallel a stage further, and to consider the route Israel took through the wilderness to the promised land.

The route of the wilderness journey

The complete journey of the children of Israel from leaving Egypt on the night of the first Passover to their encampment on the borders of the land is recorded in Numbers 33, with some additional information in Numbers 21 (see Table 11 below). The name of each place where the ark rested is given, although not all can be traced on a map today. We pick up the journey in Numbers 33:36 as they arrive at Kadeshbarnea, after wandering while a faithless generation perished. From here we can follow the later stages of the wilderness march. The reason for picking up the route here is that it marks the southern border of the land, which they should have been able to reach in 11 days from Mount Horeb.

> "(*There are* eleven days' *journey* from Horeb by the way of mount Seir unto Kadeshbarnea)" (Deut. 1:2).

The fact that it actually took them approaching 38 years is an indictment on their stubbornness and lack of faith, which necessitated that a whole generation perish in the wilderness. But for our purpose in this study the key point is that from this point on we are dealing with the Divinely ordained route that Israel should have taken all those years earlier if they had been faithful. The route would have been from Horeb to Kadeshbarnea, and then on to Jericho and the land of promise via the places we list below. What is both fascinating and amazing about these latter stages of the journey is the number of links that the various place names provide back once again into Psalm 68. These are illustrated in Table 11, and underpin yet again the fact that the wilderness journey of Israel is a type of the march of the Rainbowed Angel.

There is one complex factor about the route of the journey as set out in Numbers that is worth noting at this point before looking at the table. A careful reading of Numbers reveals that the list of places in Numbers 33 is not complete; there are actually some extra places of encampment between Ijeabarim in Numbers 33:44 and Dibongad in verse 45 (note that Iim in verse 45 is the same as Ibeajarim in verse 44). The additional places are listed in Numbers 21. The start of Numbers 22 then jumps to the final encampment, omitting three others that are listed in Numbers 33. The details, in what we believe is the order of Israel's journey, are shown in the table. Alternative meanings of place names are from Young's and Strong's Concordances.

As an aside it is worth noting that some commentators argue that the list of places given in Numbers 22 is a separate record from a different author, and thus presents an alternative route for the latter stages of the wilderness journey. We cannot concur with this reasoning. God is not the author of confusion. The places given in Numbers 21 supplement the list in Numbers 33, and fit together as a coherent whole.

Table 11 – Latter stages of Israel's wilderness journey in sequence

Numbers	Places	Meaning of place	Psalm 68
33:35	Eziongeber	Backbone of a mighty one or man	v 1 – "Let God (Elohim) arise"
33:36	Kadeshbarnea	Holy (field)	v 5, - "God in His holy habitation"
33:37	Mount Hor[1]	Mountain	v 15, 16 – "hill of God… *which* God desireth to dwell in"
33:41	Zalmonah	Terrace or Ascent	v 18 – "thou hast ascended on high"
33:42	Punon	Ore-pit or Darkness	v 6 – "rebellious dwell in a dry *land*"

Chapter 6 – Israel's wilderness march – a type for the march of the Rainbowed Angel

(cont'd) Numbers	Places	Meaning of place	Psalm 68
33:43	Oboth	Hollows or Waterskins^2	v 9 – "a plentiful rain"
33:44	Ijeabarm (also called Iim)	Heaps of the further region or Ruins of Abarim	
21:11,12	Zared^3	Willow bush or Exuberant growth	
21:13-15	Arnon	Rushing stream^4	v 12 – "kings of armies did flee apace"
21:16,17	Beer	Well^5	v 18 – "ascended on high"
21:18	Mattanah	Gift	v 18 – "thou has received gifts for men"
21:19	Nahaliel	God is splendour or Torrents of God^6	
21:19	Bamoth	High Places	
21:20	Pisgah^7	Peak or Hill or Cleft	v 15, 16 – "the hill.. *which* God desireth to dwell in"
33:45	Dibongad	River course^8 / Troop or Wasting	
33:46	Almon-diblathaim	Hiding place / double entrance	
33:47	Mountans of Abarim	Passages / Fords or Regions beyond	

(cont'd) Numbers	Places	Meaning of place	Psalm 68
33:48, 49 and 22:1 Deut.3:29	Plains of Moab by Jordan from Bethjesimoth unto Abelshittim. In the valley, over against Bethpeor.		
Summary	"by the way of mount Seir" (Deut. 1:2)[9]	Hairy	v 21 – "God shall wound the… hairy scalp of such an one as goeth on still in his trespasses"

Notes on table 11

1. Aaron died at Mount Hor (Num. 20:25-28).
2. The word seems to indicate a place or container for collecting and storing water.
3. The brook Zared or Zered was a tributary of the River Arnon. It took 38 years to get from Kadeshbarnea to here.

    "Now rise up, *said I* (i.e. Moses), and get you over the brook Zered. And we went over the brook Zered. And the space in which we came from Kadeshbarnea, until we were come over the brook Zered, *was* thirty and eight years; until all the generation of the men of war were wasted out from among the host, as the LORD sware unto them" (Deut. 2:13-14).

    From Kadeshbarnea the spies had been sent out, and ten had brought an evil report. The place is called Hazeroth in Numbers 33:17 (cf. Numbers 12:16 and 13:1-2).

4. Psalm 68:12 which is referenced here is an allusion to the victory of Deborah and Barak over Siserah. This was partly enabled by God causing the river Kishon to flood.

    "The river of Kishon swept them away, that ancient river, the river Kishon. O my soul, thou hast trodden down strength" (Judg. 5:21).

> Note however that the River Arnon is further south, to the east of the Dead Sea, and appears to be a different place from the Arnon mentioned here in Numbers.

5. When Israel encamped here God provided a well of water, hence the name of the place.

> "From thence *they went* to Beer: that *is* the well whereof the LORD spake unto Moses, Gather the people together, and I will give them water. Then Israel sang this song, Spring up, O well; sing ye unto it" (Num 21:16-17).

> The Hebrew for "spring up" is the same as for "ascended" in Psalm 68:18. The KJV margin in Numbers 21:17 has "ascend".

6. Another apparent allusion to Judges 5:21, quoted in Note 4.

7. Whilst here, Israel defeated Sihon king of Heshbon and Og king of Bashan – see Numbers 21:21-35

8. Another apparent allusion to Judges 5:21, quoted in Note 4.

9. This verse in Deuteronomy 1 summarises the journey from Egypt to Kadeshbarnea via mount Seir. "Seir" means "hairy", and thus connects with Psalm 68:21. Not only are the "issues from death" resolved at the judgment seat in Sinai for the redeemed, but there is also a fulfilment of Genesis 3:15 in that those found unworthy due to sin receive a fatal head wound.

In the Plains of Moab by Jordan from Bethjesimoth unto Abelshittim

Having arrived with the children of Israel at the plains of Moab, it is worth pausing with them there. The first reference to the camp there is in Numbers 22:1. There are then a series of references to them still encamped at this same place; Numbers 26:3, 31:12, 33:48, and 36:13, which is the very last verse of the book. So when Deuteronomy opens they are still there. It was in the Plains of Moab that Moses gave his final address to Israel, which is recorded for us as the fifth book of the Pentateuch.

> "These *be* the words which Moses spake unto all Israel on this side Jordan in the wilderness, in the plain over against the Red *sea*,

between Paran, and Tophel, and Laban, and Hazeroth, and Dizahab" (Deut. 1:1).

Thus it is from there that they send spies into Jericho, before they cross Jordan and go on to capture the city.

> "Joshua the son of Nun sent out of Shittim two men to spy secretly, saying, Go view the land, even Jericho. And they went, and came into an harlot's house, named Rahab, and lodged there" (Josh. 2:1).

It is easy to overlook from the Numbers record how much happened while Israel were encamped in the plains of Moab by Jordan, near Jericho. Whilst there they conquered Sihon, king of the Amorites, and Og, king of Bashan. Whilst they were there Balak commissioned Balaam to curse Israel, only to find that Balaam uttered words of Divinely inspired blessing, foreshadowing the victory of Messiah over his enemies.

> "His (Israel's) king shall be higher than Agag (Septuagint has "Gog"), and his kingdom shall be exalted" (Num. 24:7).

Israel then exacts vengeance on Midian and Balaam. Moses goes on to commission Joshua as his successor to lead Israel into the land promise. He also grants to the tribes of Reuben, Gad, and the half tribe of Manasseh their inheritance on the east of Jordan in Gilead, on condition that they help the other tribes to take their inheritance west of Jordan.

This series of events is highly significant in the prophetic context of this record concerning the Rainbowed Angel. The host of Israel has marched from Sinai to the borders of the land, and once there, they start the process of overcoming their enemies. This seems to be a type of the work of the Rainbowed Angel. As soon as they reach the southern borders of the land, the work of conquest of natural Israel's enemies will begin. Pointedly, they are reminded that part of the work they have come to do is to deliver Israel from the Gogian invader. For while the saints have been at Sinai, Israel will have entered the period of "dwelling safely". The Elijah mission to re-gather the remains of scattered Israel may take place during this period (or alternatively it may follow the defeat of Gog). With Israel dwelling safely, Gog comes down to take a spoil. At this point the Rainbowed Angel arrives. Firstly they will subdue the Arab enemies of Israel that surround them, typed

88

here by the Amorites, Bashan, and Midian. They will then enter the land, as we shall discover in subsequent chapters, to defeat Gog on the mountains of Israel.

Conclusion

Before we move into the prophets to consider what they have to say about the march of the Rainbowed Angel, we pause briefly to consider some other place names that are mentioned in connection with the exodus as a type, and that we shall encounter again later. The map on page 91 shows the northern part of the Sinai peninsula, the southern part of Israel, and the adjacent area to the east of the Dead Sea. Note especially the place where Israel crossed the Jordan and entered the land near Jericho, at the end of their journey. Based on the type that we have so far developed in relation to the exodus, built around a focus on Psalm 68, it is evident that the Rainbowed Angel will follow the same route from Sinai to the land of Israel.

The route passed through the area called Paran (probably a different Paran from that mentioned in Deuteronomy 1:1), went close to Teman and then passed through the territory of Edom, close to mount Seir, and then progressed along the eastern side of the Dead Sea to the plains of Moab at the northern end of the Dead Sea, across the Jordan from Jericho. Thus, the final encampment of Israel was in the plains of Moab, by the Red Sea, between Abel- Shittim and Bethjeshimoth.

As re have already noted, one of the things that takes place at this final camp is the address of Moses to the children of Israel at the very end of his life. This comprises the bulk of the book of Deuteronomy. How appropriate it is then for Moses to present to Israel, at the very end of his speech, a vision of a vast future host coming from the same direction that they had just travelled, to enter the land in triumph to fulfil Yahweh's will.

"This *is* the blessing, wherewith Moses the man of God blessed the children of Israel before his death. And he said, Yahweh came from Sinai, and rose up from Seir unto them; He shined forth from mount Paran, and He came with ten thousands of saints: from His right hand *went* a fiery law for them" (Deut. 33:1-2).

89

Here is a picture of Yahweh, manifest in a multitude, coming from Sinai and past Paran, coming to bring the blessings promised to the nations of Israel. So Deuteronomy concludes, before recording the death of Moses, with the outcome of the victory of the Rainbowed Angel for Israel. It is worth quoting here although we shall re-visit this passage later.

> "*There is* none like unto the God of Jeshurun, *Who* rideth upon the heaven in thy help, and in His excellency on the sky. The eternal God *is thy* refuge, and underneath *are* the everlasting arms: and He shall thrust out the enemy from before thee; and shall say, Destroy *them.* Israel then shall dwell in safety alone: the fountain of Jacob *shall be* upon a land of corn and wine; also his heavens shall drop down dew. Happy *art* thou, O Israel: who *is* like unto thee, O people saved by Yahweh, the shield of thy help, and Who *is* the sword of thy excellency! and thine enemies shall be found liars unto thee; and thou shalt tread upon their high places" (Deut. 33:26-29).

The opening words of Deuteronomy 33 provide a neat lead into the prophets, since the same key places are mentioned. So we close this chapter with the words of Moses, followed by the words of Habakkuk.

> "This *is* the blessing, wherewith Moses the man of God blessed the children of Israel before his death. And he said, Yahweh came from Sinai, and rose up from Seir unto them; He shined forth from mount Paran, and He came with ten thousands of saints: from His right hand *went* a fiery law for them. Yea, He loved the people; all His saints *are* in Thy hand: and they sat down at Thy feet; *every one* shall receive of Thy words" (Deut. 33:1-3).

> "God came from Teman, and the Holy One from mount Paran. His glory covered the heavens, and the earth was full of His praise" (Hab. 3:3).

Key places at the end of the wilderness journey

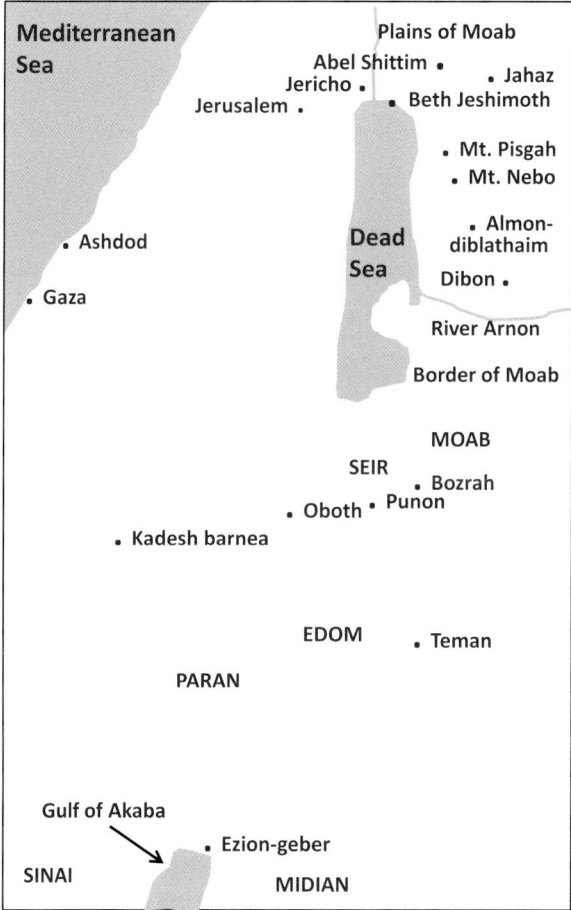

Chapter 7 – Thou wentest forth for the salvation of Thy people

Introduction

We now embark on a consideration of a series of Old Testament prophecies that detail the march of the Rainbowed Angel from the judgment at Sinai to entry into Jerusalem. Before doing this it will be helpful to summarise the progress of our exposition this far.

We first considered the vision of the Rainbowed Angel in Revelation 10. This was then linked to five other visions in the Old Testament and in Revelation (Rev. 1; Dan. 10; Zech. 14; Ezek. 1; Dan. 7), which employ similar symbols in presenting the multitudinous Christ body at successive stages of his mission. We then went on to show that the Scriptures do indeed present the concept of a military style "march" from Sinai to Jerusalem by this body of glorified saints. The foundation of this concept is the record of the journey of Israel through the wilderness from being constituted a nation at Sinai to their entry into Canaan when they crossed the Jordan near Jericho.

We have seen how this historical record is picked up in Psalm 68, and transformed into a prophecy of future events, establishing that the judgment seat will be at Sinai. In our previous chapter we have considered how even the route taken by the children of Israel was a type of the march of the Rainbowed Angel. We ended by considering some key events that took place towards the end of that journey for Israel, and how they too present a type of events to come for the glorified saints.

As we now turn to the prophets to trace the stages of this march we shall seek to place the prophecies in an approximate chronological order, as far as is possible, from the references to specific places that occur sequentially in the record of the journey of Israel.

Sequence of events from the return of Christ to the establishment of the Kingdom

A detailed consideration of Ezekiel 38 lies outside the scope of this study, except that it is now necessary to place it into a time context. The first key event will be the return of Christ from heaven to raise the dead and call those responsible to the judgment seat. A time when Israel dwells safely will then develop in Israel, as required by Ezekiel 38:8. This may be brought about by the work of Elijah in beginning to reform Israel, though Elijah's work may well take place later, once Gog has been defeated. However, the key point that is relevant to our study is that the Gogian invasion takes place after Jesus has returned to the household of faith, and after the resurrection and judgment. The saints with Christ, as the Rainbowed Angel will then enter the land to deliver Israel from the Gogian invader and from imminent annihilation. Jerusalem will then be delivered from Gentile occupation for one last time. The Rainbowed Angel will then go on to meet the challenge of the beast with its apostate woman rider, along with the ten horn kings, as outlined in Revelation 17:11-14.

The possible order of the main events may therefore be as set out below. Some of the details below are expounded and explained in more detail in succeeding chapters.

1. Return of Christ in person from heaven to the household.
2. Resurrection of the dead.
3. Those responsible to judgment gathered to Sinai.
4. The faithful rewarded with immortality; those rejected are sent back into the world to face their end.
5. The redeemed bride spends a period of time (one year?) with Christ the bridegroom in Sinai.
6. Israel dwells safely for a period.
7. Gogian confederacy invades Israel and Egypt.
8. Christ and the glorified saints comprising the Rainbowed Angel emerge from Sinai and progress northwards through Edom to the northern end of the Dead Sea, on the east of Jordan.
9. The Rainbowed Angel overcomes nations further north and east; especially Syria, and possibly also Jordan and Iraq; the treading of the winepress referred to in Isaiah 63:2-3.
10. Gogian confederacy defeated on the mountains of Israel by Christ and the glorified saints as the Rainbowed Angel. This could be described as Armageddon phase 1; the reaping of the wheat or grain harvest of the earth; Rev. 14:14-16..
11. Jerusalem delivered, and Christ proclaims himself king and demands the submission of the nations.
12. An excursion into Egypt to defeat part of Gog's army that seems to have been left there – Isaiah 19.

13. Elijah's mission to re-gather the remnant of Israel from the Gentile nations. Undertaken with the cherubim / "living creatures" of Ezekiel 1; alias the Rainbowed Angel.
14. The beast, ten horn kings and the apostate woman (false Christianity) challenge the Lamb, and are utterly defeated by Christ and those who are with him; the Rainbowed Angel again. Armageddon phase 2. The grape harvest and treading of the winepress; Rev. 14:17-19 and Rev. 19:11-16.

Our exposition of the work of the Rainbowed Angel from here on will mainly be concerned with points 8-12 in the list above.

Gog becomes aware of the Rainbowed Angel (Daniel 11)

We go first to Daniel 11, which contains a prophecy of a latter day invasion of the land of Israel, which we believe is the same invasion as that foretold in Ezekiel 38.

"The king of the north shall come against him (i.e. Israel) like a whirlwind, with chariots, and with horsemen, and with many ships; and he shall enter into the countries, and shall overflow and pass over. He shall enter also into the glorious land, and many *countries* shall be overthrown: but these shall escape out of his hand, *even* Edom, and Moab, and the chief of the children of Ammon. He shall stretch forth his hand also upon the countries: and the land of Egypt shall not escape. But he shall have power over the treasures of gold and of silver, and over all the precious things of Egypt: and the Libyans and the Ethiopians *shall be* at his steps" (Dan. 11:40-43).

The invader from the north invades suddenly and quickly conquers Israel, whilst leaving countries to the east of Israel (Jordan and Syria) alone. He passes through Israel and also conquers Egypt, apparently assisted by Libya and Ethopia (the latter may include Sudan) from further east and south. However, his victories are relatively shortlived, for Gog, the king of the north, hears of a rival force that threatens his newly gained conquests.

"But tidings out of the east and out of the north shall trouble him: therefore he shall go forth with great fury to destroy, and utterly to make away many. And he shall plant the tabernacles of his palace between the seas in the glorious holy mountain; yet he shall come to his end, and none shall help him" (Dan. 11:44-45).

94

His first reaction is to reassert his determination to hold Israel. He sets up his headquarters between the Mediterranean and Dead Seas, in the area of Jerusalem. It appears from Zechariah that he partly occupies Jerusalem itself.

> "I will gather all nations against Jerusalem to battle; and the city shall be taken, and the houses rifled, and the women ravished; and half of the city shall go forth into captivity, and the residue of the people shall not be cut off from the city" (Zech. 14:2).

Isaiah prophesied of an invasion in his days by Assyria. This seems to relate to the fourth of four Assyrian invasions which brought about the end of the northern kingdom, and threatened Judah and Jerusalem in the days of Isaiah and Hezekiah. The first three invasions are recorded in 2 Kings 15:19-20, 2 Kings 15:29, and 2 Kings 17:1-6 respectively. The fourth, led by Sennacherib, is recorded in 2 Kings 18 and 19, and was miraculously overcome by the angel of Yahweh. This destruction of the Assyrian was foretold by Isaiah.

> "Thus saith Adonai Yahweh of hosts, O My people that dwellest in Zion, be not afraid of the Assyrian: he shall smite thee with a rod, and shall lift up his staff against thee, after the manner of Egypt. For yet a very little while, and the indignation shall cease, and Mine anger in their destruction. And Yahweh of hosts shall stir up a scourge for him according to the slaughter of Midian at the rock of Oreb: and *as* his rod *was* upon the sea, so shall he lift it up after the manner of Egypt" (Isa. 10:24-26).

Isaiah then goes on to list twelve places in Israel from verses 28-32 that will be overrun by the Assyrian, who of course in this prophecy is a type of Gog, the latter day Assyrian. They are Aiath, Migron, Michmash, Geba, Ramah, Gibeah, Galim, Laish, Anathoth, Madmenah, Gebim, and Nob. They are all in the general vicinity of Jerusalem. This tallies with Daniel's prediction, that the king of the north will "plant the tabernacles of his palace between the seas in the glorious holy mountain". But Daniel also says that "he shall come to his end". The link with Isaiah continues for he goes on to say;

> "Behold, the Lord, Yahweh of hosts, shall lop the bough with terror: and the high ones of stature *shall be* hewn down, and the haughty shall be humbled... And there shall come forth a rod out of the stem

of Jesse, and a Branch shall grow out of his roots..." (Isa. 10:33 and 11:1).

The end result of the intervention of the greater Son of David will be that...

> "...they shall not hurt nor destroy in all my holy mountain: for the earth shall be full of the knowledge of Yahweh, as the waters cover the sea" (Isa. 11:9).

However, it will take time and effort to achieve this end, and this is the work of the Rainbowed Angel.

Consider now the "tidings out of the east and out of the north" that trouble Gog, king of the north, and which cause him to try to reinforce his position in Israel. He has passed through Israel into Egypt (Dan. 11:42-43). An area to the north and east of Egypt will thus encompass Sinai, Edom, Moab, and the land to the east of the Dead Sea. This is precisely the territory in which the Rainbowed Angel will be found, at the judgment seat, and on their march towards Israel, following the route taken by Israel under Moses and Joshua.

What exactly Gog hears as "tidings" we are not told. The Hebrew word means a rumour, report, or news, and is evidently something that is an accurate report about a force that is likely to challenge him. It would seem to refer to the initial movement of that force from where they have been hidden at Sinia, in preparation for their dramatic revelation to the world at large. And despite Gog's attempts to reinforce his position in Israel, he "shall come to his end, and none shall help him". So it would appear that the first public stirrings of the Rainbowed Angel will come at some point after Gog, the king of the north, arrives in Egypt, having first passed through Israel. The Rainbowed Angel will emerge from Sinai, proceed through Edom and Moab to the east of the Dead Sea, and then enter Israel from the east in the area of Jericho, prior to re-taking Jerusalem. It would appear from other prophecies that are covered in more detail later that Gog is partly destroyed in the wilderness (Isaiah 34 & 63), and partly at Jerusalem (Isaiah 30).

God came from Teman... (Habakkuk 3)

As the Rainbowed Angel moves north from Sinai, the next places on our map are Teman, Paran, and Midian. This takes us to Habakkuk 3, from which our current chapter heading is taken (verse 3), and which gives more details as the work of the Angel progresses.

> "God came from Teman, and the Holy One from mount Paran. Selah. His glory covered the heavens, and the earth was full of His praise… I saw the tents of Cushan in affliction: *and* the curtains of the land of Midian did tremble" (Hab 3:3,7).

At this stage the Rainbowed Angel is moving in a north easterly direction out of the Sinai peninsula, heading towards Teman, with Paran on the left hand, and Midian on the right hand to the south. Midian was located in the northern part of Arabia. Habakkuk mentions Cushan in connection with Midian. Cushan here appears to relate to somewhere (unknown) in Arabia. (Cush sometimes refers to Ethiopia or Sudan, or to territory in that area of north Africa. There was also a place called Cush(an) in ancient Mesopotamia, approximating to modern Iraq. However, neither of these fit the context here. (For further comments on Cushan see chapter 9).

A slight digression at this point is appropriate, in order to address the question of whether the words of Habakkuk are really a prophecy, or merely a statement of fact concerning events that happened to Israel after the exodus. Some suggest that the latter is the case on the basis of the past tense of the verbs in the opening verses of Habakkuk 3. Most versions follow the KJV in this respect, though interestingly the TRC translation has a mixture of past and present tenses. Some expositors argue that the tenses in Hebrew are not clear as they are in English, and either past, present, or future are valid. As an example of this argument it is stated that the Hebrew verb in Habakkuk 3:3 for "God came" is the same as in Habakkuk 2:3 for "it will surely come". One is translated in the past tense and one in the future.

The present author is not competent to discuss the niceties of Hebrew grammar and tenses. However, this is not necessary in order to establish conclusively that Habakkuk's words are a prophecy of future events. As shown in chapter 4 the prophet is referring back to events in the history of the nation of Israel and, under inspiration, using those as types of events still to come. We have already seen that Psalm 68 employs the same technique. God's ways are not limited by human rules of grammar. So, although expressed in the past tense (partly because they have reference to past events), these words are also a prophecy of things to come. Just as God led Israel from Sinai to

Canaan in the past, so He will again manifest Himself in the future in the Rainbowed Angel to undertake the mighty work of establishing the Kingdom.

The earth was full of His praise

This phrase connects to a relevant passage in Isaiah. In chapter 43 the prophet foretells the re-gathering of Israel as a witness to the nations that there is no other God than Yahweh. He then foretells the deliverance of Israel from Bablyon, and uses language reminiscent of the destruction of Egypt at the exodus, which is significant given the type we have noted in Habakkuk 3. Just as with Egypt, the Babylonians, along with their horses and chariots were to be utterly destroyed.

> "Thus saith Yahweh, which maketh a way in the sea, and a path in the mighty waters; Which bringeth forth the chariot and horse, the army and the power; they shall lie down together, they shall not rise: they are extinct, they are quenched as tow" (Isa. 43:16-17).

The prophet then invites the reader to consider these past events as types of something new.

> "Remember ye not the former things, neither consider the things of old. Behold, I will do a new thing; now it shall spring forth; shall ye not know it? I will even make a way in the wilderness, *and* rivers in the desert... This people have I formed for myself; they shall shew forth My praise." (Isa. 43:18,19,21).

The "new thing" is the creation of a redeemed multitude in Christ, the Rainbowed Angel, for whom there will be "a way in the wilderness". God is forming, even now, that multitude for Himself to show forth His praise. These words are an exhortation to all those who have obeyed the call of the gospel.

> "But ye *are* a chosen generation, a royal priesthood, an holy nation, a peculiar people; that ye should shew forth the praises of him who hath called you out of darkness into his marvellous light" (1 Pet. 2:9).

If we show forth the praises (KJV mg. "virtues") of our God now by manifesting His character, we shall be part of the Rainbowed Angel in the future; part of a people that God has formed for Himself to show forth His praise.

Armageddon – judgment on the nations

Verses 12 and 13 set the general theme of Habakkuk 3.

> "Thou didst march through the land in indignation, Thou didst thresh the heathen in anger. Thou wentest forth for the salvation of Thy people, *even* for salvation with Thine anointed; Thou woundedst the head out of the house of the wicked, by discovering the foundation unto the neck" (Hab. 3:12-13).

The reference to threshing the nations in anger or judgment is clearly an allusion to Armageddon – 'a heap of sheaves in a valley for threshing or judgment'. This is what we have termed the first phase of Armageddon in setting out the possible order of events at this time. It involves the destruction of Gog in order to deliver Israel and Jerusalem. The "anointed" is *mashiyach*, the Messiah, in this context it is used in the multitudinous sense; the Rainbowed Angel. His mission is to fulfil the promise of Eden, to inflict a fatal head wound in the embodiment of sin occupying God's land. The Hebrew for "head" here is *rosh*. It seems to be used simultaneously as a noun and as a proper name; in the latter sense providing a link to Ezekiel 38.

The objective of marching through the land is stated simply and succinctly; "the salvation of Thy people", that is of Israel. The mission of the Rainbowed Angel is to deliver Israel from the Gogian confederacy. On his way to destroy that confederacy of nations, the other nations through which he passes are also subdued. Verse 7 tells us that Midian will tremble. Further, Cushan will be "in affliction". The Hebrew for "affliction" is *aven*, normally translated as "iniquity". This is probably a case of cause and effect. Cushan is in affliction because of their iniquity. Their affliction and the trembling of Midian would seem to be caused by the terrifying effect of the Rainbowed Angel passing through their land. The modern equivalent of these territories would seem to be Saudi Arabia, which is therefore to be subdued by the Rainbowed Angel. If this is the case, it is interesting to note that it will involve the early subjection to the rule of Christ and the saints of two of Islam's most holy and important sites; Mecca and Medina.

99

But Saudi Arabia is just one nation. Gog heads a confederacy, as Ezekiel 38 makes clear. Thus Habakkuk speaks emphatically of how the Rainbowed Angel subdues a range of nations. Firstly the prophet uses the figure of mountains and hills brought low.

> "He stood, and measured the earth: He beheld, and drove asunder the nations; and the everlasting mountains were scattered, the perpetual hills did bow: His ways *are* everlasting… The mountains saw Thee, *and* they trembled" (Hab 3:6,10).

Mountains / hills = gentile powers

Mountains and hills represent Gentile powers in Scripture, but they will be levelled before Christ and those who are with him.

> "The voice of him that crieth in the wilderness, Prepare ye the way of Yahweh, make straight in the desert a highway for our God. Every valley shall be exalted, and every mountain and hill shall be made low: and the crooked shall be made straight, and the rough places plain: and the glory of Yahweh shall be revealed, and all flesh shall see *it* together: for the mouth of Yahweh hath spoken *it*" (Isa. 40:3-5).

Historically these words were spoken by John the Baptist to announce the first appearing of Messiah to Israel. But Messiah will be announced again to Israel by a voice in the wilderness, as Christ comes with his saints through the wilderness from Sinai to the land of promise. In the process of manifesting Divine glory, the arrogant exalted powers of the Gogian confederacy will be brought low. In contrast, the meek and downtrodden of the earth, who, in their day and generation, have submitted in meekness to the teaching of God's Word, will be exalted. Notice also the straight highway in the desert that is prepared for Yahweh our Elohim, as He moves without wavering from Sinai to Jerusalem on that march that has been foretold so long.

The point is then repeated using the figures of rivers, seas, and waters.

> "Was Yahweh displeased against the rivers? W*as* Thine anger against the rivers? *Was* Thy wrath against the sea, that Thou didst ride upon Thine horses *and* Thy chariots of salvation?... the overflowing of the water passed by: the deep uttered his voice, *and* lifted up his hands on high" (Hab. 3:8,10).

Chapter 7 – Thou wentest forth for the salvation of Thy people

Isaiah uses the symbols of both rivers and seas to represent Gentile nations, either specifically or in general.

> "Behold, the Lord bringeth up upon them the waters of the river, strong and many, *even* the king of Assyria, and all his glory: and he shall come up over all his channels, and go over all his banks" (8:7).

> "The wicked *are* like the troubled sea, when it cannot rest, whose waters cast up mire and dirt" (57:20).

When God's wrath is revealed against the kingdom of men, their arrogance will be overcome, and they will lift up their hands in acknowledgement of the greatness of the God Who goes forth for the salvation of His people.

But still Habakkuk hammers home the same message again. When the Rainbowed Angel is revealed, Gentile domination of the earth will come to an end.

> "The sun *and* moon stood still in their habitation: at the light of Thine arrows they went, *and* at the shining of Thy glittering spear" (Hab. 3:11).

Sun and moon as ruling heavenly bodies (cf. "the greater light to rule the day, and the lesser light to rule the night" (Gen. 1:16)) are used throughout Scripture to represent ruling powers among men. Before the manifestation of Yahweh in Christ and his saints they will stand still, their period of domination at an end. It is to Isaiah that we go again to confirm the interpretation of the symbol.

> "The indignation of Yahweh *is* upon all nations, and *His* fury upon all their armies: He hath utterly destroyed them, He hath delivered them to the slaughter.. all the host of heaven shall be dissolved, and the heavens shall be rolled together as a scroll: and all their host shall fall down, as the leaf falleth off from the vine, and as a falling *fig* from the fig tree" (Isa. 34:2, 4).

Whilst these words have a historical application, they are also prophetic. In that sense the context is clearly the same as Habakkuk 3; it is the indignation of Yahweh upon all nations when He marches through the land in indignation. We shall comment on Isaiah 34 again in a later chapter, but we note here that the focus of this indignation is on Edom.

101

"My sword shall be bathed in heaven: behold, it shall come down upon Idumea (i.e Edom), and upon the people of My curse, to judgment" (Isa. 34:5).

Edom sprang from Esau, the hated twin brother of Jacob; hated not by man, but by God (Mal.1:3). "Edom refused to give Israel passage through his border" (Num. 20:21) on their march to the promised land, a further confirmation that they were worthy of Divine hatred and cursing. So, as the Rainbowed Angel heads north past Paran towards Teman, they enter the territory of Edom, who now suffers Divinely ordained vengeance at the hands of Christ and his faithful saints.

But the overall message of Habakkuk is clear. By using a range of symbols to reinforce the same point, we are not left in any doubt that the Rainbowed Angel is an irresistible force before whom no nation on earth can stand.

Burning coals at his feet

At this point we must note a definite connection between Habakkuk 3 and the description of the Rainbowed Angel in Revelation. Habakkuk, speaking of God Who "came from Teman" (3:3), which we have identified as the Rainbowed Angel, says;

"Before him went the pestilence, and burning coals went forth at his feet" (Hab. 3:5).

This clearly seems to link with the statement in Revelation 10:1 concerning the angel with the rainbow on his head that "his feet (were) as pillars of fire".

Firstly we notice that the word "pestilence" in Habakkuk is the Hebrew *deber*, which comes from the root *dabar* meaning 'to speak'. The equivalent Hebrew noun is one of the Old Testament words for the Word of God. So this "pestilence" is something that comes as a result of a Divine pronouncement. This sense is picked with remarkable precision by the Spirit of inspiration in Revelation. There, the angel with the rainbow on his head "had in his hand a little book open... and (he) cried with a loud voice" (10:2,3). Here therefore is the Word of God both written and spoken to pronounce the work of judgment (symbolised by the seven thunders) that the Rainbowed Angel is to perform. Furthermore, "the seven thunders (also) uttered their voices" (verse 3), confirming the same principle.

Next, note that in both passages the feet are associated with fire. The KJV in Habakkuk has "burning coals", though the margin suggests "diseases". It is not clear what the grounds for this alternative are. The Hebrew is *resheph*, always translated by words carrying the idea of burning or heat. This seems to be correct as *resheph* comes from the root *saraph* meaning 'to burn'. So the sense of the verse in Habakkuk is that the Rainbowed Angel has a Divine commission to execute judgments signified by a hot burning fire wherever he treads with his feet.

The symbolism is identical in Revelation 10. The angel's feet were like "pillars of fire". The Greek for "pillars" is *stulos*, meaning a pillar or column. The OLB defines this as "flames rising like pillars". The unambiguous message is one of fiery judgment on those opposed to the will of God. This is confirmed by Paul.

> "To you who are troubled rest with us, when the Lord Jesus shall be revealed from heaven with his mighty angels, in flaming fire taking vengeance on them that know not God, and that obey not the gospel of our Lord Jesus Christ" (2 Thess. 1:7-8).

This imagery of judgment by fire is derived from the Old Testament.

> "Behold, the day cometh, that shall burn as an oven; and all the proud, yea, and all that do wickedly, shall be stubble: and the day that cometh shall burn them up, saith Yahweh of hosts, that it shall leave them neither root nor branch" (Mal. 4:1).

Significantly the very next verse refers to the "Sun of righteousness", which is itself part of the origin of the Rainbowed Angel figure whose "face *was* as it were the sun" (Rev. 10:1).

His brightness was as the light

> "And *his* brightness was as the light; he had horns *coming* out of his hand: and there *was* the hiding of his power" (Hab. 3:4).

Working backwards in Habakkuk 3, we now wish to consider an element of the symbolism of the Rainbowed Angel which takes us to redemption and glory rather than judgment.

However, first notice the next phrase in verse 4; "he had horns *coming* out of his hand". Here the KJV margin seems to suggest a better alternative; "bright beams out of his side". The ERV supports this, with "he hath rays *coming* forth from his hand". The Hebrew for "horns" is *qeren*, and though almost always translated as horns, it comes from the root *qaran*, meaning 'to shine'. Accepting the marginal rendering, there is an obvious connection with the beams of light which constitute the rainbow on the head of the apocalyptic angel.

Another reason for preferring the marginal alternative to "horns"[1] is that it fits better with the preceding phrase in the verse, which also focuses on light ("*his* brightness was as the light"). This first phrase leads us to the multitude of the redeemed, part of the Rainbowed Angel which manifests the glory of God. The previous verse emphasizes the One who heads the Rainbowed Angel multitude, the Lord Jesus Christ.

> "God came from Teman, and the Holy One from mount Paran" (Hab. 3:3).

"God" translates the Hebrew *Eloah*, meaning 'a Mighty One'. He is also "the Holy One". This is the leader of the multitude, God's Holy One, the Lord Jesus Christ, whose brightness will be as the light. "Brightness" in Habakkuk 3:3 translates the Hebrew *nogah*. Other uses of this word also point us to the redeemed saints. Firstly Isaiah gives a definition.

> "For Zion's sake will I not hold my peace, and for Jerusalem's sake I will not rest, until the righteousness thereof go forth as brightness, and the salvation thereof as a lamp *that* burneth" (Isa. 62:1).

Thus "brightness" is defined as "righteousness". This may then be linked to a passage in Proverbs where *nogah* is translated as "shining".

---

1. A horn has the essential idea of a protrusion. Though this is normally physical, a ray of light coming out of an object may also be described as a protrusion. An old English usage in the line of a hymn speaks of God creating the "horned moon to shine by night". This seems to refer to the idea of beams of light shining forth, though some interpret the origin as referring to the shape of the crescent moon being similar to a horn.

"But the path of the just *is* as the shining light, that shineth more and more unto the perfect day" (Prov. 4:18).

The righteous, or the just are those who are accounted righteous on the basis of their faith, and on that basis are given the gift of eternal life. The path to that promised reward is straight and sure for those who hold fast to their faith. They will attain to that "perfect day", even the Kingdom of God. In a similar context David also uses this Hebrew word in a passage where it is translated as "clear shining".

"The God of Israel said, the Rock of Israel spake to me, He that ruleth over men *must be* just, ruling in the fear of God. And *he shall be* as the light of the morning, *when* the sun riseth, *even* a morning without clouds; *as* the tender grass *springing* out of the earth by clear shining after rain" (2 Sam. 23:3-4).

The ruler over men is the Lord Jesus Christ, the Holy One of Habakkuk. David then speaks of the resurrection morning for the faithful saints. The Sun of righteousness is rising, and the joy of the kingdom morning has arrived (cf. Psa 30:5). Saints who have withered and died like the grass of the earth due to their mortality, have now sprung out of the earth, and been accounted righteous for their faith, so that they are now in their resurrected and immortal state as "clear shining" light. The rain storms of mortal life are past. Their light comes from their Saviour and Leader, who himself is the "light of the morning". Thus the multitude of saints, that along with Christ make up the Rainbowed Angel, are described by the prophet as his "brightness".

The "light of the morning", refers to Christ, and may be identified with the Morning Star. Thus, to be given the morning star is a figurative way of saying that the faithful saints will be constituted as one with the Lord Jesus Christ; made like him, immortal and incorruptible. They are the "brightness" of him who is the Sun of righteousness; they are the "bright beams (coming) out of his side".

"He that overcometh… I will give him the morning star" (Rev. 2:26,28).

Given the wonderful connections that have emerged in the preceding exposition, showing that the Messiah is the "light of the morning" or "morning star", and that his "brightness" is the light of the justified and redeemed saints that shine forth from him, it is perhaps no coincidence that in the epilogue to Revelation the Lord Jesus Christ pulls these ideas together one last time.

> "I Jesus have sent mine angel to testify unto you these things in the ecclesias. I am the root and the offspring of David, *and* the bright and morning star" (Rev. 22:16).

The salvation of Thy people

Finally in this chapter we return to the mission of the Rainbowed Angel.

> "Thou wentest forth for the salvation of Thy people" (Hab. 3:13)

As previously noted this people is natural Israel, who are to be delivered from Gentile oppression and occupation at the hands of the Gogian confederacy. If the one who goes forth in Habakkuk 3 is indeed the Lord Jesus Christ and his immortalised saints, then "Thy people" in this context must be natural Israel. It cannot refer to the saints as they have by this time already been saved.

There is in fact a remarkable proof embedded into the text of Habakkuk 3 that "Thy people" refers to natural Israel. At the end of his life Jacob uttered a prophecy to each of his twelve sons concerning the people that would be descended from them

> "Jacob called unto his sons, and said, Gather yourselves together, that I may tell you *that* which shall befall you in the last days" (Gen. 49:1).

The prophecies, or blessings are then recorded from verses 3-27. Within Habakkuk 3 there is an allusion to, or quotation from every one of those prophecies, and / or to the meaning of the names of the sons of Jacob. These are set out in the following tables. And any doubt that the connections are valid is dispelled by Habakkuk 3:9.

> "Thy bow was made quite naked, *according* to **the oaths of the tribes**, *even thy* word. Thou didst cleave the earth with rivers" (Hab. 3:9).

This truly remarkable list of connections with the twelve tribes of Israel removes any doubt that the mission of the Rainbowed Angel foretold by Habakkuk will indeed be the salvation of God's people of Israel.

Table 12 – The oaths of the tribes in Habakkuk 3

Name	Meaning of name	Gen. 49	Gen. 49 text & keywords	Hab. 3	Hab. 3 text
Reuben	**See, a son**	v3,4	Reuben, thou *art* my **firstborn**, my might, and the beginning of my **strength**, the excellency of dignity, and the excellency of **power**: Unstable as water, thou shalt not excel; because thou wentest up to thy father's bed; then defiledst thou *it*: he went up to my couch.	v 4	the hiding of His **power** (diff. Heb.)
Simeon	**Hearing**	v5-7	Simeon and Levi *are* brethren; instruments of cruelty *are in* their habitations. O my soul, come not thou into their secret; unto their **assembly**, mine honour, be not thou **united**: for in their **anger** they slew a man, and in their selfwill they digged down a wall. Cursed *be* their **anger**, for *it was* fierce; and their **wrath**, for it was cruel: I will **divide them** in Jacob, and **scatter them** in Israel.	v 2 v 16 v 2	O Yahweh, I have **heard** Thy speech (KJV mg "hearing") When I **heard** my belly trembled in **wrath** remember mercy (contrast)
Levi	**Joined**	[also see above]	[Also see above; note play on "divide / scattered" and contrast with "assembly / united" and meaning of Levi = 'joined'.]	v 6	drove asunder the nations... mountains were **scattered**

Name (cont'd)	Meaning of name	Gen 49	Gen. 49 text & keywords	Hab. 3	Hab. 3 text
Judah	Praise	v8-12	Judah, thou *art he* whom thy brethren shall **praise: thy hand *shall be* in the neck of thine enemies**; thy father's children shall **bow down** before thee. Judah *is a* lion's whelp: from the prey, my son, thou art gone up: he stooped down, he couched as a lion, and as an old lion; who shall rouse him up? The sceptre shall not depart from Judah, nor a lawgiver from **between his feet**, until Shiloh come; and unto him *shall* the gathering of the people *be*. Binding his foal unto the **vine**, and his ass's colt unto the **choice vine**; he washed his garments in **wine**, and his clothes in the blood of **grapes**: His eyes *shall be* red with **wine**, and his teeth white with milk.	v 3 v5 v4 v 13 v 17	the earth was full of His **praise** Burning coals went forth **at his feet** **horns *coming out* of his hand** **woundest the head**... of the wicked... unto the neck neither shall fruit be in the **vines** (contrast)
Zebulun	Dwelling	v13	Zebulun shall **dwell** at the haven of the sea; and he *shall be* for an haven of ships; and his border *shall be* unto Zidon.	v 11	sun... moon stood still in their **habitation** (Heb. = *zebool*)

Name (cont'd)	Meaning of name	Gen 49	Gen 49 text & keywords	Hab. 3	Hab. 3 text
Issachar	An hire	v14,15	Issachar *is* a strong ass couching down between two burdens: And **he saw that rest *was* good**, and the land that *it was* pleasant; and bowed his shoulder to bear, and became a **servant unto tribute.**	v 16	**that I might rest in the day of trouble**
Dan	Judge / Judging	v16-18	Dan shall **judge** his people, as one of the tribes of Israel. Dan shall be a serpent by the way, an adder in the path, that biteth the horse heels, so that his rider shall fall backward. I have **waited for Thy salvation** O LORD.	v 8 v 13 v 18 >>>	chariots of **salvation** Thou wentest forth for **the salvation of Thy people… salvation** with Thine anointed I will joy in **the God of my salvation** [Overall theme of judgment]
Gad	Troop	v19	Gad, **a troop shall overcome him**: but he shall overcome at the last.	v 16	**He will invade them with His troops**
Asher	Blessed / Happy	v20	Out of Asher his bread *shall be* fat, and **he shall yield royal dainties**.	v 17, 18	[contrast] **fields shall yield no meat**… Yet I will rejoice in Yahweh

Name (cont'd)	Meaning of name	Gen 49	Gen 49 text & keywords	Hab 3	Hab. 3 text
Naphtali	My wrestling	v21	Naphtali *is* a **hind let loose**: he giveth goodly words.	v 19	Yahweh Adonai… **will make my feet like hinds' feet**
Joseph	Adding	v22-26	Joseph *is* a fruitful bough, *even* a fruitful bough by a well; *whose* branches run over the wall: The **archers have sorely grieved him, and shot *at him*,** and hated him: But his **bow abode in strength**, and the **arms of his hands were made strong by the hands of the mighty *God* of Jacob;** (from thence *is* the shepherd, the stone of Israel:) *Even* by the God of thy father, Who shall help thee; and by the Almighty, Who shall bless thee with blessings of heaven above… of the deep that lieth under…of the breasts, and of the womb: The blessings of thy father have prevailed above the blessings of my progenitors unto the utmost bound of the **everlasting hills**: they shall be **on the head of Joseph, and on the crown of the head of him that was separate from his brethren**	v4 v 6 v9 v 11 v13	**horns coming out of his hand** **everlasting mountains… perpetual hills** Thy **bow** was made quite naked at the light of **Thine arrows** **woundest the head** (contrast)

Name (cont'd)	Meaning of name	Gen 49	Gen 49 text & keywords	Hab 3	Hab. 3 text
Benjamin	Son of the right hand (originally Benoni - Son of my sorrow)	v27	Benjamin shall **ravin** as a wolf: in the morning he shall **devour the prey**, and at night he shall divide the spoil.	v 14	their (the wicked v13) rejoicing as to **devour the poor** secretly

Chapter 8 – Yahweh rose up from Sinai… with ten thousands of saints

Introduction

As indicated in the title of this chapter, the next part of Scripture we wish to consider concerning the progress of the Rainbowed Angel towards the land of promise is Deuteronomy 33. Previously, in considering Habakkuk 3 we have encountered Christ and the saints at Teman, and in the vicinity of Paran, having caused Midian to tremble (Hab. 3:7) as they moved north from Sinai. They have now moved slightly further northwards, as this prophecy (Deut. 33:2) places them again in the area of Mount Paran, but also in Seir.

The geographical link is not the only connection with Habakkuk 3. We noted at the end of the previous chapter that Habakkuk refers to "the oaths of the tribes" (3:9). We also noted the number of detailed links with the prophetic blessings on the tribes given by Jacob, which are recorded in Genesis 49 (see Table 12). Moses also pronounced prophetic blessings on the tribes of Israel as they were about to enter the Land. These are recorded in the chapter we are now considering; Deuteronomy 33. Thus once again the context is in effect telling us that the prophecy of the work of the Rainbowed Angel is associated with the deliverance of the nation and land of Israel from oppression and occupation. Moses introduces the Rainbowed Angel, and then proceeds to the blessings on the tribes, which will result, finally, from the work of this multitudinous angel. Thus the chapter opens;

> "This *is* the blessing, wherewith Moses the man of God blessed the children of Israel before his death" (Deut. 33:1).

These words would be a reassurance for that generation. But they were also prophetic words. They are reassurance to any of natural Israel who will take heed that in the future, in the time of their final trouble, deliverance will come from the area of Sinai. Deliverance will arrive in the land of promise via the same route by which their fathers were led by the angel of Yahweh's presence under Moses and Joshua.

The identification of the Rainbowed Angel in Deuteronomy 33

Moses introduces the Rainbowed Angel with these words;

"Yahweh came from Sinai, and rose up from Seir unto them; He shined forth from mount Paran, and He came with ten thousands of saints: from His right hand *went* a fiery law for them" (Deut. 33:2).

"LORD" here translates the Hebrew Yahweh; 'He (who) will be". Given the statement that "He shined forth", it is clear that we are in the realm of 'God manifestation'. God manifests Himself in stages. Firstly, it is through His almighty power, for example at creation. Next it is through an individual who bears His Name and fulfils His will. Initially this is via an angel bearing the Yahweh Name, for example to Moses at the bush that burned but was not consumed.

"I *am* the God of thy father, the God of Abraham, the God of Isaac, and the God of Jacob… I will be Who I will be" (Exo. 3:6,14).

Another example is the angel that led Israel through the wilderness.

"Behold, I send an Angel before thee, to keep thee in the way, and to bring thee into the place which I have prepared. Beware of him, and obey his voice, provoke him not; for he will not pardon your transgressions: for my name *is* in him" (Exo. 23:20-21).

But these were a mere foreshadowing of the perfect personal manifestation, as recorded by John.

The Word was made flesh, and dwelt among us, (and we beheld his glory, the glory as of the only begotten of the Father,) full of grace and truth" (Jno. 1:14).

These words refer to the personal manifestation of the glory of Yahweh in the person of the Lord Jesus Christ. Moses refers to this personal manifestation in Deuteronomy 33, within his blessing on Joseph, the one of the sons of Jacob who was most like Jesus in character.

"Of Joseph he said, Blessed of Yahweh be his land… and *for* the good will of him that dwelt in the bush: let *the blessing* come upon the head of Joseph, and upon the top of the head of him *that was* separated from his brethren" (Deut. 33:13, 16).

Whilst it is clearly a blessing on the tribes of Ephraim and Manasseh that would descend from Joseph, there is also a particular focus on one man, who was not actually a descendant of Joseph, but who was typed by Joseph in so many ways, that is Jesus Christ. They were both separate from their brethren, alienated by doing God's will. Christ in particular was "separate from sinners" (Heb. 7:26), for he "did no sin" (1 Pet. 2:22). So this personal blessing pronounced by Moses through the Spirit is specifically for the one in whom "dwelleth all the fulness of the Godhead bodily" (Col. 2:9). As the perfect Nazarite the blessing will rest on the head of Christ when he is revealed and acknowledged as King of kings. The unshaven "top" or crown of the head was the outward sign of the Nazarite vow. In fulfilment of that type, Christ is now "crowned with glory and honour" (Heb. 2:9).

So it is clear that in this Mosaic blessing, the personal manifestation of Yahweh is encapsulated in the phrase "Yahweh came from Sinai, and rose up from Seir" (Deut. 33:2). But that is not the complete picture as the rest of the verse makes clear for "He came with ten thousands of saints: from His right hand *went* a fiery law for them".

The fact of the multitudinous element is self-evident. These words are echoed in other later prophecies.

> "Enoch also, the seventh from Adam, prophesied of these, saying, Behold, the Lord cometh with ten thousands of his saints, to execute judgment upon all, and to convince all that are ungodly among them of all their ungodly deeds which they have ungodly committed" (Jude verses 14-15).

Jesus himself, in the Apocalypse, picks up the same theme concerning the multitude of the redeemed, in those things he revealed to John, for he…

> "… beheld, and, lo, in the midst of the throne and of the four living creatures, and in the midst of the elders, stood a Lamb as it had been slain… and when he had taken the book, the four living creatures and four *and* twenty elders fell down before the Lamb, having every one of them harps, and golden vials full of odours, which are the prayers of saints. And they sung a new song, saying, Thou art worthy to take the book, and to open the seals thereof: for thou wast slain, and hast redeemed us to God by thy blood out of every kindred, and tongue, and people, and nation; and hast made

us unto our God kings and priests: and we shall reign on the earth. And I beheld, and I heard the voice of many angels round about the throne and the beasts and the elders: and the number of them was ten thousand times ten thousand, and thousands of thousands" (Rev. 5:6,8-11).

The four living creatures (that is the cherubim), and the twenty four elders, each representing the redeemed saints, celebrate in song their redemption through the sacrifice of the Lamb. They are also represented in the vision by a vast number of angels. These are the words that are a direct echo of Moses in Deuteronomy, and make clear that the "ten thousands of saints" that will come from Sinai is indeed a picture of the resurrected and redeemed saints.

There is a further interesting detail in the next verse in Deuteronomy that gives further support to this statement.

"Yea, he loved the people; all his saints *are* in thy hand: and they sat down at thy feet; *every one* shall receive of thy words" (Deut. 33:3).

In the spirit of prophecy Moses tells us concerning Jesus Christ, the personal manifestation of Yahweh, that "all his saints are in (his) hand". Once again the same symbolism is picked up in the Apocalypse. In the vision of the one "like unto the Son of man" John testifies that...

"...he had in his right hand seven stars" (Rev. 1:13,16).

This chapter closes with the explanation that John was given of the significance of this vision. Part of the explanation states;

"The seven stars are the angels of the seven ecclesias" (Rev. 1:20).

The following chapter then opens with the letter to Ephesus, in which the author is described, among other things as...

"...he that holdeth the seven stars in his right hand, who walketh in the midst of the seven golden candlesticks" (Rev. 2:1).

Now although many Christadelphian expositors regard the "angels" of the seven ecclesias as the spirit-guided elders in the first and early second centuries, the link with the verse in Deuteronomy 33 suggests a slightly variant, though not radically different interpretation. It would appear that the "seven stars", which are the "angels of the seven

Rev.

7 stars
7 angels } ? rep. All the saints

The March of the Rainbowed Angel

ecclesias", are equivalent to "all the saints". The "seven stars" or "angels" therefore seem to represent the true saints within the ecclesia (whether possessed of spirit gifts or not), all of whom are in the hand of the Master.

In the age to come they (and, by God's grace, we) shall "(sit) down at (his) feet" (Deut. 33:3), or, in the words of Revelation, "(fall) down before the Lamb" (5:8). These true saints, now ransomed from the power of the grave and blessed with immortality, will "receive of (the) words" of the one who is manifest in the full power and glory of the Creator, and will go forth with him to subdue the nations, deliver the remnant of Israel, and establish the righteous rule of God's promised kingdom.

These seven stars, the angels of the seven ecclesias, symbolising the true and faithful saints, together will constitute the...

> "... mighty angel come down from heaven clothed with a cloud; and [with] a rainbow... upon his head" (Rev. 10:1).

This is none other than the 'Rainbowed Angel' that we have been considering from the start of our study.

Judgment upon all... that are ungodly among them

We wish at this point to return to comment in a little more detail on Jude's reference to the prophecy of Enoch. First, we quote again the words of Jude.

> "Enoch also, the seventh from Adam, prophesied of these, saying, Behold, the Lord cometh with ten thousands of his saints, to execute judgment upon all, and to convince all that are ungodly among them of all their ungodly deeds which they have ungodly committed, and of all their hard *speeches* which ungodly sinners have spoken against him" (Jude verses 14-15).

Enoch's
prophecy

The book of Genesis does not record the prophecy of Enoch, simply recording his faithfulness, inasmuch as he "walked with God". However Jude appears to be quoting, through the Spirit, from Enoch's prophecy. The opening phrase – "the Lord cometh with ten thousands of his saints" – is apparently quoted later by Moses, when through the Spirit, he addressed Israel. The quotation is in the passage which forms the focus of this chapter.

> "Yahweh came from Sinai, and rose up from Seir unto them; He shined forth from mount Paran, and He came with ten thousands of saints" (Deut. 33:2).

This leads us to ponder upon whom the Lord with ten thousands of his saints executed their judgment? In one sense the answer may appear simple, since Jude says it will be "upon all". This implies the world at large, and this is no doubt true. Indeed, Paul indicated as much to the Corinthians.

> "Do ye not know that the saints shall judge the world? And if the world shall be judged by you, are ye unworthy to judge the smallest matters?" (1 Cor. 6:2).

However, we suggest that it is not quite as simple as this. Part of the point that Paul is making in this passage in Corinthians is that the saints have a responsibility to exercise some judgment among themselves. Consider the previous and following verses.

> "Dare any of you, having a matter against another, go to law before the unjust, and not before the saints?...Know ye not that we shall judge angels? how much more things that pertain to this life?" (1 Cor. 6:1,3).

With this in mind, we must consider again the overall situation that will obtain when the Rainbowed Angel emerges from Sinai. Those responsible will have already appeared before the judgment seat of Christ. Those found worthy will already have been made immortal and incorporated into the Rainbowed Angel. Those who have been rejected will have been sent back into the world, full of remorse and the inevitable weeping, wailing, and gnashing of teeth. There, they will have to live out a period of mortality in the chaos of a world which will be undergoing the terrible, but just judgments of the Almighty. These most unfortunate of all people will be included in those to suffer at the hands of the judgments enacted by Christ and the saints. This would appear to be the sense of Jude's phrase "all that are ungodly among them" (verse 15). If we ask 'among whom' the inevitable, and in a way, the terrible answer seems to be, 'among the ecclesia'.

117

Some will query whether this is a fair and accurate conclusion. Firstly, note that the burden of Jude's message and the warnings he gives were to the ecclesia. He is quite explicit about this.

"There are certain men crept in unawares" (verse 4).

"The angels which kept not their first estate... Likewise also these *filthy* dreamers defile the flesh, despise dominion" (verses 6, 8).

"These are spots in your feasts of charity" (verse 12).

Furthermore, this is parallel to the focus of the message of Enoch. In walking with God Enoch rebuked his generation, in much the same way that Jesus told his disciples they would rebuke their own contemporaries by their Godly way of life.

"If the world hate you, ye know that it hated me before *it hated* you. If ye were of the world, the world would love his own: but because ye are not of the world, but I have chosen you out of the world, therefore the world hateth you. Remember the word that I said unto you, The servant is not greater than his lord. If they have persecuted me, they will also persecute you; if they have kept my saying, they will keep yours also" (Jno. 15:18-20).

The generation that Enoch effectively rebuked by his own manner of life, was in fact the ecclesia of his day. He died just over 600 years before the flood, though doubtless he had spoken of that great judgment to come if the people did not repent. Noah was born not long after Enoch died, and in a sense the baton was passed to Noah. In particular Noah prophesied Divine warnings for 120 years prior to the flood. It is significant that Genesis 6 opens with a comment on how the world was adversely affecting the ecclesia as the "sons of God" (the ecclesia) married the "daughters of men" (6:2).

So we conclude that the message of Enoch and of Jude was primarily to the ecclesia of their day, and that they warned of judgments that would be executed by the "ten thousands of... saints" upon those in the ecclesia who were found to be ungodly. This does not make comfortable reading, when we realise that if we are found faithful, we may be involved, as part of the Rainbowed Angel, in executing God's judgments, which will fall on some we may have known in the days of our flesh, but who were rejected at the judgment seat. To human thinking this is difficult to comprehend or accept. But we must learn to think not as men, but as God, recalling the words of Isaiah.

"My thoughts *are* not your thoughts, neither *are* your ways My ways, saith Yahweh. For *as* the heavens are higher than the earth, so are My ways higher than your ways, and My thoughts than your thoughts" (Isa. 55:8-9).

True disciples, those who we must learn to love because they are "in Christ", are not necessarily those who we 'like' in fleshly terms, or those to whom we are related after the flesh. Instead we must develop the mind of Christ in order to prepare for a part with and in the Rainbowed Angel.

"Then one said unto him, Behold, thy mother and thy brethren stand without, desiring to speak with thee. But he answered and said unto him that told him, Who is my mother? and who are my brethren? And he stretched forth his hand toward his disciples, and said, Behold my mother and my brethren! For whosoever shall do the will of my Father which is in heaven, the same is my brother, and sister, and mother" (Matt. 12:47-50).

Yahweh… rose up

"Yahweh came from Sinai, and rose up from Seir unto them; he shined forth from mount Paran" (Deut. 33:2).

We now wish to consider the words "rose up" (a single Hebrew verb *zarach*), because this continues our focus on the multitude of redeemed saints, who will accompany and be one with the Lord Jesus Christ, the personal manifestation of Yahweh's glory. The reader is referred to chapter 7, where, in considering the "brightness" of God (*Eloah*), the Mighty One in Habakkuk 3:3-4, we made the following statement.

"The faithful saints will be constituted as one with the Lord Jesus Christ; made like him, immortal and incorruptible. They are the "brightness" of him who is the Sun of righteousness; they are the "bright beams (coming) out of his side". His "brightness" is therefore the light of the justified and redeemed saints that shine forth from him.

This brightness arises from the imputed righteousness of the saints, which emanates from him who did no sin, and who thus offered himself as a sacrifice that displayed the righteousness of God. It is referred to as "clear shining" in a passage we partly expounded on the pages referred to above.

> "*He shall be* as the light of the morning, *when* the sun riseth, *even* a morning without clouds; *as* the tender grass *springing* out of the earth by clear shining after rain" (2 Sam. 23:4).

Note now that the Hebrew for "riseth" is *zarach*, and as this passage shows, it clearly relates to the rising of the sun in its normal usage. Thus it is reasonable to map this implicit sense on to its use in Deuteronomy 33:2. We can therefore also link it to other passages that liken the future appearance of the glory of Yahweh manifest in Christ returned to the rising of the sun.

> "Behold, the darkness shall cover the earth, and gross darkness the people: but Yahweh shall arise upon thee, and His glory shall be seen upon thee. And the Gentiles shall come to Thy light, and kings to the brightness of Thy rising" (Isa. 60:2-3).

The Hebrew for "arise" is once again the verb *zarach*, while the Hebrew for "rising" is the related noun *zerach*. This latter word is qualified by "brightness", which is the same word discussed earlier (see above), and which relates to the saints, and their derived righteousness. Thus once again we are taught that when the glory of Yahweh is manifested from Sinai, it will be in the multitudinous Christ, the Rainbowed Angel. Clearly, in this passage, the darkness refers to the moral state of mankind in the last days. We are indeed now living in those days of gross darkness. There is almost universal ignorance of the Truth contained in God's Word; indeed, that Word is increasingly derided and blasphemed by the 'wise' men of the earth. But ultimately righteousness will prevail, and it will be the privilege of the saints of Christ to work with him to spread the gospel of truth and righteousness to those who survive the judgments of God out of all nations.

It is appropriate to remind ourselves at this point that the first work of the Rainbowed Angel as it arises from Sinai, Seir, and Paran is to deliver Israel from the hand of the invader. For them first of all, will the sun of righteousness arise. The deliverance of Israel is indeed the whole thrust of Isaiah 60. So it is that they are blessed with a new and

There are 6 portrayals of the role of the Rainbow Angel and they are arranged in the chronological order of their application

The Rainbowed Angel of Revelation ch.10 is not an artistic picture of an angel but is a symbol which has to be de-coded by 'letting scripture interpret scripture'

The Mighty Angel..... came from heaven,	Ephesians 1v3
clothed with a cloud,	Hebrews12:1
...and a rainbow, with...	Genesis 9:9
the face of the sun,...	Matthew 17:2
and feet of fire,	Revelation1:15
holding a book, and with the right foot on the sea	Revelation 20
...and left foot on the earth,	Daniel & Rev.13
and roared with the voice	Daniel & Rev 13
....of a lion	Joel 3 : 16

Revelation 1 : 13-18 : The Son of man at work in the Ecclesia today

Daniel 10 : The Certain Man when the saints are made immortal

Revelation 10 : 1-6 The principal vision of the Multitudinous Christ

The following are after the Angel's manifestation to the world

Zechariah 14 : 3-5 As Yahweh Elohim and the saints with him

Ezekiel 1: 1-28 : The redeemed saints go to the people of Israel

Daniel 7 : 21-27: The Ancient of Days

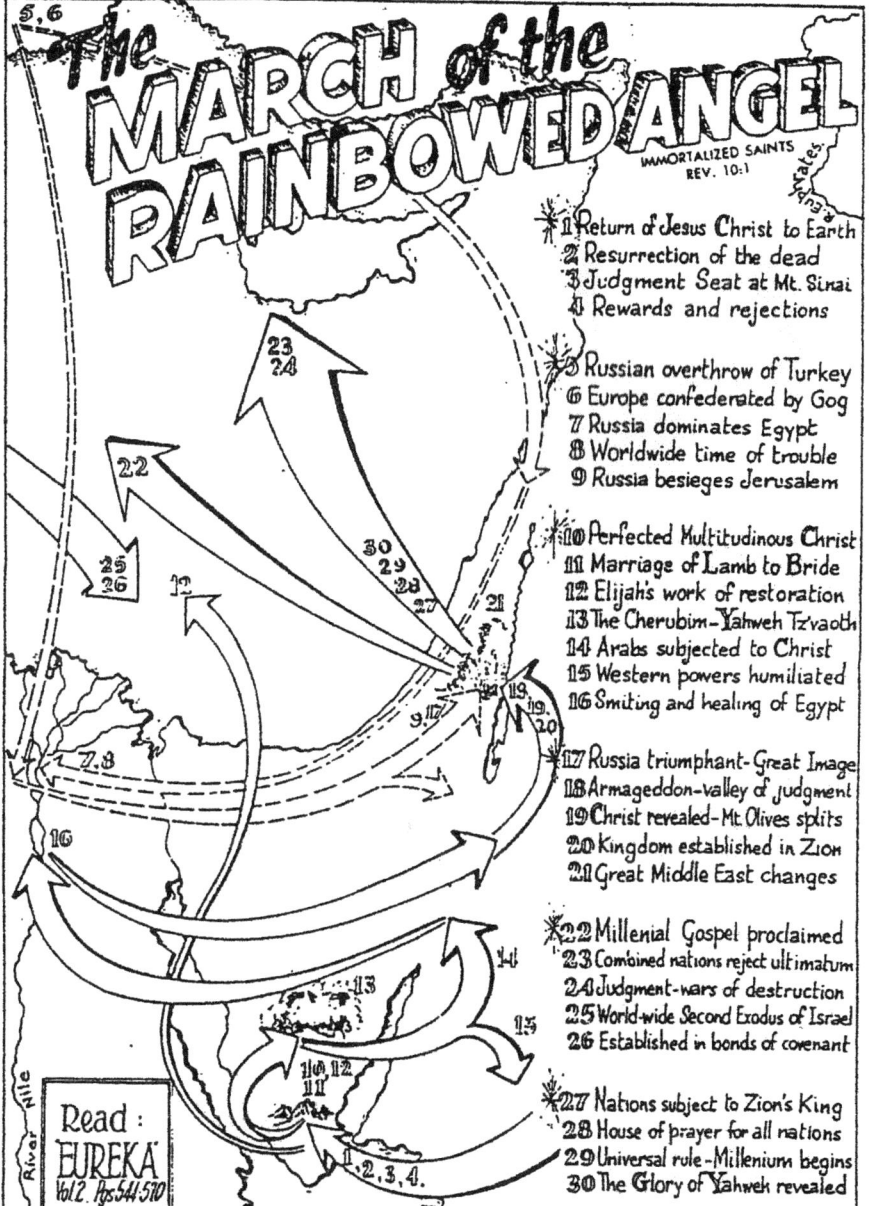

The MARCH of the RAINBOWED ANGEL

IMMORTALIZED SAINTS
REV. 10:1

1 Return of Jesus Christ to Earth
2 Resurrection of the dead
3 Judgment Seat at Mt. Sinai
4 Rewards and rejections

5 Russian overthrow of Turkey
6 Europe confederated by Gog
7 Russia dominates Egypt
8 Worldwide time of trouble
9 Russia besieges Jerusalem

10 Perfected Multitudinous Christ
11 Marriage of Lamb to Bride
12 Elijah's work of restoration
13 The Cherubim-Yahweh Tzvaoth
14 Arabs subjected to Christ
15 Western powers humiliated
16 Smiting and healing of Egypt

17 Russia triumphant-Great Image
18 Armageddon-valley of judgment
19 Christ revealed-Mt. Olives splits
20 Kingdom established in Zion
21 Great Middle East changes

22 Millenial Gospel proclaimed
23 Combined nations reject ultimatum
24 Judgment-wars of destruction
25 World-wide Second Exodus of Israel
26 Established in bonds of covenant

27 Nations subject to Zion's King
28 House of prayer for all nations
29 Universal rule-Millenium begins
30 The Glory of Yahweh revealed

Read:
EUREKA
Vol.2 Pgs 544-570

River Nile

everlasting sun, the light of the glory and righteousness of Yahweh in Christ and his saints.

> "Violence shall no more be heard in thy land, wasting nor destruction within thy borders; but thou shalt call thy walls Salvation, and thy gates Praise. The sun shall be no more thy light by day; neither for brightness shall the moon give light unto thee: but Yahweh shall be unto thee an everlasting light, and thy God thy glory. Thy sun shall no more go down; neither shall thy moon withdraw itself: for Yahweh shall be thine everlasting light, and the days of thy mourning shall be ended" (Isa. 60:18-20).

Lastly in this context we consider the words of Malachi.

> "Unto you that fear My name shall the Sun of righteousness arise (Heb. *zarach*) with healing in his wings; and ye shall go forth, and grow up as calves of the stall" (Mal. 4:2).

The healing that the Sun of righteousness will bring will be the gift of immortality for faithful saints. The Hebrew for "wings" is the word used for the wings of the cherubim, which of course we understand to be a figure for the glorified body of redeemed saints. As part of the cherubim they will have been healed from the dread disease of leprous sin. They will also be able to heal those who are prepared to respond to the preaching of the everlasting gospel, when the time for that arrives. The Hebrew verb translated "go forth" (*yatsa*) is a very common one, occurring over a thousand times. But it is nonetheless worth noting that it is used in a verse we have already considered in the context of the Rainbowed Angel.

> "Thou wentest forth (*yatsa*) for the salvation of Thy people, *even* for salvation with Thine anointed; thou woundedst the head out of the house of the wicked, by discovering the foundation unto the neck. Selah" (Hab. 3:13).

A fiery law

It is clear from the foregoing that the work of Christ and the saints when they go forth from Sinai and Paran will be one that will ultimately bring enormous blessings to the peoples of this presently troubled earth. But it is also important to remember that before that can happen, God's righteous judgments and laws have to be implemented. This will involve a process of cleansing the world of the wickedness and abominations that currently prevail. It will be a process that will involve overcoming resistance from many, not least from the Roman apostasy.

The straightforward reading of this phrase, which we believe is correct, is that any who refuse to accept and obey God's law, as set out and enforced by the Rainbowed Angel, will be consumed by fire. However, we understand that the Hebrew here is both difficult and uncertain. It appears to be a compound word made up of two other words. The word for "fiery" (*esh*) is the common word for fire, and presents no difficulty. The Hebrew for "law" is unusual, and is not the normal Old Testament word for "law". Here it is *dath*, which occurs 22 times. This usage in Deuteronomy 33:2 is the first occurrence. It is used once in Ezra, and all the other uses are in Esther. The following is a typical use.

> "If it please the king, let there go a royal commandment from him, and let it be written among the laws of the Persians and the Medes, that it be not altered, that Vashti come no more before king Ahasuerus; and let the king give her royal estate unto another that is better than she" (Est. 1:19).

It seems to refer to a royal or imperial law or decree, and because all but one occurrence are in relation to Persian kings, some commentators suggest the word may have a foreign (non-Jewish) origin. That is impossible to ascertain, and is probably irrelevant to a correct understanding of Scripture. The sense here may be the "fire of a law", which is one meaning suggested by the OLB.

There may in fact be a Scriptural example of this in practice. In the tabernacle there was a Divine law concerning the fire that was to be used to burn incense on the censers of the priests. Strict instructions were set out in Exodus 30 for the confection of the incense. It was not to be used for any other purpose than the offering of incense morning and evening by the High Priest, and anyone making such incense for any other purpose was to be cut off from Israel. The instruction concerning the burning of this incense is as follows.

> "Aaron shall burn thereon (i.e. on the altar of incense) sweet incense every morning: when he dresseth the lamps, he shall burn incense upon it. And when Aaron lighteth the lamps at even, he shall burn

incense upon it, a perpetual incense before Yahweh throughout your generations. Ye shall offer no strange incense thereon"
(Exo. 30:7-9).

Aaron's sons Nadab and Abihu chose to disobey that law, with dire consequences.

"Nadab and Abihu, the sons of Aaron, took either of them his censer, and put fire therein, and put incense thereon, and offered strange fire before Yahweh, which He commanded them not. And there went out fire from Yahweh, and devoured them, and they died before Yahweh" (Lev. 10:1-2).

We suggest that this is an example of the "fire of a law" in action, and as such is a type of some of the work of the Rainbowed Angel in the future. Although the initial tasks will be to destroy the invader of the land of Israel, deliver the remnant of Abraham's natural seed, and establish the King of kings in Zion, a later phase of the work will be to destroy the Roman apostasy. For centuries they have offered strange fire in their abominable worship and vain prayers to a false Trinitarian god; all done, blasphemously, in the name of Christ. Their defiance and idolatry will be undiminished, despite the righteous decrees of the Lord Jesus Christ. Such opposition, strange fire and false incense will not be tolerated by Yahweh any longer. The apostle John records;

"I saw heaven opened, and behold a white horse; and he that sat upon him *was* called Faithful and True, and in righteousness he doth judge and make war…. And the armies *which were* in heaven followed him upon white horses, clothed in fine linen, white and clean" (Rev. 19:11,14).

Here once again we see Christ and the glorified saints, the Rainbowed Angel. Prior to the establishment of the millennial reign of Christ, the apostate system has to be destroyed. The means of that destruction, because of their defiance of Christ's righteous laws and decrees in the Name of his Father, will be the implementation of the "fire of a law".

"And the beast was taken, and with him the false prophet that wrought miracles before him, with which he deceived them that had received the mark of the beast, and them that worshipped his image. These both were cast alive into a lake of fire burning with brimstone" (Rev. 19:20).

There is a further detail concerning this "fiery law" that is worth noting, and that confirms the foregoing exposition. The "fiery law" went forth "from His (i.e. Yahweh's) right hand" (Deut. 33:2). Similarly the Rainbowed Angel has "in his hand a little book open" (Rev. 10:2). It is this book that contains the details of the seven thunder judgments that John is commanded to "seal up… and write them not" (v 4). These are the judgments that the Rainbowed Angel will bring upon those that oppose the righteous will of Christ when he is revealed in glory and power.

The enemy thrust out of the land

Still in Deuteronomy 33, we must now consider the closing verses of the chapter. They move forward in time to the work of the Rainbowed Angel in the land of Israel, and so although considered here for convenience, this is actually taking them out of chronological sequence. In our subsequent exposition of other passages dealing with the Rainbowed Angel we shall move back again in time to pick up the progress of the march towards the land of Israel beyond Sinai, Paran, and Seir (Deut. 33:2). But it is appropriate here to consider the end of the matter as presented by the Spirit through Moses.

"*There is* none like unto the God of Jeshurun, *Who* rideth upon the heaven in thy help, and in His excellency on the sky. The eternal God *is thy* refuge, and underneath *are* the everlasting arms: and He shall thrust out the enemy from before thee; and shall say, Destroy *them*" (Deut. 33:26-27).

An alternative translation of these verses (Thomas 1902, p. 420 and p. 653) makes it clear that they refer to the Rainbowed Angel. Verse 26 is translated thus; "There is none like the Ail of Yeshurun (the Strength of Israel) riding the heavens in thy help, and with his majesty the clouds". Brother Thomas goes on to comment; "The heavenly hosts, or immortal saints, are 'the heavens' ridden by the Ail of Yeshurun". This exposition is consistent with, for example Paul's letter to the Ephesians, in which the saints are said to be "in heavenly places", or "in the heavenlies" (e.g. Eph. 1:3, KJV or Rotherham).

This is even now our exalted status in Christ as saints, and will come to full fruition in the kingdom. So this presents us with a picture of the immortalised saints under the command of the Lord Jesus Christ, who bears the name and power of the Almighty.

It has been suggested (Thomas 1902, p. 420) that a better translation of verse 27, supported by the original Hebrew, is; "The Elohim of the East a refuge, and underneath the Powers of Olahm (the Lamb with the 144,000). He shall thrust out the enemy from before thee, and shall say, Destroy!" "Eternal" in verse 27 translates the Hebrew *qedem*, which is the normal Hebrew for "east", and is translated as such (or similar) in the KJV on 50 of its 87 occurrences. Linked with *Elohim*, translated "God", this phrase thus becomes 'the Mighty Ones of the east'. This is clearly linked with "the kings of the east" (Rev. 16:12) which is also a reference to the saints. This would imply that the phrase in Deuteronomy refers to the saints manifest as an army prepared for conquest. A further confirmation comes from an examination of the usage of the Hebrew word *zeroah*, translated as "arms" in the KJV, and as "Powers" by Bro. Thomas. The word seems to refer either to the arms (limbs) of a man, as a symbol of strength, and also to armaments, according to context. Indeed this latter sense is the way the word is first used in Jacob's blessing on Joseph.

> "But his bow abode in strength, and the arms (Heb. *zeroah*) of his hands were made strong by the hands of the mighty *God* of Jacob; (from thence *is* the shepherd, the stone of Israel)" (Gen. 49:24).

These two verses therefore present the Rainbowed Angel as a military force under Christ, endued with Divine power, ready to destroy the Gogian invader on the mountains of Israel. This is exactly in line with the words of the later prophets.

> "I will call for a sword against him throughout all my mountains, saith the Lord Yahweh" (Ezek. 38:21).

> "He shall plant the tabernacles of his palace between the seas in the glorious holy mountain; yet he shall come to his end, and none shall help him" (Dan. 11:45).

The result of this military victory will be the deliverance of the remnant of Israel who are prepared to accept Jesus as their Messiah. They will enter into a time of wonderful blessing.

> "Israel then shall dwell in safety alone: the fountain of Jacob *shall be* upon a land of corn and wine; also his heavens shall drop down

dew. Happy *art* thou, O Israel: who *is* like unto thee, O people saved by Yahweh, the shield of thy help, and Who *is* the sword of thy excellency! and thine enemies shall be found liars unto thee; and thou shalt tread upon their high places" (Deut. 33:28-29).

One feature of this time of blessing is worthy of note here; "his heavens shall drop down dew". As noted earlier in this chapter, the "heavens" here relates to the saints. The doctrine refers to the Word and teaching of God. The previous chapter in Deuteronomy provides the definition.

"My doctrine shall drop as the rain, My speech shall distil as the dew, as the small rain upon the tender herb, and as the showers upon the grass" (Deut. 32:2).

So it would appear that the saints will have the task of educating the remnant of Israel in the land concerning God's law and commands.

Deborah and Barak, and the Rainbowed Angel

As we continue to attempt to track the march of the Rainbowed Angel northwards from Sinai, we turn next to the song of Deborah in Judges 5, celebrating her victory, along with Barak, over Sisera and the Canaanites. The key verses which link with our theme are as follows.

"Yahweh, when Thou wentest out of Seir, when Thou marchedst out of the field of Edom, the earth trembled, and the heavens dropped, the clouds also dropped water. The mountains melted from before Yahweh, *even* that Sinai from before Yahweh God of Israel" (Jud. 5:4-5).

As with other passages we have considered, there is here the consistent theme of a march from Edom and Seir, indicating northward movement. Clearly these words are partly intended as a reference back to Israel's journey from Sinai to Canaan under Moses. But the similarity of the language and place names to Deuteronomy 33 and Habakkuk 3 indicate that the words are also prophetic, and concern the glorified saints.

The song is introduced with words which indicate high praise to Yahweh God of Israel.

"Praise ye Yahweh for the avenging of Israel, when the people willingly offered themselves. Hear, O ye kings; give ear, O ye princes; I, *even* I, will sing unto Yahweh; I will sing *praise* to Yahweh God of Israel" (Jud. 5:2-3).

The victory for which Yahweh is here being praised was over Sisera and his army. They represent worldly, fleshly powers, referred to as the "earth" (which trembled) and the "mountains" (which melted), as shown in verses 2 and 3 quoted above.

"Yahweh sold (Israel) into the hand of Jabin king of Canaan, that reigned in Hazor; the captain of whose host *was* Sisera, which dwelt in Harosheth of the Gentiles" (Jud. 4:2).

Sisera, to whom reference was made earlier, was the very embodiment of fleshly, Gentile rebellion against, and oppression of the people of God. As such it was highly symbolic that he was slain by a nail hammered through his head. This was accomplished by Jael, wife of Heber the Kenite, who stands for the seed of the woman in this context. Using this nail she foreshadowed the ultimate fulfilment of Genesis 3:15, and the fatal head wound to be inflicted on the seed of the serpent by the true seed of the woman, the Lord Jesus Christ. The instrument of Sisera's death also represented Christ, for he is the nail.

"I will fasten him *as* a nail in a sure place; and he shall be for a glorious throne to his Father's house" (Isa. 22:23).

That victory accomplished by Christ at his crucifixion was one stage, albeit a crucial stage, in the process of the conquest and destruction of sin and all its consequences. Thus, the victory of Deborah and Barak over Sisera and his army also points to the victory of the Rainbowed Angel over the fleshly hosts and armies that will oppose the Lamb when he is revealed as the Lion of the tribe of Judah.

Not surprisingly therefore there are a whole series of connections to other passages concerned with the Rainbowed Angel. The fact that the same geographical locations (Edom, Seir) are mentioned in Deuteronomy 33 (Seir, Paran) and Habakkuk 3 (Teman, Paran) establishes the link. But there are also at least seven verbal links between Judges 5 and Psalm 68, a psalm which, as we have already clearly seen, deals with the judgment of the saints at Sinai, prior to their constitution as the Rainbowed Angel. These connections are set out in Table 10, and need not be repeated here. We can therefore state categorically, on the basis of our foregoing exposition, that the victory over Sisera, and Deborah's resultant song of victory foreshadow the work of the Rainbowed Angel.

It is also fascinating to note that there are some oblique references to the judgment in Judges 5, confirming the link with Psalm 68, which deals with the judgment seat. Firstly there are two references to those of Israel who had willingly joined with Deborah and Barak in the war against Sisera.

"Praise ye Yahweh for the avenging of Israel, when the **people willingly offered themselves**… My heart *is* toward the governors of Israel, that **offered themselves willingly among the people**. Bless ye Yahweh" (Jud. 5:2,9).

We suggest that these willing servants represent the saints who will be approved at the judgment at Sinai; willing servants of the Lord Jesus Christ. It prompts us to ask ourselves whether we are prepared to willingly hazard our lives for our Master in fighting the good fight of faith.

In contrast, there were those in Israel at that time who were not prepared to follow Deborah and Barak.

"For the divisions of Reuben *there were* great thoughts of heart. Why abodest thou among the sheepfolds, to hear the bleatings of the flocks? For the divisions of Reuben *there were* great searchings of heart. Gilead abode beyond Jordan: and why did Dan remain in ships? Asher continued on the sea shore, and abode in his breaches" (Jud. 5:15-17).

The Reubenites were divided over whether to commit themselves to Deborah; those who dwelt in Gilead stayed at home, as did the Danites and the Asherites. Similarly, at the judgment seat, some will be revealed as disloyal or half-hearted disciples.

There is a final issue arising from this incident that we wish to consider in relation to the Rainbowed Angel. Although Yahweh is described as coming out Seir and Edom (Judg. 5:4), in the actual historical event, the Israelites were already dwelling in the land, and this battle took place in the northern part of the land. Jabin, whom Sisera served, was king of Hazor, which is north of Galilee. Sisera himself is described as dwelling in "Harosheth of the Gentiles" (Jud. 4:2), which is west of Galilee, close to Mount Carmel. The battle in which Sisera's army was overcome by Deborah, Barak, and the elements of heaven, was at Mount Tabor and in the region of the brook Kishon (Jud. 4:12-13). These places are south west of Galilee. So if this incident is indeed prophetic of the work of the Rainbowed Angel, we see that the Angel will venture considerably further north to defeat these oppressing enemies, possibly even before entering Jerusalem.

It might be argued that since this victory is achieved much further north, it occurs after Jerusalem is conquered and the King of kings is settled on his throne. It seems to the present writer that the evidence is inconclusive, and could be interpreted either way. On the one hand, the manifestation of Yahweh marching forth is seen coming out of Seir and Edom, implying that the Rainbowed Angel is still concentrated at this stage south and east of Jerusalem, although venturing north to defeat the challenge from other nations in the vicinity (e.g. Jordan, Syria, Iraq). On this basis we have put the prophetic exposition of Judges 5 regarding the Rainbowed Angel at this chronological point in his work of judgment and conquest.

On the other hand, there are two pieces of evidence which could be used to suggest the victory of Deborah types a later stage of the work of the Rainbowed Angel. The victory of Deborah took place near mount Tabor. The Hebrew for "Tabor" comes from a root meaning something "broken in pieces". This calls to mind the destiny of the image of Daniel 2, which will stand again in the last days, but will be broken by the stone cut out of the mountain without hands.

> "… the stone… brake in pieces the iron, the brass, the clay, the silver, and the gold" (Dan. 2:45).

Furthermore, following Deborah's victory "the land had rest forty years" (Jud. 5:31). Could this type the Millennial rest established once Christ's enemies have been overcome?

There is clearly a case to be made either way, but we have decided to place Judges 5 at this chronological point in the march. Readers may also like to note that subsequent exposition (in chapter 10) will examine some of the final events prior to Israel's entry into the land of promise, which also show that Israel undertook a military foray further north (to defeat Sihon king of Heshbon, and Og king of Bashan) before crossing the Jordan into Canaan. This indicates that the Rainbowed Angel may do the same, linking once again with the type provided by Deborah and Barak.

We shall also return later, briefly, to the issue of the work of the Rainbowed Angel **after** the occupation and conquest of Jerusalem.

Chapter 9 – Who is this that cometh from Edom, with dyed garments from Bozrah?

Introduction

The Rainbowed Angel will continue his inexorable march northwards from Sinai to Jerusalem. We last encountered the multitudinous angel at Paran and Mount Seir (Deut.33). We now wish to consider Isaiah 63, where we learn that he has now left Edom, and has also left Bozrah, one of Edom's chief cities behind. It would appear that the angel is now in the vicinity of the Dead Sea, and sufficiently far north for the remaining inhabitants of Jerusalem who have not been removed or killed by the Gogian invader to be aware of him. They question who it is that is approaching from the south.

> "Who *is* this that cometh from Edom, with dyed garments from Bozrah? " (Isa. 63:1).

Edom, Moab, and Ammon have escaped the ravages of Gog, the king of the north (Dan. 11:41). Thus the Rainbowed Angel can move freely north through Edom, and into Moabite and Ammonite territory to the east of the Red Sea on his way to encounter and destroy the Gogian host on the mountains of Israel.

The king's highway

The context for the opening words of Isaiah 63 is back in chapter 62, and so we must go there first before examining chapter 63 in detail. Isaiah states quite plainly that it is God's absolute and determined purpose to deliver Jerusalem from the hand of the enemy, and to make her a praise and a joy in the earth.

> "For Zion's sake will I not hold My peace, and for Jerusalem's sake I will not rest, until the righteousness thereof go forth as brightness, and the salvation thereof as a lamp *that* burneth... Yahweh hath sworn by His right hand, and by the arm of His strength, Surely I will no more give thy corn *to be* meat for thine enemies; and the sons of the stranger shall not drink thy wine, for the which thou hast laboured" (Isa. 62:1,8).

The words could not be more definite. God has sworn to deliver Zion from her enemies, and will not rest until He has done so. Furthermore it is clear that the thrust of these words concerns events yet future, including the final destiny of Jerusalem, rather than any historical events. The following words can only apply to the future and final fulfilment of this prophecy.

> "The Gentiles shall see thy righteousness, and all kings thy glory… Thou shalt also be a crown of glory in the hand of Yahweh, and a royal diadem in the hand of thy God" (Isa. 62:2-3).

So the enemy from which Zion is to be delivered by the fulfilment of this prophecy is Gog, the northern invader, the last power that will ever be allowed to trample on the soil of God's chosen city. Thus the command will be given to those Jews who remain in Jerusalem after Gog's invasion ("the residue of the people (that) shall not be cut off from the city" (Zech. 14:2)), to prepare for the arrival of the Rainbowed Angel, who is their deliverer.

> "Go through, go through the gates; prepare ye the way of the people; cast up, cast up the highway; gather out the stones; lift up a standard for the people. Behold, Yahweh hath proclaimed unto the end of the world, Say ye to the daughter of Zion, Behold, thy salvation cometh; behold, his reward *is* with him, and his work before him. And they shall call them, The holy people, The redeemed of Yahweh: and thou shalt be called, Sought out, A city not forsaken" (Isa. 62:10-12).

The initial instruction is to prepare a "way", path or road by which the multitudinous deliverer may approach and enter into the city. To what extent this will be fulfilled literally is debatable, given that Jerusalem will be a partially occupied city, so that the Jews who remain there will presumably have limited freedom of action. We suggest that there is primarily a metaphorical meaning to the words. The residue of the people will be commanded to prepare themselves to welcome their Messiah; something that will require a complete change of heart on their part. This change is demanded by the proclamation that their "salvation cometh", and that the one who is coming is bringing a "reward" for those who will welcome him in sincerity and truth. The metaphor is however entirely appropriate, for they are being told to prepare for the climax of the march of the Rainbowed Angel, as he

Chapter 9 – Who is this that cometh from Edom, with dyed garments from Bozrah?
comes northwards from Edom, along the route of what in ancient times was called "the kings' highway".

The inhabitants are also told in verse 11 that the one who is coming, who we believe is the Rainbowed Angel, has a "work before him" which he must carry out. The KJV margin renders "work" as "recompense". The Hebrew *peullah* has the sense of 'wages', that is, a just payback for work done. The payback could be a reward for good, parallel with the "reward (that is) with him" in the same verse. But the Hebrew can also have the sense of payback in punishment, which we suggest is the sense here. An example of its use in this way is as follows.

"Let them be before Yahweh continually, that He may cut off the memory of them from the earth... *Let* this *be* the reward (Heb. *peullah,* translated "work" in Isaiah 62:11) of mine adversaries from Yahweh, and of them that speak evil against my soul" (Psa 109:15,20).

So there will be a good reward for the residue of the Jews who genuinely welcome the Rainbowed Angel and accept Christ as their Messiah. But for Gog, the enemy, there will be recompense in punishment. Their graves will be on the mountains of Israel.

Verse 12, the final verse of Isaiah 62 quoted above, seems to address two distinct groups of people. The second group is perhaps the easiest to identify. "Thou shalt be called, Sought out, A city not forsaken". Since this section is addressed to the Jews in the city, commanding them to "prepare... the way", they may be identified as the "thou" of this verse. They will have been sought out by the Rainbowed Angel. Their city will not have been forsaken, but will have been delivered from the oppressor.

The other group addressed are called "The holy people, The redeemed of Yahweh". These, we suggest, are the saints, who with Christ as the Rainbowed Angel, deliver Jerusalem and the residue of the Jews there from the Gogian invader. The "redeemed" also appear in Isaiah 35 which we consider later.

The words of Isaiah 62:10 are an echo of earlier words from the inspired pen of the same prophet. On an earlier occasion he spoke words of comfort to Jerusalem in preparation for the first appearing of

Messiah. On that occasion the people were prepared ("prepare ye the way") by the work of John the Baptist.

> "Comfort ye, comfort ye My people, saith your God. Speak ye comfortably to Jerusalem, and cry unto her, that her warfare is accomplished, that her iniquity is pardoned: for she hath received of Yahweh's hand double for all her sins. The voice of him that crieth in the wilderness, Prepare ye the way of Yahweh, make straight in the desert a highway for our God. Every valley shall be exalted, and every mountain and hill shall be made low: and the crooked shall be made straight, and the rough places plain" (Isa. 40:1-4).

We know that this prophecy refers to John the Baptist because it is so applied by all the gospel writers. Clearly, in those days, there was not a physical roadway prepared for the Lord. It was a work to prepare the hearts and minds of Israel for the first coming of their Messiah. What they were to prepare for is stated thus.

> "The glory of Yahweh shall be revealed, and all flesh shall see *it* together: for the mouth of Yahweh hath spoken *it*" (Isa. 40:5).

In those days the glory of Yahweh was revealed in the person of the Word made flesh, the only begotten Son of God. However, there is no doubt that these words have a second application parallel with Isaiah 62. They also apply to the approach of the Rainbowed Angel to Jerusalem. Indeed they reveal an additional, beautiful aspect of the preparation for the arrival of the Rainbowed Angel.

> "O thou that tellest good tidings to Zion, get thee up into the high mountain: O thou that tellest good tidings to Jerusalem, lift up thy voice with strength; lift it up, be not afraid; say unto the cities of Judah, Behold, your God! Behold, the Lord GOD will come as a mighty one ("with strong hand", KJV), and his arm shall rule for him: behold, his reward is with him, and his recompense before him" (Isa. 40:9-10 ERV).

We have quoted these verses from the Revised Version as they seem to make better sense. They speak of good tidings being brought to Zion instead of Zion itself bringing good tidings. This fits the context of the Rainbowed Angel delivering Zion from oppression far better, and indeed is the alternative reading given in the KJV margin. It almost seems as if messengers are sent on in advance of the Rainbowed

Chapter 9 – Who is this that cometh from Edom, with dyed garments from Bozrah?
Angel in order to announce to Jerusalem that relief and deliverance is on the way, from the God of Israel, no less! Zion and the cities of Judah are told to expect the arrival of their "Elohim" ("Behold your God"). These mighty ones will be revealed as a multitude of Divine rulers ("Behold, the Lord GOD will come"; Heb. *Adonai Yahweh*), to rule in righteousness, to reward those who accept him as Messiah, and to punish the invader with a recompense.

These advance messengers are an indication of the inherent compassion of the God of Jacob, Who still wishes to lead His people like a flock, despite their centuries of rebellion and pride. God has never forgotten His promises to the fathers of His chosen people, even during those times when He has had to bring just punishment upon them.

> "Why sayest thou, O Jacob, and speakest, O Israel, My way is hid from Yahweh, and my judgment is passed over from my God?" (Isa 40:27).

All their ways have been known to Him throughout their history. Despite all that often terrible history, His ultimate purpose is still to have compassion on them if they will accept Him.

> "He shall feed His flock like a shepherd: He shall gather the lambs with His arm, and carry *them* in His bosom, *and* shall gently lead those that are with young" (Isa. 40:11).

The intervening verses between those quoted above present the supreme and almighty strength of the God of Israel, the Creator. It is as if the words of the prophet through those advance messengers of the Rainbowed Angel are reminding the nation of Israel that they have never been forgotten by the supreme power of the universe Who calls the stars by name, and before Whom all nations are but the merest drop in a bucket!

But who is this coming from Bozrah?

Despite the announcements of the advance messengers, and despite an increasing awareness that Jerusalem was about to witness a dramatic arrival from the south east, the remaining inhabitants will apparently find it difficult to believe what they have been told. Given the time of distress that the Jews will be experiencing at the hands of

Gog and their other enemies among the surrounding nations, this is perhaps not surprising. It therefore appears from the opening of Isaiah 63 that they will pose a series of questions, possibly addressed to the same advance messengers, who presumably were the ones who will tell them "to prepare… the way of the people (and to) cast the highway". Whether or not the questions are asked of the advance messengers, they are answered either by the Rainbowed Angel himself, or by the messengers speaking on behalf of, and with the authority of the Rainbowed Angel. We have set out the opening verses of Isaiah 63 in a way that shows these questions and their respective answers.

Q "Who *is* this that cometh from Edom, with dyed garments from Bozrah? this *that is* glorious in his apparel, travelling in the greatness of his strength?"

A "I that speak in righteousness, mighty to save."

Q "Wherefore *art thou* red in thine apparel, and thy garments like him that treadeth in the winefat?"

A "I have trodden the winepress alone; and of the people *there was* none with me: for I will tread them in mine anger, and trample them in my fury; and their blood shall be sprinkled upon my garments, and I will stain all my raiment. For the day of vengeance *is* in mine heart, and the year of my redeemed is come. And I looked, and *there was* none to help; and I wondered that *there was* none to uphold: therefore mine own arm brought salvation unto me; and my fury, it upheld me. And I will tread down the people in mine anger, and make them drunk in my fury, and I will bring down their strength to the earth" (verses 3-6).

It is perhaps reasonable to pause at this point and examine whether the assumption that we have made hitherto, that the one seen approaching Jerusalem at the opening of Isaiah 63 is indeed the Rainbowed Angel. We believe there are at least five pieces of Scriptural evidence for identifying the one coming from Edom as the Rainbowed Angel.

- The one that is approaching brings "salvation" and a "reward" (Isa. 62:11)

Chapter 9 – Who is this that cometh from Edom, with dyed garments from Bozrah?

- He is "glorious in his apparel" (Isa. 63:1). We shall comment in more detail on this phrase below. It is sufficient to note here that this relates to royal apparel. It is a king who is approaching.
- He speaks "in righteousness" (Isa. 63:1). This indicates that he is a manifestation of the Divine character.
- He is coming in "the day of vengeance" (Isa. 63:4). This phrase also occurs in Isaiah 61:2 - "To proclaim the acceptable year of Yahweh, and the day of vengeance of our God" – a passage which Christ applied to himself when he read it aloud in the synagogue at Nazareth (Lk. 4:18-21).
- The titles he is given – "The holy people, The redeemed of Yahweh" (Isa. 62:12) – show that he is actually a multitude.

The second question we wish to address regarding this passage concerns the time period or periods to which it relates. There appears to have been some past judgmental activity by the Rainbowed Angel which has resulted in blood-stained garments. This is indicated by the past tense at the start of verse 3 (the second answer above). But from the end of that verse onwards the future tense is used, including the statement "I **will** stain all my raiment". Since the destruction of the Gogian forces in Israel and the deliverance of the nation have not yet taken place, how have the garments become blood-stained?

One solution to this problem caused by the different tenses is that adopted by, for example, the RV and the RSV, which use the future tense throughout the passage. On the other hand, Young's Literal Translation uses exactly the same mixture of tenses as the KJV. The present writer is not competent to comment from a linguistic perspective which is the correct rendering of the Hebrew. However, viewed from both an expositional and logical perspective, the KJV would appear more likely to be correct. Those viewing the approach of what we believe to be the Rainbowed Angel from the direction of Edom are hardly likely to ask why the garments will, in the future become stained red with blood. How would they know that this would happen? It seems more reasonable to accept the mix of past and future tenses as in the KJV.

But this begs a further question. If the treading and trampling of Gog's forces which "will stain all my raiment" is still in the future when the residue of Jews in the land see the Rainbowed Angel approaching, what has already happened at that point to cause the Angel's garments to be blood-stained? We believe that the answer to this problem lies in the march of Israel of old through the wilderness to Canaan, which, as previously discussed, is a type of the march of the Rainbowed Angel. The reader is referred back to Table 11, and in particular the places listed in Numbers 21.

In that stage of their journey Israel arrived at Pisgah. Pisgah is located some 8-10 miles east of, and in line with the northern end of the Dead Sea. The remainder of that chapter in Numbers recounts two battles fought by the children of Israel. Firstly they overcame the Amorites under their king Sihon, and took possession of their capital city, Heshbon, which is around 5 miles north east of Pisgah. This is recorded in Numbers 21:21-30. Next is the record of their defeat of Og king of Bashan at Edrei. Edrei is located some 60 miles further north, and is about 30 miles east-south-east of the southern end of the Sea of Galilee.

Two facts emerge from this record, which is a type. Firstly, Israel fought and won two key battles **before** the end of their wilderness march, and **before** they crossed Jordan near Jericho, and entered the land west of the river. Secondly, one of these battles, at Edrei, involved a brief expedition some miles further north, before returning to the camp at Pisgah.

We conclude therefore that, in fulfilment of the type, the Rainbowed Angel will, prior to entering the land to relieve and occupy Jerusalem, engage in a preliminary battle considerably further north. It will be in this battle that the Angel's garments are first stained with blood, prompting the questions at the start of Isaiah 63.

It is interesting also to consider where this early battle might take place. Edrei was in Bashan, which is in modern Syria. Edom, Moab, and Ammon escape the attention of the northern invader, as previously noted from Daniel 11:41. They equate to modern Jordan, and part of Saudi Arabia. So it would seem that Syria does not escape from Gog, which may explain why it is necessary for the Rainbowed Angel to subdue the enemy there, before going to Jerusalem.

Further than this, there is an interesting verse in Habakkuk 3, which we have previously alluded to only briefly.

Chapter 9 – Who is this that cometh from Edom, with dyed garments from Bozrah?
"I saw the tents of Cushan in affliction: *and* the curtains of the land of Midian did tremble" (Hab. 3:7).

There is some difficulty in identifying the location of Cush. Sources consulted by the author seem to point to three possibilities. One is that Cush equates to Ethiopia or Sudan. This seems unlikely in this context, given that the Rainbowed Angel is moving northwards from Sinai. Secondly, there is the suggestion that it relates to an area west of the Red Sea, in present-day Egypt. This would balance with Midian, also mentioned in this verse, which is located on the east of the Gulf of Aqaba, opposite the Sinai peninsula. This is possibly correct, as no doubt the activity of the Rainbowed Angel in Sinai will cause consternation in the whole region, including in an area south and west of Sinai.

The third possibility is that Cushan is in Mesopotamia, or present-day Iraq. This is based on the name of Cushan-rishathaim, a king of Mesopotamia, mentioned in Judges 3:8,10, on the basis that kings sometimes gave their names to places where they ruled. In support of this is the fact that Nimrod was the son of Cush. Nimrod founded Babylon, and Asshur went forth from the territory of Babylon to found Nineveh, the capital of Assyria; (see Gen. 10:8-11). All these places are in Mesopotamia. Bearing in mind the exposition above concerning the Rainbowed Angel and Bashan / Syria based on the type in Numbers 21, we have the intriguing possibility that the Rainbowed Angel may also venture even further north than Syria, into Iraq, before moving back south to take Jerusalem. It would be during this period of activity in Syria (and possibly Iraq) that his garments initially become blood-stained. Hence the questions posed by the inhabitants of Jerusalem in the opening verses of Isaiah 63.

Returning to the questions posed and answers given in the opening of Isaiah 63 there are two other matters we wish to examine. One thing that puzzles the onlookers is that the one approaching is "glorious in his apparel" (v 1). The Hebrew adjective for "glorious" is *hadar*, and conveys the sense of 'honour' bestowed on the wearer of such apparel. The equivalent noun *hadar* is used of the honour or glory that comes from God, and that pertains to royalty, even the royalty of Christ the king. The words are highlighted in the following verses.

"(The wilderness) shall blossom abundantly, and rejoice even with joy and singing: the glory of Lebanon shall be given unto it, the **excellency** of Carmel and Sharon, they shall see the glory of Yahweh, *and* the **excellency** of our God" (Isa. 35:2).

"Gird thy sword upon *thy* thigh, O *most* mighty, with thy glory and thy **majesty**. And in thy **majesty** ride prosperously because of truth and meekness *and* righteousness; and thy right hand shall teach thee terrible things" (Psa. 45:3-4).

The Hebrew for "apparel" (*leboosh*) is used to describe royal garments. For example it is used repeatedly in Esther of the garments that Haman wished to wear and that were eventually worn by Mordecai. Haman recommends to Ahasuerus;

"Let the royal **apparel** be brought which the king *useth* to wear, and the horse that the king rideth upon, and the crown royal which is set upon his head: and let this **apparel** and horse be delivered to the hand of one of the king's most noble princes, that they may array the man *withal* whom the king delighteth to honour, and bring him on horseback through the street of the city, and proclaim before him, Thus shall it be done to the man whom the king delighteth to honour. Then the king said to Haman, Make haste, *and* take the **apparel** and the horse, as thou hast said, and do even so to Mordecai the Jew, that sitteth at the king's gate: let nothing fail of all that thou hast spoken. Then took Haman the **apparel** and the horse, and arrayed Mordecai, and brought him on horseback through the street of the city, and proclaimed before him, Thus shall it be done unto the man whom the king delighteth to honour." (Esth. 6:8-11).

So the one who is described in Isaiah 63:1 as "glorious in his apparel" is indeed one whom the King delights to honour. It is the Lord Jesus Christ in his glory, along with the multitude represented by Mordecai, who are faithful, and who have been accounted righteous. They are clothed with glory and beauty, even with immortality.

In answer to how their garments are "red", or blood-stained, this multitudinous one replies "I have trodden the winepress alone; and of the people there *was* none with me" (v 3). There are two issues to consider here. Firstly, it may seem curious to some that the words "alone" and "none with me" can be applied to a multitude. The answer

Chapter 9 – Who is this that cometh from Edom, with dyed garments from Bozrah?

is of course that it is the Rainbowed Angel that is "alone", but that angel is the symbol of a multitude, even the redeemed saints. We refer back to our exposition in chapter 2 of the original vision of the Rainbowed Angel in Revelation 10. For example the symbol of being "clothed with a cloud" is linked to the "great… cloud of witnesses" mentioned by the Apostle Paul. It is a multitude represented by one.

The other question is who is referred to by the "people" in the phrase "of the people there *was* none with me"? There are two possible answers. The Hebrew *am* is almost always translated "people", and occasionally "nation" (1,836 times compared to 17). Its most frequent application is to the people of Israel, though it can refer to other nations. So in this passage it may mean that no Jews (in the sense of natural Israel as opposed to individual Jews who would be among the redeemed saints on the basis of faith) had been with the Rainbowed Angel in his work hitherto. Alternatively it may mean that as a corporate body the Rainbowed Angel acts alone, with no assistance from any other nation or people. The author is inclined to the latter view, though a case can be made either way.

The year of my redeemed is come

This phrase is taken from Isaiah 63:4 to describe the significance of the time when the Rainbowed Angel appears to the residue of Jews in Jerusalem. We have earlier applied the phrase "The redeemed of Yahweh" (Isa. 62:12) to the redeemed saints comprising the multitudinous element of the Rainbowed Angel. We believe that is the correct exposition of that word in its context at the end of chapter 62.

However, in the context of Isaiah 63:4 we believe that it applies to natural Israel, and is referring to the greatest jubilee year of all, when all Israel will finally be re-gathered. There is clearly a connection between the relevant verse in Isaiah 63 and the verse from Isaiah 61 quoted by Christ and applied to himself.

"For the day of vengeance *is* in mine heart, and the year of my redeemed is come" (Isa. 63:4).

"To proclaim the acceptable year of Yahweh, and the day of vengeance of our God; to comfort all that mourn" (Isa. 61:2).

This "acceptable year" of God's redeemed is surely a reference to the principle of the jubilee years. After counting seven Sabbaths of years (i.e. 49) the Law of Moses states;

> "Then shalt thou cause the trumpet of the jubile to sound on the tenth *day* of the seventh month, in the day of atonement shall ye make the trumpet sound throughout all your land. And ye shall hallow the fiftieth year, and proclaim liberty throughout *all* the land unto all the inhabitants thereof: it shall be a jubile unto you; and ye shall return every man unto his possession, and ye shall return every man unto his family. A jubile shall that fiftieth year be unto you: ye shall not sow, neither reap that which groweth of itself in it, nor gather *the grapes* in it of thy vine undressed. For it *is* the jubile; it shall be holy unto you: ye shall eat the increase thereof out of the field. In the year of this jubile ye shall return every man unto his possession" (Lev. 25:9-13).

We need to note a number of features of this law which are relevant to the context of Isaiah 63 and the impending work of the Rainbowed Angel, to free Israel from foreign oppression once and for all. Firstly, the jubilee year began on the Day of Atonement. It thus signified spiritual salvation, forgiveness and redemption. It is therefore not without coincidence that after speaking of judgment and vengeance, Isaiah picks up the atonement theme.

> "I will mention the lovingkindnesses of Yahweh, *and* the praises of Yahweh, according to all that Yahweh hath bestowed on us, and the great goodness toward the house of Israel, which He hath bestowed on them according to His mercies, and according to the multitude of His lovingkindnesses. For He said, Surely they *are* My people, children *that* will not lie: so He was their Saviour" (Isa. 63:7-8).

Next, notice that it was a year when a trumpet was blown, and "liberty" was proclaimed. It was a year when every man could return to his possession and reclaim it, even if he had previously had to sell it due to poverty or adverse circumstances. These points take us back, we suggest, to an earlier chapter in Isaiah. In chapter 11 Messiah is presented in all his holiness. He evicts all foreigners (portrayed as wild beasts) from Jerusalem leading to the conclusion stated in verse 9.

Chapter 9 – Who is this that cometh from Edom, with dyed garments from Bozrah?

> "They shall not hurt nor destroy in all My holy mountain: for the earth shall be full of the knowledge of Yahweh, as the waters cover the sea" (Isa. 11:9).

This is of course the outcome of the work of the Rainbowed Angel at Jerusalem. Although we are jumping ahead somewhat from the events of Isaiah 63, that chapter nonetheless points forward to the "year of My redeemed", this great year of jubilee.   It is therefore interesting to note in passing the events that follow on from the liberation and cleansing of Jerusalem. These will be events which will, no doubt, be directed by the Rainbowed Angel, somewhat later, once the march from Sinai to Jerusalem is completed.

> "In that day there shall be a root of Jesse, which shall stand for an ensign of the people; to it shall the Gentiles seek: and his rest shall be glorious. It shall come to pass in that day, *that* the Lord shall set His hand again the second time to recover the remnant of His people, which shall be left, from Assyria, and from Egypt, and from Pathros, and from Cush, and from Elam, and from Shinar, and from Hamath, and from the islands of the sea. And He shall set up an ensign for the nations, and shall assemble the outcasts of Israel, and gather together the dispersed of Judah from the four corners of the earth" (Isa. 11:10-12).

Whilst an "ensign", mentioned twice in the verses quoted abive, is a visible signal, in contrast to the audible signal of the trumpet, blown to announce the year of jubilee, they are parallel in that both serve the same purpose. They both proclaim the arrival of the Messiah in Zion and the final jubilee freedom that that signifies. Thus, just as in the year of jubilee "every man… (was to return) unto his possession", so the ensign represents the focal point for the final re-gathering of the dispersed of Judah.

The Hebrew for "ensign" (*nec*) in Isaiah 11 is, very significantly, the word translated "pole" in Numbers; the pole on which the brasen serpent was fixed.

> "Yahweh said unto Moses, Make thee a fiery serpent, and set it upon a pole: and it shall come to pass, that every one that is bitten, when he looketh upon it, shall live. And Moses made a serpent of brass, and put it upon a pole, and it came to pass, that if a serpent

had bitten any man, when he beheld the serpent of brass, he lived" (Num. 21:8-9).

In fact, the word has already appeared in the life of Moses. Israel, under Joshua, and with Yahweh's help, had defeated the Amalekites, while Aaron and Hur held up Moses's hands. This victory was memorialised by an altar named "Yahweh-nissi" (Exo. 17:15); where "nissi" is actually the Hebrew *nec*, combined with Yahweh. This takes us back to Numbers 21 and the commentary by Jesus on the incident that is recorded there.

"As Moses lifted up the serpent in the wilderness, even so must the Son of man be lifted up" (Jno. 3:14).

This shows that the brasen serpent, lifted up, represented Christ as Yahweh manifest in flesh, in which sin had been rendered dead and powerless. The Jews who crucified Christ utterly failed to recognise this. However, when the same pole or ensign is lifted up again, they will…

"… look upon me whom they have pierced, and they shall mourn for him, as one mourneth for *his* only *son*, and shall be in bitterness for him, as one that is in bitterness for *his* firstborn" (Zech. 12:10).

The circle is completed by noting that "look upon" translates the same Hebrew as "behold" in Numbers 21:9. This time they will look, not upon a brasen serpent, but on the Messiah, with marks in his hands, and they will truly recognise him for who he is.

There is another interesting parallel between the march of the Rainbowed Angel and the outcome of the later phases of his work as portrayed in Isaiah 11. As the Angel approaches Jerusalem the command goes out to the remaining Jews there to "prepare ye the way of the people; cast up, cast up the highway" (Isa. 62:10). Similarly, once Messiah is established in Jerusalem, and the final re-gathering of Israel is underway;

"There shall be an highway for the remnant of His people, which shall be left, from Assyria; like as it was to Israel in the day that he came up out of the land of Egypt" (Isa. 11:16).

Chapter 9 – Who is this that cometh from Edom, with dyed garments from Bozrah?

Say ye to the daughter of Zion, salvation cometh

There is one further feature of Isaiah 62/63 we wish to develop. This concerns parallels with historical events, plus a further insight into the work of the Rainbowed Angel. The subtitle above is taken from the following verse.

> "Behold, Yahweh hath proclaimed unto the end of the world, Say ye to the daughter of Zion, Behold, thy salvation cometh; behold, his reward *is* with him, and his work before him" (Isa. 62:11).

Very similar words occur in Zechariah in a prophecy that was initially fulfilled by Jesus when he rode into Jerusalem a week before his crucifixion.

> "Rejoice greatly, O daughter of Zion; shout, O daughter of Jerusalem: behold, thy King cometh unto thee: he *is* just, and having salvation; lowly, and riding upon an ass, and upon a colt the foal of an ass" (Zech. 9:9).

However, typical of many of Zechariah's prophecies, whilst they are rooted in events that are historical (to us), their thrust is towards events that are still future. The following verse goes on to describe the objective of the second coming of the King.

> "…he shall speak peace unto the heathen: and his dominion *shall be* from sea *even* to sea, and from the river *even* to the ends of the earth" (Zech. 9:10).

The next few verses then reveal something of how this objective will be accomplished, and contain a distinct indication, we believe, of the involvement of the Rainbowed Angel.

> "Yahweh shall be seen over them, and His arrow shall go forth as the lightning: and the Lord Yahweh shall blow the trumpet, and shall go with whirlwinds of the south" (Zech. 9:14).

Note first the connections with other passages that we have already considered. The phrase likening arrows to lightning links with the phrase "the light of Thine arrows" in Habakkuk 3:11, another Rainbowed Angel passage. Secondly, there seems to be another allusion to the final jubilee trumpet being blown, by God Himself, linking to Isaiah 11. Thirdly, we must consider the phrase "whirlwinds of the south". "South" translates the Hebrew *teman*, which can be a proper name, or simply the word meaning 'south'. Teman, as a proper name, is one of the places from where Habakkuk saw the Rainbowed Angel appear ("God came from Teman" (Hab. 3:3)).

Lastly, note the word "whirlwinds". In Zechariah this is a noun, but the equivalent Hebrew verb is also used in Habakkuk 3; "they came out as a whirlwind" (v 14). So the series of links with Habakkuk 3 is a strong indication that in speaking of God going with "whirlwinds of the south", Zechariah is referring to the Rainbowed Angel. But there is further evidence that clinches this beyond reasonable doubt. The Hebrew for "whirlwind" (*caar*) is used by Ezekiel to refer to the cherubim, another Scriptural symbol of the body of redeemed saints.

> "I looked, and, behold, a whirlwind came out of the north, a great cloud, and a fire infolding itself, and a brightness *was* about it, and out of the midst thereof as the colour of amber, out of the midst of the fire. Also out of the midst thereof *came* the likeness of four living creatures. And this *was* their appearance; they had the likeness of a man" (Ezek. 1:4,5).

Surely the four living creatures likened to a man, and appearing like a whirlwind are none other than the Rainbowed Angel.

A brief digression is perhaps appropriate here. Ezekiel sees the cherubim coming from the north, whereas in the rest of our study, the Rainbowed Angel is coming from the south, towards the north. Is there a contradiction between these passages? In fact there are two possible explanations. It may be that the sense of "out of the north" in Ezekiel is purely symbolic. It may be linked with the fact that the northern encampment of Israel (and the cherubim) was headed by Dan, whose name means judgment. Ezekiel may therefore simply be signifying that the cherubim (alias the Rainbowed Angel) is, in this context, coming in judgment. Another possible explanation is that the Hebrew word translated "north" sometimes means "northward", that is, towards the north. It is translated "northward" on 24 occasions out of a total of 153 occurrences; a minority, but a significant minority. Two of these are worth quoting, since they are in the context of the march of the children of Israel towards the promised land, as a type of the Rainbowed Angel.

Firstly, there is God's command to leave Sinai just over a year after leaving Egypt.

Chapter 9 – Who is this that cometh from Edom, with dyed garments from Bozrah?

> "Ye have compassed this mountain long enough: turn you northward" (Deut. 2:3).

Then there is God's instruction to Moses when Israel were on the borders of the land.

> "Get thee up into the top of Pisgah, and lift up thine eyes westward, and northward, and southward, and eastward, and behold *it* with thine eyes: for thou shalt not go over this Jordan" (Deut. 3:27).

So perhaps Ezekiel saw the four living creatures moving northwards, as we would expect of the Rainbowed Angel, instead of coming "out of the north"?

Whether or not one of these explanations is correct, or whether Ezekiel did indeed see them coming from the north, there is no doubt that Zechariah sees the same body as a whirlwind moving north to deliver Israel, God's people. Speaking for Yahweh manifest in the Lord Jesus Christ, he first announces a message of hope to a people partly held captive by the enemy, indicating recompense will be rendered to their enemies, and that deliverance is ultimately based on the blood of his covenant, shed at the first coming of Messiah.

> "As for thee also, by the blood of thy covenant I have sent forth thy prisoners out of the pit wherein *is* no water. Turn you to the strong hold, ye prisoners of hope: even today do I declare *that* I will render double unto thee" (Zech. 9:11,12).

He next indicates that not only will he deliver Israel, but he will actually use them, in effect as his weapons of war, against their enemies. Judah is likened to a bow, and Ephraim to an arrow.

> "When I have bent Judah for Me, filled the bow with Ephraim, and raised up thy sons, O Zion, against thy sons, O Greece, and made thee as the sword of a mighty man… and his arrow shall go forth as the lightning… Yahweh of hosts shall defend them" (Zech. 9:13-15).

We learn therefore from these verses that the Rainbowed Angel will work with natural Israel to bring about the downfall of their enemies.

Zechariah 9 ends with the conclusion of the matter, including a heartfelt exclamation in praise of the goodness and mercy of God.

"Yahweh their God shall save them in that day as the flock of His people: for *they shall be as* the stones of a crown, lifted up as an ensign upon His land. For how great *is* His goodness, and how great *is* His beauty!" (Zech. 9:16-17).

How remarkable it is that once again the words take us back to earlier passages we have expounded. The remnant of Israel in the land, who have been delivered from Gog, serve as an ensign, commanding the remainder of their scattered brethren to return and acknowledge their Messiah. They are also described as the "stones of a crown". Are these perhaps the same stones that the advance messengers of the Rainbowed Angel said should be gathered out of the highway (Isa. 62:10)? Are they individuals from the residue of the Jews in Jerusalem after Gog's invasion who now accept their Messiah in truth? Like the living stones of the Gentile era that become precious stones (cf. 1 Pet. 2:4-9), these stones are now jewels in a crown.

Whirlwinds in the south again

Our excursion into Zechariah introduced us to the "whirlwinds of the south". An almost identical phrase occurs in Isaiah, and before we complete this chapter we need to look at the passage concerned. The historical context of the prophecy was a prediction of the conquest of Babylon by Medo-Persia. Media was told to "besiege", and Elam (Persia) was told to "Go up", with the result that Isaiah declares "Babylon is fallen, is fallen" (Isa. 21:2,9). However, the prophecy clearly has a latter day application regarding the fall of "Babylon the Great", since the words of verse 9 are quoted in Revelation 18:2; "Babylon the great is fallen, is fallen".

In its latter day application, Isaiah 21 also deals with Armageddon (stage 2 that we have earlier referred to). Verse 10 has the phrase "O my threshing, and the corn of my floor", which is a play on the meaning of "Armageddon". Thus, we conclude that this chapter has to do with the final demise of Babylon the Great, and the completion of God's Armageddon work. Given that this is so, it is interesting to note how the chapter begins, introducing this phase of Divine judgment.

"The burden of the desert of the sea. As whirlwinds in the south pass through; *so* it cometh from the desert, from a terrible land" (Isa. 21:1).

Chapter 9 – Who is this that cometh from Edom, with dyed garments from Bozrah?

It would appear that in the latter day context it is the "whirlwinds of the south", that is, the Rainbowed Angel, that undertakes this judgment on Babylon the Great. We have actually jumped ahead chronologically of the point we had earlier reached on the march of the Rainbowed Angel. Judgment on the great apostasy represented by Babylon the Great, and by the whore that rides the scarlet-coloured beast, will take place after the destruction of Gog and the establishment of the Lord Jesus Christ as king in Jerusalem. But it seemed appropriate to digress slightly at this point to link together the passages dealing with the "whirlwinds of the south", and to emphasize that it will be the Rainbowed Angel who will undertake this work also. In fact this seems to be confirmed in Revelation. The opening verse of the chapter, which is immediately before the statement that "Babylon the great is fallen" reads thus:-

"After these things I saw another angel come down from heaven, having great power; and the earth was lightened with his glory" (Rev. 18:1).

We suggest that this is none other than the Rainbowed Angel!

There is one final footnote on this exposition. The Hebrew for "south" in Zechariah, as noted earlier, is *teman*, consistent with the march of the Rainbowed Angel from that area. In Isaiah 21 the Hebrew for "south" is *negeb*, referring to the Negev, in the south of Judah. In this later stage of its work the Rainbowed Angel is operating out of the land of Israel itself, which is precisely what we would expect.

In the purpose of God the Rainbowed Angel will play a role in bringing to true salvation the remnant of Abraham's fleshly seed, and in the destruction of the great apostasy which has deceived the nations of the earth. What a wonderful prospect for us to look forward to in these dark days of the Gentiles!

Chapter 10 – Armageddon and treading the winepress

Introduction

In our previous chapter we left the Rainbowed Angel located to the east of the Dead Sea on his march northwards; destination Jerusalem. We also noted an excursion further north to overcome the two Amorite kings, Sihon of Heshbon, and Og of Bashan. We now wish, in this chapter, to discuss an apparent problem that arises from Isaiah 63, which was expounded in our last chapter. We shall then pick up once again the march of the Rainbowed Angel in chapter 11.

When was the winepress trodden?

The verses in Isaiah 63 which give rise to the apparent problem are as follows:-

> "Wherefore *art thou* red in thine apparel, and thy garments like him that treadeth in the winefat? I have trodden the winepress alone; and of the people *there was* none with me: for I will tread them in mine anger, and trample them in my fury; and their blood shall be sprinkled upon my garments, and I will stain all my raiment" (verse 2-3).

At this stage in his progress, the Rainbowed Angel treads out grapes in the winefat or winepress. As a result his garments become stained red with wine, representing the blood shed during this phase of God's judgments. The same metaphor is used in the Apocalypse, as quoted below. This begs the question whether the two passages concern the same event. The present writer believes that they are not about the same event, but it requires some detailed exposition to tease out this conclusion. The apostle John records in Revelation 14:-

> 14. "And I looked, and behold a white cloud, and upon the cloud *one* sat like unto the Son of man, having on his head a golden crown, and in his hand a sharp sickle."

> 15. "And another angel came out of the temple, crying with a loud voice to him that sat on the cloud, Thrust in thy sickle, and reap: for the time is come for thee to reap; for the harvest of the earth is ripe."

> 16. "And he that sat on the cloud thrust in his sickle on the earth; and the earth was reaped."

150

17. "And another angel came out of the temple which is in heaven, he also having a sharp sickle."

18. "And another angel came out from the altar, which had power over fire; and cried with a loud cry to him that had the sharp sickle, saying, Thrust in thy sharp sickle, and gather the clusters of the vine of the earth; for her grapes are fully ripe."

19. "And the angel thrust in his sickle into the earth, and gathered the vine of the earth, and cast *it* into the great winepress of the wrath of God."

The first point to note is that verse 14 begins John's record of a new vision. That verse begins "And I looked…"; and this vision runs through to the end of chapter 14 (i.e. verse 20). Similarly, chapter 14 opens with the start of a new vision, using the same statement "And I looked…" (verse 1). Likewise, chapter 15 then begins yet another vision with the words "And I saw another sign in heaven" (verse 1). So, in terms of determining chronology, Revelation 14:14-20 stands alone as a separate vision.

Next, when we look carefully at the vision, we realise that it is in fact a vision of the Rainbowed Angel. The "white cloud" (v. 14) is the multitude of saints, the cloud of faithful witnesses. They are ruled over by one like the Son of Man. This is a phrase we have encountered early in our study; it speaks both of Jesus as a person, and of Jesus as a multitude. Here he wears a crown, which tells us that the vision belongs to a time after the judgment seat, for the saints are now kings and priests with Christ. Also, since the one like the Son of Man has a sharp sickle in his (their) hand, it is clear that they are ready and prepared to execute God's righteous judgments.

The command is then given to wield the sickle for the harvest is ripe, and so "the earth was reaped". This first reaping is clearly of a grain harvest. This work is completed in verses 15 and 16.

In verses 17 and 18 two more angels appear. The first also has a sickle, and the second has power over fire, and comes out of the altar. This indicates that the second angel comes to manifest the wrath of the Almighty in fiery judgments that will uphold the righteousness of Yahweh. He commands the other angel to wield his sickle. However this time it is to cut down grapes, not grain, for the earth's "grapes are fully ripe". So the grapes are cut down and gathered into the winepress of the wrath of God.

The sequence of events in this vision is not arbitrary. It matches the sequence in God's natural creation in His chosen land. The grain harvests of barley and wheat were gathered in the period from April to June. Fruit, including grapes, was harvested later, in September. It would seem therefore that this vision is teaching us that the judgments referred to will be carried out in two distinct phases.

We suggest that the grain harvest relates to Armageddon, involving the destruction of the forces of the Gogian confederacy, and the establishment of Christ as King of kings in Jerusalem. This we have termed elsewhere, Armageddon phase 1. Further, we suggest that the treading of the gathered grapes relates to the judgment and fall of Babylon the Great, the perdition of the European beast system and the whore that rides her, and might be termed Armageddon phase 2, though admittedly this is not strictly in line with the literal meaning of "Armageddon". It may however be argued that it does fit the semantic context.

It is well to remind ourselves here of the meaning of the Hebrew language word "Armageddon"; 'a heap of sheaves in a valley (ready) for threshing'. Hence it readily ties in with Revelation 14:14-16; the ripe grain is cut down and reaped. In the context of the Rainbowed Angel's march, this therefore relates to the destruction of Gog on the mountains of Israel once the Angel arrives in the land. This will be followed by the occupation of Jerusalem, never again to be trodden down by either Gentiles or apostate Jews. Once in Jerusalem Christ will demand the submission of all nations.

> "Yet have I set my king upon my holy hill of Zion. I will declare the decree: Yahweh hath said unto me, Thou *art* My Son; this day have I begotten thee. Ask of Me, and I shall give *thee* the heathen *for* thine inheritance, and the uttermost parts of the earth *for* thy possession" (Psa. 2:6-8).

But the nations will not readily submit.

> "The kings of the earth set themselves, and the rulers take counsel together, against Yahweh, and against His anointed, *saying,* Let us break their bands asunder, and cast away their cords from us." (verses 3-4).

Chapter 10 – Armageddon and treading the winepress

However, God's response will be devastating.

> "He that sitteth in the heavens shall laugh: the Lord shall have them in derision… Thou shalt break them with a rod of iron; Thou shalt dash them in pieces like a potter's vessel" (verses 4,9).

These events tie in with Revelation 17 which portrays the challenge against the Lord Jesus Christ and his followers from the beast system.

> "Here *is* the mind which hath wisdom. The seven heads are seven mountains, on which the woman sitteth. And there are seven kings: five are fallen, and one is, *and* the other is not yet come; and when he cometh, he must continue a short space. And the beast that was, and is not, even he is the eighth, and is of the seven, and goeth into perdition. And the ten horns which thou sawest are ten kings, which have received no kingdom as yet; but receive power as kings one hour with the beast. These have one mind, and shall give their power and strength unto the beast. These shall make war with the Lamb, and the Lamb shall overcome them: for he is Lord of lords, and King of kings: and they that are with him *are* called, and chosen, and faithful" (Rev. 17:9-14).

Note that it is the beast-plus-ten-kings alliance which take the initiative; "these shall make war with the Lamb". This clearly implies that the Lamb has asserted his authority, and that this alliance is not prepared to submit to that authority. This exactly fits the patterns of Psalm 2. Note also that in defeating this challenge to his authority the Lamb is not alone. "They that are with him are called, and chosen, and faithful". These are the glorified saints, the Rainbowed Angel that continues to work with Christ in establishing his kingdom even after Gog has been defeated and Christ has been installed in Jerusalem on David's throne.

This second phase of victory over the nations is, we believe, that which is portrayed in Revelation 14 as the treading of the grapes gathered into the winepress of the wrath of God. A later chapter in Revelation pulls together the various threads we have been considering; the saints with Christ, smiting the nations with a rod of iron, and treading the grapes in the winepress of God's anger.

> "I saw heaven opened, and behold a white horse; and he that sat upon him *was* called Faithful and True, and in righteousness he doth judge and make war. His eyes *were* as a flame of fire, and on his

head *were* many crowns; and he had a name written, that no man knew, but he himself. And he *was* clothed with a vesture dipped in blood: and his name is called The Word of God. And the armies *which were* in heaven followed him upon white horses, clothed in fine linen, white and clean. And out of his mouth goeth a sharp sword, that with it he should smite the nations: and he shall rule them with a rod of iron: and he treadeth the winepress of the fierceness and wrath of Almighty God" (Rev. 19:11-15).

This passage then concludes with a statement of the accomplishment of the Divine object behind the work of Christ with the Rainbowed Angel. The one on the white horse…

"… hath on *his* vesture and on his thigh a name written, KING OF KINGS, AND LORD OF LORDS" (Rev. 19:16).

This now takes us back to the question posed at the beginning of this section. Does the treading of the winepress in Isaiah 63 relate to these events set out in Revelation 14 and 19? If it does, it presents a problem, for in Isaiah 63 the Rainbowed Angel is only just emerging from Bozrah in Edom, and is still east of the Red Sea. He has not yet entered the land of Israel, or the city of Jerusalem.

An earlier battle

We believe that the reference to treading the winepress in Isaiah 63 relates to different events; to a phase in the work of the Rainbowed Angel before he enters the land of Israel west of Jordan and approaches Jerusalem. In other words, the figure of treading grapes in the winepress is used to refer to two different sets of events. What is the evidence for this?

We have concluded in earlier exposition that the Rainbowed Angel in his work and march follows the pattern and type set by Israel in their progress through the wilderness to the land of promise. We further noted in the previous chapter that, in line with this type, the Rainbowed Angel will apparently overcome and subdue modern Jordan, Syria, and possibly Iraq while still based east of the Dead Sea. The type is recorded in Numbers 21 in the victories over Sihon king of Heshbon and Og king of Bashan.

Chapter 10 – Armageddon and treading the winepress

In his final speech to Israel before his death (the book of Deuteronomy) Moses recounts the significance of these victories. He recalls what happened to Israel as they moved north of Edom and away from mount Seir. (The fulfilment of this type is in the prophecies of the Rainbowed Angel coming from the same area in Deuteronomy 33, Habakkuk 3, and Isaiah 63.) They were told to pass through the land of the Moabites and Ammonites, but not to attack them as they too were related to Abraham, as children of Lot.

> "When we passed by from our brethren the children of Esau, which dwelt in Seir, through the way of the plain from Elath, and from Eziongaber, we turned and passed by the way of the wilderness of Moab. And Yahweh said unto me, Distress not the Moabites, neither contend with them in battle: for I will not give thee of their land *for* a possession; because I have given Ar unto the children of Lot *for* a possession… Thou art to pass over through Ar, the coast of Moab, this day: and *when* thou comest nigh over against the children of Ammon, distress them not, nor meddle with them: for I will not give thee of the land of the children of Ammon *any* possession; because I have given it unto the children of Lot *for* a possession" (Deut. 2:8,9,18,19).

It is significant that Israel were not to attack or attempt to subdue Moab and Ammon at this time. This ties in with the latter day type, for when Gog invades Israel, he will pass through to Egypt, but will leave Moab and Ammon untouched (cf. Dan. 11:41). Hence the Rainbowed Angel, whose chief initial objective is to free Israel from Gentile dominion, has no need to oppose the latter day Moab and Ammon, for they are not under foreign dominion, and may even be providing a refuge for some Jews who have fled from Israel (cf. Isa. 16:4,5). Note also the command from God to Israel that they were not to "distress" Moab or Ammon. We shall comment further on the significance of this below.

In contrast, God's command to Israel through Moses was that the Amorite kings were to be overthrown, and their land taken.

> "Rise ye up, take your journey, and pass over the river Arnon: behold, I have given into thine hand Sihon the Amorite, king of Heshbon, and his land: begin to possess *it*, and contend with him in battle" (Deut. 2:24).

When Israel approached the territory of Sihon, they requested safe passage, but this was refused, and so Sihon was overcome in battle, and his land possessed.

> "I sent messengers out of the wilderness of Kedemoth unto Sihon king of Heshbon with words of peace, saying, Let me pass through thy land: I will go along by the high way, I will neither turn unto the right hand nor to the left. Thou shalt sell me meat for money, that I may eat; and give me water for money, that I may drink: only I will pass through on my feet; (As the children of Esau which dwell in Seir, and the Moabites which dwell in Ar, did unto me;) until I shall pass over Jordan into the land which Yahweh our God giveth us. But Sihon king of Heshbon would not let us pass by him: for Yahweh thy God hardened his spirit, and made his heart obstinate, that he might deliver him into thy hand, as *appeareth* this day. And Yahweh said unto me, Behold, I have begun to give Sihon and his land before thee: begin to possess, that thou mayest inherit his land. Then Sihon came out against us, he and all his people, to fight at Jahaz. And Yahweh our God delivered him before us; and we smote him, and his sons, and all his people. And we took all his cities at that time, and utterly destroyed the men, and the women, and the little ones, of every city, we left none to remain" (Deut. 2:26-34).

The same fate was to befall Og King of Bashan and his people.

> "Then we turned, and went up the way to Bashan: and Og the king of Bashan came out against us, he and all his people, to battle at Edrei. And Yahweh said unto me, Fear him not: for I will deliver him, and all his people, and his land, into thy hand; and thou shalt do unto him as thou didst unto Sihon king of the Amorites, which dwelt at Heshbon. So Yahweh our God delivered into our hands Og also, the king of Bashan, and all his people: and we smote him until none was left to him remaining. And we took all his cities at that time, there was not a city which we took not from them, threescore cities, all the region of Argob, the kingdom of Og in Bashan" (Deut. 3:1-4).

It is worth noting the extent of this territory that Israel conquered, as stated by Moses; a pattern for the work of the Rainbowed Angel, before he approaches Jerusalem.

> "We took at that time out of the hand of the two kings of the Amorites the land that *was* on this side Jordan, from the river of Arnon unto mount Hermon" (Deut. 3:8).

The river Arnon flows into the eastern side of the Dead Sea, approximately half way between its northern and southern ends. Mount Hermon is around 40 miles north east of the northern end of the Sea of Galilee. So this military expedition involved an incursion much further north than the main camp of Israel, and as indicated earlier, we believe the same will be true for the Rainbowed Angel. The initial historical record of these events is in Numbers 21. Once the victories were completed the next chapter records where Israel was then encamped.

> "The children of Israel set forward, and pitched in the plains of Moab on this side Jordan *by* Jericho" (Num. 22:1).

This tallies with the comment of Moses following his account of the same victories in his speech to Israel

> "So we abode in the valley over against Bethpeor" (Deut. 3:29).

They were now at the northern end of the Dead Sea, near the eastern shore of Jordan, opposite Jericho; their last encampment before crossing Jordan. (See Table 11.)

We therefore conclude that the reference in Isaiah 63 to the Rainbowed Angel treading the winepress refers to his conquest of territories to the east and north of Israel, in line with the typical conquest of the Amorite kings recorded in Numbers 21. In modern terms, this conquest may well focus on Syria, but could also include Jordan and / or Iraq.

Balaam's prophecies

Having arrived at the borders of the land, Israel, led by Moses, caused consternation among the various peoples in that area. Midian is singled out as being troubled by their arrival. As a result, Balak king of Moab hired Balaam to curse Israel, in the superstitious hope that this might save Moab and the Midianites.

> "Balak the son of Zippor saw all that Israel had done to the Amorites. And Moab was sore afraid of the people, because they *were* many: and Moab was distressed because of the children of Israel. And Moab said unto the elders of Midian, Now shall this

company lick up all *that are* round about us, as the ox licketh up the grass of the field" (Num. 22:2-4).

The misplaced trust in Balaam, and the request from Balak that he should curse Israel is expressed thus:-

"Come now therefore, I pray thee, curse me this people; for they *are* too mighty for me: peradventure I shall prevail, *that* we may smite them, and *that* I may drive them out of the land: for I wot that he whom thou blessest *is* blessed, and he whom thou cursest is cursed" (Num. 22:6).

It is interesting that Moab is described as being "distressed" because of Israel's arrival. Although the Hebrew for "distress" is different from the word used by God to Moses in Deuteronomy 2, quoted above, the sense is very similar, describing the effects of fear and terror. Even this detail is a type. Note that the fear was felt by Moab and the elders of Midian. The fulfilment of the type is set out in Habakkuk, as they see the Rainbowed Angel approach.

"I saw the tents of Cushan in affliction: *and* the curtains of the land of Midian did tremble" (3:7).

They did well to fear in the past, and they will similarly be justified in their fear in the future. Like Israel of old, the Rainbowed Angel will come to conquer.

Balaam did indeed utter prophetic words concerning Israel at Balak's behest. But despite being richly paid with the "rewards of divination", his prophecies contained abundant blessings for Israel, not curses. Balaam is obliged by the spirit of inspiration from the Almighty to describe the nation of Israel in terms that are clearly intended to depict not merely the mortal nation of Israel in times past, but the Rainbowed Angel, spiritual Israel, in future glory. Their victory over Gog is foretold, as well as something of the glory of the kingdom. We quote below some samples from the four prophecies of Balaam, which enlighten us further concerning the work of the Rainbowed Angel, now encamped on the borders of the land. In the first prophecy (Num. 23:7-10) Balaam says:-

"For from the top of the rocks I see him, and from the hills I behold him: lo, the people shall dwell alone, and shall not be reckoned among the nations. Who can count the dust of Jacob, and the number of the fourth *part* of Israel?" (Num. 23:9-10).

From an elevated place, in one of the "high places of Baal" (Num. 22:41), Balaam was able to see the whole encampment of Israel. They are so numerous that not even one quarter of the foursquare camp could be numbered. There is clearly an echo here of the promises to Abraham; "if a man can number the dust of the earth, *then* shall thy seed also be numbered" (Gen. 13:16). But this is now the foursquare camp of the saints that Balaam sees. Interestingly he foretold that "the people shall dwell alone". This in turn is echoed in Isaiah 63, for the Rainbowed Angel says he has "trodden the winepress alone; and of the people *there was* none with me"

The second prophecy runs from Numbers 23:19-24, and includes the following verse:-

"He hath not beheld iniquity in Jacob, neither hath He seen perverseness in Israel: Yahweh his God *is* with him, and the shout of a king *is* among them" (Num. 23:21).

If further proof were needed that these prophecies refer to the redeemed saints in the future, we surely have it here! It is very clear from the Old Testament that there was iniquity and perverseness in abundance in Israel, even in the days of Moses. These words must refer to the redeemed saints, spiritual Israel, the Rainbowed Angel. They will be a body amongst whom there will indeed be the shout of a king, as they give praise and glory to the one who redeemed them from all nations on earth, and who is the King of kings, the lion of the tribe of Judah. This latter point seems to be alluded to in the last verse of this second prophecy, which should be compared to Jacob's prophetic blessing on Judah. We quote them side by side in the table below.

Table 13 – Comparison of Balaam's prophecies and Jacob's blessing on Judah

Balaam's prophecies	Jacob's blessing on Judah
2nd prophecy:- "Behold, the people shall rise up as a great lion, and lift up himself as a young lion: he shall not lie down until he eat *of* the prey, and drink the blood of the slain" (Num. 23:24). 3rd prophecy:- "He couched, he lay down as a lion, and as a great lion: who shall stir him up?" (Num. 24:9)	"Judah *is* a lion's whelp: from the prey, my son, thou art gone up: he stooped down, he couched as a lion, and as an old lion; who shall rouse him up? The sceptre shall not depart from Judah, nor a lawgiver from between his feet, until Shiloh come; and unto him *shall* the gathering of the people *be*. Binding his foal unto the vine, and his ass's colt unto the choice vine; he washed his garments in wine, and his clothes in the blood of grapes: His eyes *shall be* red with wine, and his teeth white with milk" (Gen. 49:9-12).

The third prophecy (Numbers 24:5-9) also portrays the encampment of the saints, and foretells the conquest of Gog.

"How goodly are thy tents, O Jacob, *and* thy tabernacles, O Israel... He shall pour the water out of his buckets, and his seed *shall be* in many waters, and his king shall be higher than Agag, and his kingdom shall be exalted" (Num. 24:5,7).

Agag, later in Israel's history, was the king of Amalek, whom Samuel hewed in pieces. Of this nation it is recorded that, because of their opposition to Israel who had newly come out of Egypt,

"… Yah hath sworn *that* Yahweh *will have* war with Amalek from generation to generation" (Exo. 17:16).

Further, Haman, the enemy of the Jews in Persia in the days of Esther, is also described as an Agagite, possibly a descendant of Agag, king of Amalek.

The name "Agag" thus stands as the personification of Israel's and God's enemies, and here in Numbers 24, which is a latter day prophecy, may well stand for Gog. Indeed, the name is rendered as

"Gog" in the Septuagint. If this is so, and it does not seem unreasonable, then Balaam was made to predict that Israel's king would be exalted over Gog. This is entirely consistent with our thesis that these prophecies of Balaam have a latter day thrust, and that their context relates to the Rainbowed Angel. This is strongly indicated by the fact that in their historical context they fit precisely with events in which Israel typed the Rainbowed Angel.

This third prophecy of Balaam closes with a remarkable verse which has another link to Jacob's prophetic blessing on Judah quoted above, and also echoes the blessing promised to Abraham and his seed.

> "He couched, he lay down as a lion, and as a great lion: who shall stir him up? Blessed *is* he that blesseth thee, and cursed *is* he that curseth thee" (Num. 24:9).

The fourth and final prophecy of Balaam (Numbers 24:16-24) also foretells the coming of Messiah and again fits exactly with the appearing and work of the Rainbowed Angel. The key verses in this respect are quoted here.

> "I shall see him, but not now: I shall behold him, but not nigh: there shall come a Star out of Jacob, and a Sceptre shall rise out of Israel, and shall smite the corners of Moab, and destroy all the children of Sheth. And Edom shall be a possession, Seir also shall be a possession for his enemies; and Israel shall do valiantly. Out of Jacob shall come he that shall have dominion, and shall destroy him that remaineth of the city" (Num. 24:17-19).

This is really quite a remarkable prophecy in the context of our study. Firstly, Balaam is explicit that he was speaking of the future, and not of things relating to his own time. He speaks of a "Star", thus taking us right to the end of God's revelation in the Scriptures, for twice in Revelation Jesus is referred to as the "morning star" (Rev. 2:28 and 22:16). Yet again he takes us back to Jacob's words to Judah with his reference to the "Sceptre" that shall rise out of Israel. He reinforces his previous prophecies indicating that Messiah, this Star and Sceptre, shall have "dominion", referring to the restoration of Divine dominion that was lost in Eden (cf. Gen. 1:26). And lastly, he takes us to the context of the Rainbowed Angel, who has emerged from Edom and Mount Seir, by confirming that Messiah will possess Edom and will also smite Moab, those very territories through which the Rainbowed Angel has passed.

Conclusion

In conclusion, we summarise again what we believe to be the answer to the question posed at the start of this chapter regarding the treading of the winepress referred to in the early verses of Isaiah 63. We feel that this relates to an earlier phase of the work of the Rainbowed Angel, when he conquers lands to the east and north of Israel, comprising modern Syria, and possibly also Jordan and Iraq, prior to entering the land itself en route to Jerusalem. It does not relate to the destruction of Babylon the Great, although the same metaphor is used in relation to that in Revelation 14 and 19.

Chapter 11 – The year of recompenses for the controversy of Zion

Edom again

The previous chapter was a slight digression. We now pick up once again the route of the march of the Rainbowed Angel as he emerges from Edom, as discussed in relation to Isaiah 63. The same prophet has earlier dealt with Divine anger against Edom, showing that the Rainbowed Angel is God's instrument in enacting these judgments. The context is of a developing process of judgment on all nations.

> "The indignation of Yahweh *is* upon all nations, and *His* fury upon all their armies: He hath utterly destroyed them, He hath delivered them to the slaughter" (Isa. 34:2).

But Isaiah then focuses this phase of judgment on Edom or Idumaea.

> "My sword shall be bathed in heaven: behold, it shall come down upon Idumea, and upon the people of My curse, to judgment. The sword of Yahweh is filled with blood, it is made fat with fatness, *and* with the blood of lambs and goats, with the fat of the kidneys of rams: for Yahweh hath a sacrifice in Bozrah, and a great slaughter in the land of Idumea... their land shall be soaked with blood, and their dust made fat with fatness. For *it is* the day of Yahweh's vengeance, *and* the year of recompenses for the controversy of Zion" (Isa. 34:5-8).

The references to judgment and slaughter in Idumaea and Bozrah clearly place this prophecy in the same context as Isaiah 62. As we have noted earlier, the Rainbowed Angel is now nearing the end of his march to Jerusalem, and will cross from Edom into Israel, following the type of the children of Israel under Joshua. It is perhaps fitting that this is so, and that Edom is the last land to be dealt with in judgment before arrival in the chosen land, as Edom often represents the nations at large who oppose God's will. The name "Edom" has the same root origin as "Adam", and thus stands for flesh. Esau, the archetypal man of flesh, is clearly identified with Edom. Genesis states this repeatedly; "Esau, who *is* Edom" (36:1; see also verses 8 and 19). Esau, and thus Edom also, are hated by God, because they represent those who oppose Him and despise His promises (cf. Gen. 25:34 and Heb. 12:16-17. So God says "I loved Jacob, and I hated Esau" (Mal. 1:1-2).

163

Psalm 137 provides a further example of this principle, setting Edom alongside Babylon as Israel's great enemies, and those who were the first to seek the desolation of Jerusalem when Babylon invaded.

> "By the rivers of Babylon, there we sat down, yea, we wept, when we remembered Zion... Remember, O Yahweh, the children of Edom in the day of Jerusalem; who said, Rase *it*, rase *it, even* to the foundation thereof. O daughter of Babylon, who art to be destroyed; happy *shall he be*, that rewardeth thee as thou hast served us" (Psa 137:1, 7-8).

The desolation of the fleshly enemy Edom is the precursor to the climax to this stage of the march; the entry to Jerusalem. The destruction of their land is complete and final, representing the complete triumph over his enemies that Christ is accomplishing, through the Rainbowed Angel.

> "The land thereof shall become burning pitch. It shall not be quenched night nor day; the smoke thereof shall go up for ever: from generation to generation it shall lie waste; none shall pass through it for ever and ever" (Isa. 34:9-10).

The highway for the redeemed

In contrast, Isaiah then presents the multitude of saints that constitute the Rainbowed Angel.

> "Seek ye out of the book of Yahweh, and read... for My mouth it hath commanded, and His spirit it hath gathered them. And He hath cast the lot for them, and His hand hath divided it unto them by line: they shall possess it for ever, from generation to generation shall they dwell therein" (Isa. 34:16-17).

This is surely Yahweh's "book of remembrance" (Mal. 3:16), and when it is read, there will be found therein the names of the faithful saints of all ages. At God's command they have been gathered from the dust, raised to immortal life, and are now about to be given their long promised inheritance in God's land, which was covenanted to Abraham and his seed so long ago.

> "The wilderness and the solitary place shall be glad for them; and the desert shall rejoice, and blossom as the rose... and... they shall

164

see the glory of Yahweh, *and* the excellency of our God" (Isa. 35:1-2).

The succeeding verses give encouragement to the weak and fearful. These words of exhortation may be applicable to the saints now in the days of their mortality. But it is also possible, given the context of this vision, that they are words of encouragement to those Jews still in Jerusalem, under the rule of the Gogian conqueror. They are words of assurance that deliverance is imminent, for the highway that we have encountered previously is about to be trodden by the Rainbowed Angel.

"An highway shall be there, and a way, and it shall be called The way of holiness; the unclean shall not pass over it; but it *shall be* for those: the wayfaring men, though fools, shall not err *therein*. No lion shall be there, nor *any* ravenous beast shall go up thereon, it shall not be found there; but the redeemed shall walk *there*" (Isa. 35:8-9).

The first half of verse 8 is easily understood. The highway is the way prepared for those who have walked in the narrow way of life, now embodied in the Rainbowed Angel, who is now marching towards Jerusalem. It is a way of holiness, reserved for people who are holy. Therefore the unclean will not be allowed to walk therein. Like the enemies of Zerubbabel and Nehemiah, they have no portion or right or memorial in Jerusalem. The sense of the rest of the verse seems to be that fools will not be allowed to "trespass" (NEB) on that highway, but it is only for those who are called "wayfaring men" in the KJV. These we suggest are in fact the saints who comprise the Rainbowed Angel, who have been strangers and pilgrims in their mortal lives. What is the justification for this latter interpretation?

"Wayfaring men" translates a single, common Hebrew verb, *halak*. It occurs 500 times, and is normally (373 times) translated as either "go" or "walk". As is often the case, an examination of the first or early uses of a word in Scripture gives a clear indication of the sense in which it is normally, or at least often used. In this case the first use is not especially helpful. It is in Genesis 2:14, and refers to the river Hiddekel which "**goeth toward** the east". However, a series of subsequent occurrences in Genesis confirms our suggestion above, that it refers to the glorified saints; the Rainbowed Angel. The following are examples, comprising the 2nd, 3rd, 4th, 7th, 8th, and 10th occurrences of the word.

"They heard the voice of the LORD God (Yahweh Elohim) **walking** in the garden in the cool of the day: and Adam and his wife hid themselves from the presence of Yahweh Elohim amongst the trees of the garden" (Gen. 3:8).

"Enoch **walked** with God after he begat Methuselah three hundred years, and begat sons and daughters" (Gen. 5:22).

"Enoch **walked** with God: and he *was* not; for God took him" (Gen. 5:24).

"These *are* the generations of Noah: Noah was a just man *and* perfect in his generations, *and* Noah **walked** with God" (Gen. 6:9).

"Abram journeyed, **going on** still toward the south" (Gen. 12:9).

"Arise, **walk** through the land in the length of it and in the breadth of it; for I will give it unto thee" (Gen. 13:17).

The word is used of Yahweh manifest in the angels, walking in the garden, of men walking faithfully in fellowship with God, and of Abraham travelling to, and walking through the land promised to him as an inheritance. There is therefore a very sound basis for arguing that the "wayfaring men" of Isaiah 35:8 are indeed the complete body of faithful men and women marching to fulfil God's purposes in the earth.

The next verse (9) in Isaiah 35 is consistent with this. The "highway" from Sinai to Jerusalem, to be trodden by the Rainbowed Angel will have no wild or ravenous beasts on it. Such beasts represent the wild, untamed and un-Godly nations of the earth. The lion mentioned here is used, for example, to represent both Assyria and Babylon in Scripture. A related passage shows that the wild nations will be completely tamed in Messiah's kingdom.

"The wolf also shall dwell with the lamb, and the leopard shall lie down with the kid; and the calf and the young lion and the fatling together; and a little child shall lead them. And the cow and the bear shall feed; their young ones shall lie down together: and the lion shall eat straw like the ox. And the sucking child shall play on the hole of the asp, and the weaned child shall put his hand on the cockatrice' den. They shall not hurt nor destroy in all My holy mountain: for the earth shall be full of the knowledge of Yahweh, as the waters cover the sea" (Isa. 11:6-9).

Chapter 11 – The year of recompenses for the controversy of Zion

In contrast to the wild beasts, and in confirmation of our exposition of the "wayfaring men", the prophet tells us that "the redeemed shall walk *there*". It is the highway for Christ and the saints as they come to deliver Jerusalem once and for all from Gentile down-treading.
The final verse of the chapter is then set in interesting juxtaposition to verse 9.

> "The ransomed of Yahweh shall return, and come to Zion with songs and everlasting joy upon their heads: they shall obtain joy and gladness, and sorrow and sighing shall flee away" (Isa. 35:10).

Are "the redeemed" of verse 9 and "the ransomed of Yahweh" of verse 10 the same group of people? It is difficult to be dogmatic, but we suggest that they are not the same. "The ransomed of Yahweh" may be those of natural Israel, who are delivered from Gentile oppression by the arrival of the Rainbowed Angel. Many will have fled or been taken into exile at the time of the Gogian invasion (cf. Zech. 14:2 – "half of the city shall go forth in to captivity"). The survivors will now be able to return to Jerusalem, ransomed from their captivity by their Messiah. There is actually an Old Testament historical precedent for this. In their original setting many of these chapters of Isaiah had an application in the days of Hezekiah, when Judah was under threat from the Assyrians. Prior to Sennacherib's arrival in Judah to threaten Jerusalem, Hezekiah had kept a great Passover celebration. To this he had invited remaining Israelites from the ten tribes still living in the north of the land, and some did indeed respond.

> "Nevertheless divers of Asher and Manasseh and of Zebulun humbled themselves, and came to Jerusalem" (2 Chron. 30:11).

Moreover, consistent with the "songs", "joy", and "gladness" of Isaiah 35:10, the Chronicles record continues:-

> "All the congregation of Judah, with the priests and the Levites, and all the congregation that came out of Israel, and the strangers that came out of the land of Israel, and that dwelt in Judah, rejoiced. So there was great joy in Jerusalem: for since the time of Solomon the son of David king of Israel *there was* not the like in Jerusalem" (30:25-26).

Readers are referred back chapter 9 where we noted in Isaiah 62:12 a similar distinction between the redeemed saints and those of natural Israel who are delivered from oppression.

In relation to the final verse of Isaiah 35, we therefore suggest that in the context of the approach of Christ and the saints to Jerusalem, it looks forward to the joyful consequences for Israel of the final arrival of the Rainbowed Angel in the city.

Who is this that cometh out of the wilderness?

Once again we refer readers to the fact that in this chapter we are continuing the theme of chapter 9 which addressed the question posed in Isaiah 63:1; "Who *is* this that cometh from Edom...?" Before leaving this theme we have now to deal with two very similar passages in the Song of Solomon, which appear to refer to the same event and corporate personage.

"Who *is* this that cometh out of the wilderness like pillars of smoke, perfumed with myrrh and frankincense, with all powders of the merchant?" (Song 3:6).

"Who *is* this that cometh up from the wilderness, leaning upon her beloved? I raised thee up under the apple tree: there thy mother brought thee forth: there she brought thee forth *that* bare thee" (Song 8:5).

We do not have the space here to attempt a full, or even brief exposition of the complex Song of Solomon. Despite that, the present writer is satisfied that these verses do refer to the same things as Isaiah 63. The similarity in terminology is one indication, but there are others that will emerge as we seek to unravel these verses in their immediate context.

Before starting to examine these passages in detail it is perhaps worth stating the obvious; that the general theme of the Song of Solomon concerns the future relationship between the Lord Jesus Christ, the bridegroom, and his chaste ecclesial bride. The book is surely all about their union as one spirit, as expressed by the inspired apostle.

"For this cause shall a man leave his father and mother, and shall be joined unto his wife, and they two shall be one flesh. This is a great mystery: but I speak concerning Christ and the ecclesia" (Eph. 5:31-32).

This is important because these are the same two parties that comprise the corporate entity that is the overall subject of our study; the Rainbowed Angel.

The exact English phrase "who is this that cometh" occurs only 4 times in the KJV. One is in Jeremiah and relates to Egypt, and may be ignored for the purposes of this exposition. The others are those quoted above from the Song of Solomon, along with Isaiah 63:1. However, the Hebrew in these three is not the same; Isaiah uses a different verb. The verb in the Song of Solomon is common and seems to have the sense of coming or going up, and is used of offering up sacrifices. Isaiah's word is also very common and is the normal word for 'come'. However despite these differences it is difficult to discern a dissimilar overall meaning between the passages. They all seem to refer to the bride and bridegroom emerging from the wilderness of Edom en route to Jerusalem.

The next point worth noting is that both these verses are preceded by an almost identical verse giving a charge to the daughters of Jerusalem.

"I charge you, O ye daughters of Jerusalem, by the roes, and by the hinds of the field, that ye stir not up, nor awake *my* love, till he please" (Song 3:5).

"I charge you, O daughters of Jerusalem, that ye stir not up, nor awake *my* love, until he please" (Song 8:4).

These verses present us with a number of questions. Who are the daughters of Jerusalem? Who is giving them this charge? What exactly is the "charge"? And who is asking the question in the following verses about the one emerging from the wilderness?

The Scriptural evidence about the "daughters of Jerusalem" seems to be that it can refer to either natural or spiritual Israel. The sense will normally be determined by the context, though of course there can sometimes be more than one level of meaning. We suggest that in these verses in the Song the phrase refers to natural Israel. Consider the following passages in which the phrase is used in this sense.

Firstly, Isaiah, speaking God's words, uses the phrase to describe Judah in Hezekiah's days as she stood against the Assyrian threat. Notice also that the phrase seems be paralleled with "daughter of Zion".

> "This *is* the word which Yahweh hath spoken concerning him (Sennacherib and the Assyrians); The virgin, the daughter of Zion, hath despised thee, *and* laughed thee to scorn; the daughter of Jerusalem hath shaken her head at thee" (Isa. 37:22).

Jeremiah similarly uses both phrases to describe the way in which Judah has been brought low by the Babylonians.

> "How hath the Lord covered the daughter of Zion with a cloud in his anger, *and* cast down from heaven unto the earth the beauty of Israel, and remembered not his footstool in the day of His anger!... What thing shall I take to witness for thee? what thing shall I liken to thee, O daughter of Jerusalem? what shall I equal to thee, that I may comfort thee, O virgin daughter of Zion? for thy breach *is* great like the sea: who can heal thee?... All that pass by clap *their* hands at thee; they hiss and wag their head at the daughter of Jerusalem, *saying, Is* this the city that *men* call The perfection of beauty, The joy of the whole earth?" (Lam. 2:1,13,15).

It is true that in these passages "daughter" is in the singular, rather than in the plural as in the Song of Solomon passages. However this simply seems to be presenting Israel as a nation, made of many individuals. Speaking of the same nation, natural Israel, Jesus himself uses the plural form.

> "But Jesus turning unto them said, Daughters of Jerusalem, weep not for me, but weep for yourselves, and for your children" (Lk. 23:28).

The answer to the first question therefore seems to be that the "daughters of Jerusalem" refers to Israel after the flesh. So who is giving this charge to the daughters of Jerusalem? Given the overall bridegroom / bride theme of the book, it is clearly the bride. The instruction or charge is to be adhered to until "**he** please", that is the bridegroom. But what is the charge?

The key to answering this question is, we suggest, in the fact that the word "*my*" is in italics on both occasions. The inclusion of that pronoun makes "*my* love" refer to a person, the "he" of the next phrase. In fact this cannot be so, as the Hebrew for "love" in both verses is in the feminine form (*ahabah*). It is referring to love as an abstract quality, and not to a person. Further, note that it is the same Hebrew verb that is translated as both "stir up" and "awake". It is repeated, but in a different grammatical form, the second apparently more intensive than the first. The word has the sense of 'to arouse or excite'. The sense of the "charge" therefore seems to be an instruction that the celebration of the consummation of the love between the bride and bridegroom is not to be aroused or undertaken until the time of the bridegroom's choosing. It is not easy to grasp quite why natural Israel needs to be given this charge. Perhaps it is because that when they realise that the one who is approaching is indeed their Messiah, along with his bride, they will want the celebration of the completion of His purposes to happen immediately. In fact, this cannot happen until he has finally reached Jerusalem, until the enemy has been removed and destroyed, and until Israel truly acknowledges that the Jesus Christ whom their fathers crucified is indeed their Messiah.

Thus we suggest that the question posed in the Song of Solomon 3:6 and 8:4 is asked by the remnant of the Jews who are left in Jerusalem by the Gogian invader.

It would appear that the consummation of the marriage of Christ and his ecclesia takes place at Sinai when they become one Spirit, when the redeemed bride becomes a partaker of the Divine nature. This is the resolution of the issues from death mentioned in Psalm 68:20. However we believe that the celebration of the marriage at the marriage supper of the Lamb will not take place until Christ and the saints are in Jerusalem. We shall develop the evidence for this further in chapter 14.

Pillars of smoke out of the wilderness

The first time Israel after the flesh question the identity of the one coming out of the wilderness in the Song of Solomon, they see the Rainbowed Angel coming "like pillars of smoke" (3:6). This phrase is reminiscent of the pillar of cloud and fire above the tabernacle in the wilderness when Israel came out of Egypt. It must be acknowledged however that the Hebrew words used in all the passages referring to the Exodus are different to that in the Song of Solomon. The following is just one example.

> "Yahweh went before them by day in a pillar of a cloud, to lead them the way; and by night in a pillar of fire, to give them light; to go by day and night: He took not away the pillar of the cloud by day, nor the pillar of fire by night, *from* before the people" (Exo. 13:21-22).

Despite the fact the words are different, other Scriptural connections show that it is legitimate to link the pillars in Exodus and the Song of Solomon. The pillar of cloud is referred to in Numbers.

> "The cloud of Yahweh *was* upon them by day, when they went out of the camp" (10:34).

When the pillar of cloud moved, Israel broke camp and followed. Thus the passage continues:-

> "It came to pass, when the ark set forward, that Moses said, Rise up, Yahweh, and let Thine enemies be scattered; and let them that hate Thee flee before Thee. And when it rested, he said, Return, O Yahweh, unto the many thousands of Israel" (verses 35-36).

Verse 35 is quoted at the opening of Psalm 68, which we have earlier shown to be prophetic of the saints at the judgment seat in Sinai. This is based on the type of Israel in the wilderness being constituted a nation of kings and priests at Sinai. So it is entirely reasonable to connect the pillars between these passages. Even though different words are used, there is an identity of context which confirms the connection.

When Israel emerged from the wilderness they entered the land of promise initially as a conquering force. This is precisely the way they are portrayed in the Song of Solomon.

> "Behold his bed, which *is* Solomon's; threescore valiant men *are* about it, of the valiant of Israel. They all hold swords, *being* expert in war: every man *hath* his sword upon his thigh because of fear in the night" (Song 3:7-8).

Here is a picture of the bridegroom, represented by Solomon, accompanied by valiant men ready for war. This is the multitudinous element of the Rainbowed Angel. The word "valiant" in this verse translates the Hebrew *gibbor* on both occasions. Interestingly, this is the same word used to describe David's mighty men of war in 2 Samuel 23 and 1 Chronicles 11, there translated as "mighty". We suggest that these mighty men may be a type of the multitude of redeemed saints in the initial phase of their immortal career during which they go to war with the King of Kings to remove the desolators from the land of Israel, and then to rid the earth of rebellious opposition to the righteous rule of the Lord Jesus Christ. With this suggestion in mind it is interesting to consider the verse that introduces then in Chronicles.

> "These also *are* the chief of the mighty men whom David had, who strengthened themselves with him in his kingdom, *and* with all Israel, to make him king, according to the word of Yahweh concerning Israel" (1 Chron. 11:10).

Their role was identical to that which the saints will perform as part of the Rainbowed Angel; to establish and strengthen Christ in his kingdom according to the Word of Yahweh.

It is only fair to acknowledge that there are some in-exactitudes in the type. 1 Chronicles 11 lists 52 mighty men, and 2 Samuel 23 lists 37[1], neither of which tallies with the 60 ("threescore") of the Song of Solomon.

In addition, the "mighty men" in the historical record accompanied David rather than Solomon. It was David who was a "man of war" (1 Chron. 28:3), whereas Solomon typed the Prince of Peace, in accordance with his name, which means "peace". But in the Song of Solomon the "valiant" men are companions of Solomon. Perhaps the reason for this is that the focus of the Song of Solomon is on the conclusion of the work of the Rainbowed Angel. This will be the

---

1.   It is a remarkable fact that in Romans 16 the apostle Paul commends or greets 37 individuals. Of these, 35 are named. He also mentions the sister of Nereus in verse 15. Further, in verse 13, after naming Rufus, he goes on, "and his mother and mine". Assuming that this latter phrase refers to one lady only, there are 37 individuals mentioned. This would mean that the mother of Rufus was a sort of spiritual mother to Paul. It must be acknowledged that this phrase could refer to two people; the mothers of both Rufus and the apostle. It is however tempting to assume that it refers to just one person, and is therefore a remarkable evidence of Divine inspiration. Paul mentions precisely 37 individual mighty men and women of faith!

worldwide peace (the 'Solomon' phase), which will follow the defeat of all Messiah's enemies (in the 'David' phase). In the Song, the peace phase is exemplified by the celebration of the union of the bride and bridegroom; in New Testament language, the "marriage supper of the Lamb" (Rev. 19:9).

There is another possible facet to the significance of the "threescore valiant men". We have already noted that the imagery in this passage is an allusion to the children of Israel in the wilderness, and to the pillar of cloud and fire over the tabernacle. There were in fact 60 pillars that supported the curtains around the outer court of the tabernacle (see Exo. 27:9-16). As a whole, the tabernacle represented the way to salvation and the body of the redeemed. Thus the 60 valiant men around Solomon may represent the completed number of the redeemed. Finally in this context we note that the "myrrh and frankincense" of Song 3:6 may be a further allusion back to the tabernacle and all that it represented.

The marriage of the Lamb

The passage we have been considering in the Song of Solomon chapter 3 concludes with an invitation, apparently to natural Israel, addressed as the "daughters of Zion", to go out of the city to see the king. The invitation seems to be given by the bride, and to relate to the time after the warfare of the Rainbowed Angel is over.

> "Go forth, O ye daughters of Zion, and behold king Solomon with the crown wherewith his mother crowned him in the day of his espousals, and in the day of the gladness of his heart" (Song 3:11).

Firstly, note that the Hebrew word for "espousals" only occurs here, and means 'marriage'. It would seem therefore that the remnant of natural Israel in Jerusalem are invited to witness the joy of the Lamb and his bride, after Christ has secured the city and established himself on the throne of David.

Next, note that historically, the mother of Solomon was Bathsheba. Although she did not literally crown her son as king, it was she and Nathan the prophet who intervened with David when Adonijah tried to seize the throne, and ensured that, in line with the declared will of God, Solomon was crowned king by Zadok the priest, along with Nathan (cf.

Chapter 11 – The year of recompenses for the controversy of Zion

1 Kgs. 1:5-40). The significance of this in connection with the Song of Solomon passage is that Bathsheba means "daughter of the oath". The oath referred to would seem to be the revealed will of God that Bathsheba's son Solomon should be king. As king it was he that was chosen to build the temple for the ark of the covenant. This is a different Hebrew word to that for "oath", but there is clearly a semantic link.

"Then David the king stood up upon his feet, and said, Hear me, my brethren, and my people: *As for me*, I *had* in mine heart to build an house of rest for the ark of the covenant of Yahweh, and for the footstool of our God, and had made ready for the building: But God said unto me, Thou shalt not build an house for My name, because thou *hast been* a man of war, and hast shed blood… And of all my sons, (for Yahweh hath given me many sons,) He hath chosen Solomon my son to sit upon the throne of the kingdom of Yahweh over Israel. And He said unto me, Solomon thy son, he shall build my house and my courts: for I have chosen him *to be* My son, and I will be his father" (1 Chron. 28:2-3, 5-6).

When Solomon was anointed king, Scripture records that the people acclaimed him and rejoiced with him. This is surely a type of the celebration of the union of the bride and bridegroom at the marriage supper of the Lamb, when Christ is established as king.

"And all the people said, God save king Solomon. And all the people came up after him, and the people piped with pipes, and rejoiced with great joy, so that the earth rent with the sound of them" (1 Kgs. 1:39-40).

In Song of Solomon 3, in response to the question about the identity of the one coming from the wilderness, the answer deals with both the warfare and the marriage. The question is repeated in chapter 8, and in the answer given there, there are two differences to be noted. The focus is on the identity of the bride, and there is no mention of anything connected with warfare.

"Who *is* this that cometh up from the wilderness, leaning upon her beloved? I raised thee up under the apple tree: there thy mother brought thee forth: there she brought thee forth *that* bare thee" (Song 8:5).

175

The second half of the verse seems to be spoken by the bridegroom identifying the one who is leaning upon him. It would appear from the following verse that this is the time when the marriage is finally sealed.

> "Set me as a seal upon thine heart, as a seal upon thine arm" (Song 8:6).

In verse 5 the bridegroom refers to the apple tree, and by this symbol appears to be referring to himself. There are two other passages of Scripture that indicate that this is so. In an earlier chapter in the Song the bride refers to her beloved using this symbol.

> "As the apple tree among the trees of the wood, so *is* my beloved among the sons. I sat down under his shadow with great delight, and his fruit *was* sweet to my taste" (Song 2:3).

But probably even more interesting is the reference to the apple tree in Proverbs.

> "A word fitly spoken *is like* apples of gold in pictures of silver" (Prov. 25:11).

The Hebrew for "apples" is the same as for "apple tree" in the Song of Solomon. Thus, the apple and apple tree is now linked with the Word. Since it is linked with the bridegroom in Song of Solomon 2:3, we may conclude that the apple tree represents the Word made flesh. We also note, incidentally, that the figure may also be extended to the sliver, which can also represent the Word, and to the gold, which represents faith which comes by hearing the Word of God. Thus:-

> "The words of Yahweh *are* pure words: *as* silver tried in a furnace of earth, purified seven times" (Psa. 12:6).

> "So then faith *cometh* by hearing, and hearing by the word of God" (Rom. 10:17).

More interesting still however is the KJV marginal rendering for Proverbs 25:11. Instead of a "word fitly spoken" it offers a "word spoken upon his wheels". The word "fitly" translates the Hebrew *ophan*, which is translated as "wheel" on every other occurrence in the KJV, and is one of the words used by Ezekiel in his visions of the living creatures. It is easy to see why the translators have opted for "fitly" so that the verse may seem to make sense, and indeed the author has not found a version that does not follow the lead of the KJV text in this respect. Yet the KJV margin, in drawing attention to the literal rendering of the Hebrew here is actually highlighting a wonderful and profound point. The "wheels" in Ezekiel's vision are intimately associated with the "living creatures" or the cherubim, which represent the saints in their future immortal glory. As such they are energised by the spirit of Yahweh, and move in perfect synchronism with the living creatures. In a sense, the wheels symbolise the spirit in motion, and the living creatures and wheels together have been defined by one Christadelphian speaker as representing "the aggregate of the redeemed from the nations in their resurrection state".

> "Now as I beheld the living creatures, behold one wheel upon the earth by the living creatures, with his four faces… And when the living creatures went, the wheels went by them: and when the living creatures were lifted up from the earth, the wheels were lifted up. Whithersoever the spirit was to go, they went, thither *was their* spirit to go; and the wheels were lifted up over against them: for the spirit of the living creature *was* in the wheels" (Ezek. 1:15, 19-20).

How marvellous that this takes us back to the core of our study; the march of the Rainbowed Angel. This is the symbol of the spirit-energised, immortal saints, in motion with the Lord Jesus Christ heading towards Jerusalem. It is a symbol of the manifestation of the glory of Yahweh throughout the earth.

Conclusion

In this chapter we have jumped ahead somewhat in the chronology of the march of the Angel. We have done so because we chose to deal at this point with the passages in the Song of Solomon that pose the same question as that asked in Isaiah 63:1, expounded in chapter 9. Our consideration of the Song of Solomon has led us to Jerusalem and the marriage of the Lamb and his wife. We shall return to that later, but we must now take a step back, for there is still the final stage of the march to consider, and also the arrival of the Rainbowed Angel at Jerusalem. These points are considered in the next two chapters.

Chapter 12 – The Name of Yahweh cometh from far

Introduction

The title of this chapter is taken from Isaiah 30. We shall argue below that it refers to the approach of the Rainbowed Angel to Jerusalem. The succeeding verses, especially verse 31, make it clear that the passage has to do with the destruction of "the Assyrian". This we believe has both a historical application in the days of the prophet, and also an application to Gog, the latter day Assyrian.

Despite that, it may seem a little presumptuous, in terms of exposition, to assume that this passage has anything to do with the Rainbowed Angel. In fact, this can be justified if we quickly take a broad view of Isaiah's prophecy, particularly the first 39 chapters. A broad view will have to suffice; there is not space here to undertake anything more.

Chapters 1-12 deal with the sins of Judah at the time of the Assyrian destruction of the northern kingdom of Israel, events which were contemporary with Ahaz and Hezekiah kings of Judah. These chapters also portray the deliverance of Judah and Jerusalem at that time. As latter day prophecies, they lead up to the establishment of Messiah in his kingdom with his throne in Jerusalem. The chapters that follow, from 13 to 35, then portray the judgments that were to be brought on the various nations around Israel, along with Israel and Judah themselves. These judgments include the fall of Babylon, whom God used to bring the kingdom of Judah to an end. In latter day terms, these same prophecies cover the wide sweep of the effect of Gog's invasion, followed by the establishment of Messiah's kingdom, climaxing in chapter 35. They also portray the eventual fall of Babylon the Great. Chapters 36-39 then have a specific focus on the Assyrian threat in the days of Hezekiah, though here also there is a latter day, Messianic level of meaning.

So both the broad context, and the mention of the destruction of "the Assyrian" validate the application to the Rainbowed Angel of the verses we shall now consider from Isaiah 30.

Burning anger

The complete passage we wish to consider is set out below.

"Behold, the name of Yahweh cometh from far, burning *with* His anger, and the burden *thereof is* heavy: His lips are full of indignation, and His tongue as a devouring fire: and His breath, as an overflowing stream, shall reach to the midst of the neck, to sift the nations with the sieve of vanity: and *there shall be* a bridle in the jaws of the people, causing *them* to err. Ye shall have a song, as in the night *when* a holy solemnity is kept; and gladness of heart, as when one goeth with a pipe to come into the mountain of Yahweh, to the Mighty One of Israel. And Yahweh shall cause His glorious voice to be heard, and shall shew the lighting down of His arm, with the indignation of *His* anger, and *with* the flame of a devouring fire, *with* scattering, and tempest, and hailstones. For through the voice of Yahweh shall the Assyrian be beaten down, *which* smote with a rod. And *in* every place where the grounded staff shall pass, which Yahweh shall lay upon him, *it* shall be with tabrets and harps: and in battles of shaking will He fight with it. For Tophet *is* ordained of old; yea, for the king it is prepared; He hath made *it* deep *and* large: the pile thereof *is* fire and much wood; the breath of Yahweh, like a stream of brimstone, doth kindle it" (Isa. 30:27-33).

The language of these verses makes it crystal clear that they are speaking of God's judgments on "the Assyrian". However, beyond that general statement we need to note the detailed connections with our foundation passage in Revelation 10 dealing with the judgment role of the Rainbowed Angel via the warfare that he will wage. The verses quoted from Isaiah 30 mention "anger" of Yahweh twice, and His "indignation" once. This may be compared to the language applied to the actions of the Rainbowed Angel.

"(He) cried with a loud voice, as *when* a lion roareth: and when he had cried, seven thunders uttered their voices" (Rev. 10:3).

These are actions associated with Divine judgments. This is clear from similar language used in Joel.

"Yahweh also shall roar out of Zion, and utter his voice from Jerusalem; and the heavens and the earth shall shake: but Yahweh *will be* the hope of His people, and the strength of the children of Israel" (Joel 3:16).

The voice of the Lord roaring like a lion is a symbol of judgments that will both literally and figuratively shake the Gentile nations. Note therefore the links between these two key elements of Isaiah 30 and the description of the Rainbowed Angel in Revelation 10.

Table 14 – Anger and judgment – Isaiah 30 and Revelation 10

Isaiah 30	Revelation 10
v 27 – "burning with His anger"	v 1 – "pillars of fire"
v 27 – "devouring fire"	
v 30 – "flame of a devouring fire"	
v 33 – "fire and much wood"	
v 33 – "a stream of brimstone doth kindle"	
v 33 – "Tophet" ('place of fire')	
v 30 – "scattering" ('driving storm' – OLB Hebrew Lexicon)	v 3 – "seven thunders"
v 30 – "tempest"	
v 30 – "hailstones"	

These linguistic connections make it clear that the Isaiah 30 passage is indeed concerned with the Rainbowed Angel, whose work and progress we can therefore develop a little further.

The Name from far

"Behold, the name of Yahweh cometh from far" (30:27).

The prophet is apparently speaking from the vantage point of Jerusalem. We know that Isaiah dwelt in Jerusalem, for it is clear from both the Kings and Chronicles records, as well as Isaiah's prophecy, that he lived in close proximity to Hezekiah. This is further confirmed by the mention of Tophet in verse 33. "Tophet" means" a place of fire", and relates to that part of the valley of the son of Hinnom to the south of Jerusalem in which the rubbish of the city was burned. It is called Gehenna in the New Testament. So Isaiah sees the "Name of Yahweh" coming to Jerusalem from afar.

We suggest that this connects with Zechariah 14, where Yahweh has arrived at Jerusalem, along with a multitude ("Yahweh my God shall come, *and* all the saints with Thee" (v 5)). Once established in Jerusalem Zechariah states that;

Chapter 12 – The Name of Yahweh cometh from far

"Yahweh shall be king over all the earth: in that day shall there be one Yahweh, and His name one" (Zech. 14:9).

This Name is described (Thomas 1909, p. 550) as follows:- "One Yahweh and one Name… (that is) the eternal Spirit, by Spirit incorporate in Jesus and his brethren". In other words, this defines Christ and his immortal saints in glory; the Rainbowed Angel. In the context of the chapter, this describes Christ and the saints established in Jerusalem after they have destroyed the Gogian host.

Although this is jumping slightly ahead of the chronology of the Rainbowed Angel's march as portrayed in Isaiah 30, we will digress here into Zechariah 14, partly because they both refer to the corporate "Name" with respect to Jerusalem, and partly because, for reasons which will become obvious later in the chapter, it is appropriate to consider them together.

This corporate Name coming from far is coming for war against the alliance of nations under Gog who have come against Jerusalem, looted the city, raped the women, and taken half of the inhabitants into captivity.

"Then shall Yahweh go forth, and fight against those nations, as when He fought in the day of battle" (Zech. 14:3).

This is the same God Who brought the Israelites out of Egypt and destroyed the army and chariots of Pharaoh in the Red Sea.

"Yahweh *is* a man of war: Yahweh *is* his name. Pharaoh's chariots and his host hath he cast into the sea: his chosen captains also are drowned in the Red sea" (Exo. 15:3-4).

As noted above this is the Yahweh Name manifest in a multitude; "Yahweh my Elohim shall come, *and* all the saints with thee… one Yahweh, and His Name one" (Zech. 14:5,9).

His feet shall stand on the Mount of Olives

Of this multitudinous manifestation of the Yahweh Name it is stated by the prophet that:

"His feet shall stand in that day upon the mount of Olives, which *is* before Jerusalem on the east, and the mount of Olives shall cleave in the midst thereof toward the east and toward the west" (Zech. 14:4).

181

It is clear from this exposition that the pronoun "his" in the phrase "his feet" does not refer to the Lord Jesus Christ as an individual person. Rather, it refers to the multitudinous Christ, the Rainbowed Angel. Initially the angel's feet will be planted on the Mount of Olives as he causes a cataclysmic earthquake to take place. Ezekiel describes it as "a great shaking in the land of Israel" (38:19) which will destroy the Gogian host. He will then "set his right foot upon the sea, and *his* left *foot* on the earth" (Rev. 10:2) as he embarks on carrying out God's judgment on all nations throughout the earth.

There is here, in Zechariah 14:4, an allusion to Acts 1, where it is recorded that Jesus ascended to heaven from the Mount of Olives. The angels told the watching disciples that he "shall so come in like manner as ye have seen him go into heaven" (Acts 1:11). This is an absolute truth, but once we understand the Old Testament prophets we can see that this will be fulfilled in two stages. He will come personally to the disciples when the dead are raised, and the living and the dead are taken to the judgment seat. It is also true that he will come again to the Mount of Olives, but at a later date, when he appears there with the saints in glory, the Rainbowed Angel.

This may seem a novel and strange idea to some, but is we believe absolutely Scriptural and true. It is in fact supported by other references to the feet of Jesus personally, and to the feet of the disciples as a body, showing that "his feet" can apply to the feet of a multitude, specifically to the saints in Christ as a multitudinous, corporate man.

First consider the words of Isaiah (duplicated in Nahum) where the "feet" are applied to Christ personally.

"How beautiful upon the mountains are the feet of **him** that bringeth good tidings, that publisheth peace; that bringeth good tidings of good, that publisheth salvation; that saith unto Zion, Thy God reigneth!" (Isa. 52:7).

The apostle Paul, through the Spirit, picks up this verse and applies it to disciples in Christ preaching the gospel.

"How shall they preach, except they be sent? as it is written, How beautiful are the feet of **them** that preach the gospel of peace, and bring glad tidings of good things!" (Rom. 10:15).

So we are sure that the feet standing on the Mount of Olives in Zechariah 14 are the feet of the Rainbowed Angel. The sense of the words "in like manner" in Acts 1:11 probably refers to the fact that, when Christ comes again, both individually and manifest in a multitude, it will be a visible and bodily appearing.

Yahweh shall cause His glorious voice to be heard

We now return to another thematic link between Isaiah 30 and Revelation 10. In both it is clear that the primary agency carrying out God's judgments is His voice crying forth His Word. Thus there are repeated references to breath (necessary for speaking), crying, lips and tongue, as the following table shows.

Table 15 – The voice of judgment – Isaiah 30 and Revelation 10

Isaiah 30	Revelation 10
v 27 – "His lips are full of indignation"	v 3 – "Cried with a loud voice, as *when* a lion roareth: and when he had cried, seven thunders uttered their voices."
v 27 – "His tongue as a devouring fire"	v 4 – "When the seven thunders had uttered their voices, I was about to write: and I heard a voice from heaven saying unto me, Seal up those things which the seven thunders uttered, and write them not."
v 28 – "His breath, as an overflowing stream"	
v 30 – "cause His glorious voice to be heard"	
v 31 – "through the voice of Yahweh shall the Assyrian be beaten down"	
v 33 – "the breath of Yahweh…"	

When Yahweh causes His glorious voice to be heard through Christ and the immortal saints, it will be like a lion roaring, but unlike any lion that has ever hunted its prey in the natural world. This voice will probably constitute the seven thunders of Revelation 10:3-4, which John was told not to write. The reason why John was instructed not to write the details of the seven thunder judgments is not given. One possible reason is that the effects of these judgments will be so terrible that Divine mercy has withheld the details. If this is so, it is surely a sobering lesson to us to be sure we hold fast the Truth so that we are not rejected at the judgment at Sinai, and sent back into a world of chaos to endure the consequences of this climax of God's anger against human wickedness. The breath and word of God, when so directed, are a creative force for good.

> "By the word of Yahweh were the heavens made; and all the host of them by the breath of His mouth... For He spake, and it was *done*; He commanded, and it stood fast" (Psa. 33:6,9).

But it will also be by that same Word of God that the wicked will be judged, both personally, and nationally, throughout the earth.

> "But with righteousness shall he judge the poor, and reprove with equity for the meek of the earth: and he shall smite the earth with the rod of his mouth, and with the breath of his lips shall he slay the wicked" (Isa. 11:4).

When "the breath" of the "name" of Yahweh, the Rainbowed Angel goes forth as an "overflowing stream", it will "sift the nations with the sieve of vanity" (Isa. 30:28). The language here links to Armageddon, for it uses the same figures of speech as "a heap of sheaves in a valley (prepared) for judgment". The Hebrew for "sift" is the word used for "wave" in relation to the wave offerings under the Law of Moses. This would be a grain offering, for example the "sheaf of the firstfruits of your harvest" (Lev. 23:10). Further, the word "sieve" (Heb. *naphah*) is derived from the verb for "sift, wave", and is defined among other things by the Online Bible Lexicon as meaning a "winnowing implement". This is none other than Armageddon itself, a judgment that will reveal the nations who will have invaded Israel, along with all their philosophies, as worthless "vanity".

Fire in Tophet

"Tophet" means "a place of fire", and it is in that pre-ordained place that the "breath of Yahweh" will "kindle" a fire that will destroy the power of Gog (Isa. 30:33). We know from elsewhere in Scripture that Tophet was located in the valley of the Son of Hinnom to the south of the old city of Jerusalem, the Gehenna of the gospels (see also the comments earlier in the chapter in the section headed "The Name from far"). Does this therefore mean that the site of Armageddon, and the place where Gog will be burned, is at Jerusalem?

Firstly note that Jeremiah clearly indicates the location of Tophet, when condemning Israel for their idolatry in making their sons pass through the fire in this valley.

> "Behold, the days come, saith Yahweh, that it shall no more be called Tophet, nor the valley of the son of Hinnom, but the valley of slaughter: for they shall bury in Tophet, till there be no place. And the carcases of this people shall be meat for the fowls of the heaven, and for the beasts of the earth; and none shall fray *them* away" (Jer. 7:32-33).

Historically this referred to the Babylonian invasion of Judah, but we believe also has a latter day application to Gog. It would appear that the carcases of the Gogian host will not merely be buried in Tophet, but also burned there, given that Isaiah says the "pile thereof *is* fire and much wood" (30:33) to be kindled by Yahweh. In that context, the passage should be linked to Ezekiel 39, concerning the destruction of the Gogian invader.

> "Thou shalt fall upon the mountains of Israel, thou, and all thy bands, and the people that *is* with thee: I will give thee unto the ravenous birds of every sort, and *to* the beasts of the field to be devoured… And it shall come to pass in that day, *that* I will give unto Gog a place there of graves in Israel, the valley of the passengers on the east of the sea: and it shall stop the *noses* of the passengers: and there shall they bury Gog and all his multitude: and they shall call *it* The valley of Hamongog" (Ezek. 39:4,11).

Let us assume for the moment that "The valley of Hamongog" is the same place as Tophet. The passage does not limit the destruction of the Gogian host to taking place at Jerusalem. That is accomplished

185

more broadly on "the mountains of Israel". The more specific location refers to the place where the corpses of the Gogian host are buried and burned. It does not refer to a location where the Armageddon judgments themselves are carried out. The meaning of Armageddon seems to indicate that it is not so much a specific, identifiable, geographical location, but rather the process of these terrible Divine judgments.

But is "The valley of Hamongog" (KJV margin – "the multitude of Gog"), "on the east of the sea" the same as Tophet, which is to the south of Jerusalem? On the face of it, it would seem not. However, we must remember that when the Rainbowed Angel intervenes in Israel, to challenge and overcome Gog, there will be a huge earthquake, probably of a severity unprecedented in human experience.

> "In My jealousy *and* in the fire of My wrath have I spoken, Surely in that day there shall be a great shaking in the land of Israel" (Ezek. 38:19).

> "His feet shall stand in that day upon the mount of Olives, which *is* before Jerusalem on the east, and the mount of Olives shall cleave in the midst thereof toward the east and toward the west, *and there shall be* a very great valley; and half of the mountain shall remove toward the north, and half of it toward the south… And it shall be in that day, *that* living waters shall go out from Jerusalem; half of them toward the former sea, and half of them toward the hinder sea: in summer and in winter shall it be" (Zech. 14:4,8).

The whole topography of the land around Jerusalem will be radically changed in ways that we can only partly conceive. It is not impossible that Ezekiel's description of the location of the valley of Hamongog will be accurate in relation to what in former times has been Tophet. We cannot be sure; but we can be certain that things will be so changed that from our present perspective it is not wise to be dogmatic on these details.

Assyria, Babylon, Gog, and Babylon the Great

We wish at this point to make another digression to address a potential difficulty that arises from the foregoing exposition.

Chapter 12 – The Name of Yahweh cometh from far

Earlier in this chapter we made a connection between the "name of Yahweh (coming) from far" (Isa. 30:27), and the one "name" and "one Yahweh" established as king in Jerusalem (Zech. 14:9). Since we know that Isaiah was writing in the context of the Assyrian invasion of Judah, and since we have also expounded Zechariah 14 as applying to Gog and Ezekiel 38, it follows that we are regarding the Old Testament Assyrian as a type of the latter day Gog. However, does this type hold up? There is one crucial difference that inevitably causes us to question the type. In the days of Isaiah and Hezekiah Assyria did **not** take Jerusalem. Isaiah was told to tell Hezekiah;

"Therefore thus saith Yahweh concerning the king of Assyria, **He shall not come into this city**, nor shoot an arrow there, nor come before it with shields, nor cast a bank against it. By the way that he came, by the same shall he return, and **shall not come into this city**, saith Yahweh" (Isa. 37:33-34, my emphasis).

Yet in Zechariah 14, the invader, which we take to be Gog, **does indeed enter Jerusalem**.

"I will gather all nations against Jerusalem to battle; and **the city shall be taken**, and the houses rifled, and the women ravished; and half of the city shall go forth into captivity, and the residue of the people shall not be cut off from the city" (Zech. 14:2, my emphasis).

How do we explain this apparent contradiction? Is Assyria perhaps not a type of Gog after all?

One possible solution that might seem plausible at first sight is to see Zechariah 14 typed by the Babylonian invasion of Nebuchadnezzar, which after all did take Jerusalem and destroy the temple. This would mean that we would have to link Zechariah 14 as a latter day prophecy, with the latter day confederation led by Babylon the Great, as portrayed in Revelation 17. This confederacy is described as quite deliberately making war, not on Israel, but on the Lamb of God and his companions.

"These shall make war with the Lamb, and the Lamb shall overcome them: for he is Lord of lords, and King of kings: and they that are with him *are* called, and chosen, and faithful" (Rev. 17:14).

This clearly takes place later than the Gogian invasion. By definition, since this confederacy makes war on the Lamb who is identified as

"King of kings", it must take place after the establishment of Christ as King in Jerusalem, and after he has issued his decree to the nations to submit as set out in Psalm 2.

> "I will declare the decree: Yahweh hath said unto me, Thou *art* my Son; this day have I begotten thee… Be wise now therefore, O ye kings: be instructed, ye judges of the earth. Serve Yahweh with fear, and rejoice with trembling" (verses 7,10-11).

Zechariah 14 cannot be fulfilled after this, and at the same time as Revelation 17. Once Christ is established with his saints, the "called, and chosen, and faithful", it is inconceivable that any enemy or apostate rebels will ever again be allowed to enter even part of the city. From that time onwards any rebellion will immediately be put down.

So the problem remains. How do we reconcile Assyria as a type of Gog / Zechariah 14, when the former did not enter Jerusalem, and the latter will take half of the city for a time? We suggest that the problem may be resolved if we view Assyria and Babylon as essentially two parts of a single whole in the Old Testament; two phases of a power that opposed Israel and Judah, while at the same time carrying out God's will. We can then apply the principle of inversion as set out below, a principle which, incidentally, is often used in the Companion Bible in relation to the structure of chapters or books of Scripture. We begin and end with Jerusalem **not** taken by Gentile powers.

- Assyrian invasion in Hezekiah's reign. Jerusalem not taken.
  - Babylonian invasion. Jerusalem captured.
  - Gogian invasion (Ezek. 38 / Zech. 14). Half city taken.
- Babylon the Great's confederacy (Rev. 17). Jerusalem not taken.

A feast of rejoicing

Although the burden of the closing verses of Isaiah 30, which have been the focus of the exposition in this chapter, is one of judgment, there is also a positive message. The Rainbowed Angel "shall have a song" (verse 29), which would appear to be one of celebration for the defeat of the enemies of Yahweh and of Israel. Christ and the saints have come to the "mountain of Yahweh, the mighty One of Israel" (verse 29; the Hebrew for "mighty One" is *tsoor*, meaning "rock", as it is normally translated). Having arrived at Jerusalem, and evicted the

188

northern invader, they will presumably prepare to celebrate the marriage supper of the Lamb, of which more in chapter 14. But there are also hints in the language used that they celebrate the Feast of Tabernacles.

The word translated "solemnity" in verse 29 is the word used in the Law of Moses for "feast". It first occurs in Exodus 10 when Moses demands that Pharaoh let Israel go to keep a "feast" to Yahweh in the wilderness. The next occurrence is in Exodus 12 concerning the Passover. So it would seem we are being pointed at the feasts. But the word translated "gladness" is very close to that for "rejoice" with regard specifically to the celebration and thanksgiving at the Feast of Tabernacles, the feast to celebrate the ingathering of the harvests.

> "Thou shalt observe the feast of tabernacles seven days, after that thou hast gathered in thy corn and thy wine: and thou shalt **rejoice** in thy feast… Seven days shalt thou keep a solemn feast unto Yahweh thy God in the place which Yahweh shall choose: because Yahweh thy God shall bless thee in all thine increase, and in all the works of thine hands, therefore thou shalt surely **rejoice**" (Deut. 16:13-15).

If this suggestion regarding the Feast of Tabernacles is correct in relation to the context of Isaiah 30, then there is surely a connection to Revelation 7. John saw a great multitude of redeemed. The fact that they are carrying palm branches tells us that they are in effect celebrating the ultimate fulfilment of the Feast of Tabernacles; the ingathering of the redeemed saints to God's holy mountain in Jerusalem. They cry "Salvation to our God which sitteth upon the throne, and unto the Lamb" (verse 10). One of the elders then answers John's query about the identity of this multitude, confirming indeed that they are the redeemed saints.

> "He said to me, These are they which came out of great tribulation, and have washed their robes, and made them white in the blood of the Lamb. Therefore are they before the throne of God, and serve him day and night in his temple: and he that sitteth on the throne shall dwell among them" (Rev. 7:14-15).

Given this link into Revelation, it is also interesting to note that the Hebrew noun translated "pipe" in Isaiah 30:29, played as part of this celebration, is used elsewhere in connection with the anointing of kings.

189

It only occurs four times outside Isaiah 30; of these occurrences, one relates to the anointing of Saul as king, and another to the anointing of Solomon.

> "Zadok the priest took an horn of oil out of the tabernacle, and anointed Solomon. And they blew the trumpet; and all the people said, God save king Solomon. And all the people came up after him, and the people piped with pipes, and rejoiced with great joy, so that the earth rent with the sound of them" (1 Kgs. 1:39-40).

The link to Revelation is appropriate, for there the saints acknowledge Christ as their king.

Conclusion

We began this chapter with the Name of Yahweh approaching Jerusalem from far. We have briefly seen that Name incorporate in Christ and the saints already in Jerusalem, with the saints celebrating the eviction of the Gentile intruder. In our next chapter we shall consider in more detail the actual arrival of the Rainbowed Angel at Jerusalem. Meanwhile we conclude this chapter with a continuation of the passage in Isaiah. The end of chapter 31 restates the demise of the historical Assyrian and the latter day Gog, whom the Assyrian types.

> "Then shall the Assyrian fall with the sword, not of a mighty man; and the sword, not of a mean man, shall devour him: but he shall flee from the sword, and his young men shall be discomfited. And he shall pass over to his strong hold for fear, and his princes shall be afraid of the ensign, saith Yahweh, Whose fire *is* in Zion, and His furnace in Jerusalem" (Isa. 31:8-9).

Assyria was not defeated by human hand; the angel slew their host in one night. Similarly Gog will be overthrown by Divine power. The end result of that destruction will be the establishment of the kingdom of God. Thus the very next verse that opens Isaiah 32 reads:-

> "Behold, a king shall reign in righteousness, and princes shall rule in judgment" (verse 1).

Chapter 13 – Lift up your heads, O ye gates, and the King of glory shall come in

Introduction

When we last considered the Rainbowed Angel on his march to Jerusalem, he was near enough to be seen from the city. This prompted the watchers to declare that "the Name of Yahweh cometh from far, burning *with* His anger" (Isa. 30:27). We now turn to Psalm 24 which we believe presents the arrival of the Angel at the gates of the city. By way of introduction, we quote the last four verses of the Psalm which will be examined in detail in this chapter, as they relate to the Rainbowed Angel. Note first that the early verses of the Psalm, which will also be considered later, examine the characteristics of those who will be allowed to enter the city as part of the multitudinous element of the Angel. This will be the focus of a concluding exhortation in our final chapter, to all who desire an eternal inheritance in the kingdom of God. The Psalm then continues:-

"Lift up your heads, O ye gates; and be ye lift up, ye everlasting doors; and the King of glory shall come in.

Who *is* this King of glory?

Yahweh strong and mighty, Yahweh mighty in battle. Lift up your heads, O ye gates; even lift *them* up, ye everlasting doors; and the King of glory shall come in.

Who is this King of glory?

Yahweh of hosts, he *is* the King of glory. Selah" (Psa. 24:7-10).

Note that we have set out these verses in a way that distinguishes the instructions and responses given by the Rainbowed Angel, from the questions put to the Angel by the trembling inhabitants of Jerusalem. We shall analyse this discourse in due course, but first must consider some background.

Historical background to Psalm 24

The first occasion on which the ark arrived at Jerusalem is recorded in 2 Samuel 6. This was accomplished under the supervision of David, who wrote Psalm 24, inspired by the Holy Spirit. However, it is important to go back even further, and set this arrival in Jerusalem against the background of the wilderness journey of the children of Israel, for as we have seen, that journey was itself a type of the march of the Rainbowed Angel. From the time that the tabernacle was completed, just before Israel left Sinai, the ark and the mercy seat, overshadowed by the cherubim, was the dwelling place of the glory and presence of Yahweh. This presence was in the person of an Angel sent by Yahweh, Who declared "My Name *is* in him" (Exo 23:20-21). The final chapter of Exodus reveals the start of the time when this Angel of Yahweh's presence began to dwell with the ark.

"(Moses) took and put the testimony into the ark, and set the staves on the ark, and put the mercy seat above upon the ark: and he brought the ark into the tabernacle, and set up the vail of the covering, and covered the ark of the testimony; as Yahweh commanded Moses... Then a cloud covered the tent of the congregation, and the glory of Yahweh filled the tabernacle. And Moses was not able to enter into the tent of the congregation, because the cloud abode thereon, and the glory of Yahweh filled the tabernacle. And when the cloud was taken up from over the tabernacle, the children of Israel went onward in all their journeys... For the cloud of Yahweh *was* upon the tabernacle by day, and fire was on it by night, in the sight of all the house of Israel, throughout all their journeys" (Exo. 40:20-21, 34-36, 38).

Note that last phrase; God dwelt with the ark "throughout all their journeys". There is surely a parallel here with the march of the Rainbowed Angel. Yahweh will dwell with, and journey with the multitude of redeemed saints throughout their journey from Sinai to Jerusalem in the person of His beloved Son.

However this was not intended to be a permanent arrangement. God revealed to Moses that He would choose a place in the land of Israel in which to dwell. Moses explained this to the nation when they were on the borders of the land, just before his own death.

"When ye go over Jordan, and dwell in the land which Yahweh your God giveth you to inherit, and *when* He giveth you rest from all your enemies round about, so that ye dwell in safety; then there shall be a place which Yahweh your God shall choose to cause His name to dwell there; thither shall ye bring all that I command you" (Deut. 12:10-11).

Chapter 13 – Lift up your heads, O ye gates, and the King of glory shall come in

Whether or not it was revealed to Moses that the chosen location was Jerusalem we are not told, though it would seem unlikely as the record is totally silent about that detail. All that is stated is that it would be "over Jordan", that is to the west of the river Jordan. Indeed, initially, the tabernacle and the ark, and thus the presence of the Yahweh Angel, was at Shiloh. Joshua 18:1 records that it was "at Shiloh (that Israel) set up the tabernacle of the congregation". It was there that Joshua "cast lots for (Israel) before Yahweh in Shiloh" (verse 8) in order to divide the land among the tribes. The same situation still obtained some years later, for Elkanah, Samuel's father "went up... yearly to worship and to sacrifice unto Yahweh of hosts in Shiloh" (1 Sam. 1:3).

From the later records it becomes clear that Shiloh was but a staging-post on the way to Jerusalem. When we get to 2 Samuel 6, at least 7 years into the reign of David, we reach, in one sense at least, the end of the journey of the nation of Israel and the ark, which began at Sinai in the second month of the second year after Israel came out of Egypt. That journey had now ended with the arrival of the ark in Jerusalem. It is of course true that in another sense the journey did not finally end until the ark was placed in the temple that Solomon built.

Even at the end of the journey all was not straightforward. The first attempt to bring the ark into Jerusalem failed when Uzzah was struck dead. He touched the ark to steady it, when the oxen, which were pulling the cart on which the ark rested, stumbled. This reflected a failure on the part of David and the priests to follow the precise instructions of God concerning how the ark should be moved.

"When Aaron and his sons have made an end of covering the sanctuary, and all the vessels of the sanctuary, as the camp is to set forward; after that, the sons of Kohath shall come to bear *it*: but they shall not touch *any* holy thing, lest they die. These *things are* the burden of the sons of Kohath in the tabernacle of the congregation" (Num. 4:15).

The sons of Kohath were to carry the ark, taking care "not (to) touch any holy thing". This would be achieved by carrying the ark using the staves inserted through the rings in its sides. It should not have been on an ox-drawn cart. "Kohath" means "assembly". So the ark was to be carried by the "sons of the assembly", or, the "sons of the ecclesia". They were not to touch it because it represented immortality, and the assembly or ecclesia was still mortal. The type will be fulfilled when the redeemed "sons of the ecclesia" join with their Master as the

Rainbowed Angel to move as the embodiment of Yahweh's presence and glory to Jerusalem. The prohibition on touching the ark will no longer apply, for the "sons of the ecclesia" will then be immortal, partakers of the Divine nature.

It would seem that Psalm 24 in its historical setting refers to both the unsuccessful attempt to bring the ark to Jerusalem, and David's later faithful adherence to the Law of Moses, which resulted in success. With Uzzah struck dead for touching the ark, David is caused to question;

> "Who shall ascend into the hill of Yahweh? or who shall stand in His holy place? He that hath clean hands, and a pure heart; who hath not lifted up his soul unto vanity, nor sworn deceitfully" (Psa. 24:3-4).

It may be that these words were prompted by the attitude of mind of Uzzah, and possibly some of the other priests as well, since they had not properly advised David concerning the manner in which the ark should be transported. It may be that Uzzah, as a representative of the priests, did not have a pure heart, and therefore his hands were defiled and unclean when he touched the ark, however well-intentioned his instinctive reaction to the oxen stumbling may have been.

Reflecting on this incident David had been caused to examine himself and his own motives, and also to recognise the supreme power and prerogative of His God. Thus he opens the Psalm "The earth is Yahweh's, and the fullness thereof" (verse 1). Then, accepting the conditions set out in verse 4, quoted above, he confesses who it is that will be blessed by Yahweh. Such blessed people will comprise a single generation of faithful ones, drawn from each epoch of human existence.

> "He shall receive the blessing from Yahweh, and righteousness from the God of his salvation. This *is* the generation of them that seek Him, that seek Thy face, O God of Jacob. Selah" (Psa. 24:5-6, KJV margin).

On the basis of these reflections, David embarks on the second, and this time successful venture to bring the ark into Jerusalem.

Chapter 13 – Lift up your heads, O ye gates, and the King of glory shall come in

The ark of Yahweh enters the city of David

We wish first to examine the historical record of this event. We quote it in full as there are remarkable details in this inspired record which merit careful examination.

> "It was told king David, saying, Yahweh hath blessed the house of Obededom, and all that *pertaineth* unto him, because of the ark of God. So David went and brought up the ark of God from the house of Obededom into the city of David with gladness. And it was *so*, that when they that bare the ark of Yahweh had gone six paces, he sacrificed oxen and fatlings. And David danced before Yahweh with all *his* might; and David *was* girded with a linen ephod. So David and all the house of Israel brought up the ark of Yahweh with shouting, and with the sound of the trumpet… they brought in the ark of Yahweh, and set it in his place, in the midst of the tabernacle that David had pitched for it: and David offered burnt offerings and peace offerings before Yahweh. And as soon as David had made an end of offering burnt offerings and peace offerings, he blessed the people in the name of Yahweh of hosts. And he dealt among all the people, *even* among the whole multitude of Israel, as well to the women as men, to every one a cake of bread, and a good piece *of flesh*, and a flagon *of wine*" (2 Sam. 6:12-15, 17-19).

Given that this forms part of the background to Psalm 24, our interest in this passage is from the perspective of seeing these events as being a type of events relating to the entry of the Rainbowed Angel into Jerusalem.

Firstly, note that the ark was brought into the city of David with "gladness". This is reminiscent of a passage considered in the last chapter. In Isaiah 35:10, the "ransomed of Yahweh", return to Zion with "gladness" and "joy". In fact the word "joy" translates the same Hebrew as "gladness" in 2 Samuel 6, with "gladness" there translating a different Hebrew word with a similar meaning. We identified these ransomed people as natural Israel, delivered by the arrival of the Rainbowed Angel. This is present in the type, with the gladness displayed in the city of David by the arrival of the ark.

Secondly, notice the behaviour of David, who danced before Yahweh, girded with a linen ephod. The Hebrew for "danced" is only used in this passage, so it is difficult to compare it with any other behaviour. Whilst it may seem the kind of behaviour that is strange to many readers, indeed behaviour with which we would be uncomfortable, it was clearly acceptable to God. All we can therefore say with any certainty is that these actions certainly did not glorify the flesh, as with much modern dancing that we are acquainted with. Nor was it something in which David indulged for his own pleasure. It glorified God, and as such was acceptable to Him. Without further details, we simply have to accept what the record says, but also acknowledge that we do not know enough of what was involved to be able to try and imitate David in this regard.

What is perhaps even more interesting is the fact that David, who was of the tribe of Judah, was wearing a linen ephod, which was a priestly garment. We suggest that this indicates that David was acting as a priest, but not a Levitcal priest. Rather he seems to have been acting in a way that anticipated the great high priest to come, who would be of the order of Melchisedec, for "our Lord sprang out of Juda" (Heb. 7:14). More remarkable still is the linen ephod. The Hebrew for "linen" here is *bad*. This is not the word used of the fine twined linen in the garments that were for glory and beauty. Rather it is the word used of the coarse linen garments that the high priest alone wore on the Day of Atonement, when he went into the most holy place to sprinkle blood on the mercy seat. Once again this emphasizes that David was certainly not glorifying the flesh. Rather he was acting in a way which called to mind the fact that flesh required atonement, cleansing, and forgiveness. Furthermore, as another Christadelphian expositor has suggested (Barling 1952) the ritual of the Day of Atonement was in a sense outside the law, for by going beyond the vail, the Levitical high priest was anticipating the work of Christ as the priest after the order of Melchisedec.

It may also be significant that the Day of Atonement on the 10th day of the 7th month, preceded the Feast of Tabernacles, which began on the 15th of that same month. This is once again consistent with our suggestion in the previous chapter that the language of Isaiah 30 seems to suggest that once the Rainbowed Angel arrives in Jerusalem, the Feast of Tabernacles will be celebrated.

Next, we comment on the fact that David brought the ark to Jerusalem with "shouting, and with the sound of the trumpet". It is worth noting in

Chapter 13 – Lift up your heads, O ye gates, and the King of glory shall come in

passing that there may be an allusion to this phrase in the New Testament.

> "For the Lord himself shall descend from heaven with a shout, with the voice of the archangel, and with the trump of God: and the dead in Christ shall rise first" (1 Thess. 4:16).

This verse refers of course to an earlier event than the arrival of Christ and the saints at Jerusalem. This refers to the return of Christ from heaven to earth to raise the dead and take all who are responsible to judgment to appear before him. But it is probably not a coincidence that this later phase of the work of Christ, now accompanied by those approved and rewarded at the judgment seat, is also announced by a shout and the sound of the trumpet.

The Hebrew word for "trumpet" in 2 Samuel 6 is *shophar*, the ram's horn trumpet. This is only used in two contexts in the books of the Law. The first is Exodus 19 in relation to terrifying manifestation of the glory of God to Israel at Sinai. There of course it was a Divine trumpet that sounded from the mountain. Interestingly, that chapter may also form part of the Old Testament background to 1 Thessalonians 4:16.

The other occurrence of the *shophar* in the Law relates to the law of the jubilee year. (Elsewhere in the Law, the trumpets are either silver trumpets used to call the assembly or to signal war, or the word "trumpet" is inferred from a Hebrew word for blowing, to make a sound. In both the cases the Hebrew is different from *shophar*.)

> "Then shalt thou cause the trumpet of the jubile to sound on the tenth *day* of the seventh month, in the day of atonement shall ye make the trumpet sound throughout all your land. And ye shall hallow the fiftieth year, and proclaim liberty throughout *all* the land unto all the inhabitants thereof: it shall be a jubile unto you; and ye shall return every man unto his possession, and ye shall return every man unto his family" (Lev. 25:9-10).

The significant connection here with the events recorded in 2 Samuel 6 relates to the proclamation of the jubilee, of liberty, and of the freedom for every man to return to his rightful possession of land. Thus, when the Rainbowed Angel enters Jerusalem, as typed by the entry of the ark, the trumpet sound will signal deliverance for Israel, and they will be free to return to their land previously overrun by the northern invader.

Once the ark was in the tabernacle in Jerusalem we read that David offered sacrifices. The record is quite specific. He offered burnt and peace offerings. Note that there were no sin or trespass offerings made at that time. This we believe is significant in terms of the type. The Rainbowed Angel will not be in need of those offerings. The only sacrifices needed will be total dedication to the righteous service of the King of kings (the burnt offering), with whom the saints will be in perfect fellowship (the peace offering, which also signifies thanksgiving).

That perfect fellowship is further emphasized by what appears to be a type, enacted by David, of the Breaking of Bread.

> "He dealt among all the people, *even* among the whole multitude of Israel, as well to the women as men, to every one a cake of bread, and a good piece *of flesh*, and a flagon *of wine*. So all the people departed every one to his house" (2 Sam. 6:19).

It is only fair to observe that the Hebrew here appears to be difficult, and some might therefore doubt whether there really is a type. The cake of bread is straightforward. However, the Hebrew for the "flagon of wine" is less clear. It is always so translated in the KJV, but the word apparently literally means a 'cake of raisins", and this is the translation that, for example, the ERV and RSV opt for. Youngs Literal translation, (as quoted in the OLB), recognises the difficulty and simply transliterates the Hebrew word (as it also does for "a good piece of flesh"). Raisins (i.e. grapes) are clearly the key raw material for wine. Furthermore, the word only occurs in three other passages. One is the parallel record in Chronicles. The others are in the Song of Solomon and Hosea, and in both these cases a "flagon of wine" would appear to be a more reasonable translation than a "cake of raisins". So on balance we believe that the KJV rendering is sound.

But if this event is a type of the Breaking of Bread, why is an extra element apparently introduced; the "good piece *of flesh*"? Again, the Hebrew seems difficult, and only occurs in the two records of this event. However, any difficulty may be more imagined than real. There is no direct Hebrew equivalent of the words "*of flesh*", hence they are in italics. So the "good piece" may simply be referring to the bread suggesting that David gave a generous portion. If however a piece of flesh was also provided, it does not really undermine the type, since in the memorial feast bread represents the body of Christ, and his nature of sinful flesh, which he overcame and conquered.

So, if this celebratory meal that David provided was indeed a type, the fulfilment will be when Christ's promise to his disciples becomes a reality.

> "But I say unto you, I will not drink henceforth of this fruit of the vine, until that day when I drink it new with you in my Father's kingdom" (Matt. 26:29).

It would seem that he will drink of the fruit of the vine anew with his disciples, the Rainbowed Angel, in Jerusalem, in his Father's kingdom.

Finally with regard to this type, we note that the bread, flesh and wine was dealt "among the whole multitude of Israel" (2 Sam. 6:19). If we substitute the meaning of "Israel" in this phrase, it reads "among the whole multitude of the Prince of Ail" (cf. Gen. 32:28). The Prince of, or with Ail is the Lord Jesus Christ, enthroned as God's anointed ruler and king. The multitude with him ultimately refers to the redeemed saints. So in this phrase we have another description of the Rainbowed Angel, confirming our belief that this chapter in 2 Samuel is indeed a type of the arrival of the Rainbowed Angel at Jerusalem. That takes us back to Psalm 24.

Lift up your heads O ye gates

As we saw in the last chapter, when the Rainbowed Angel enters the land and approaches Jerusalem, there will be a huge earthquake, which is spoken of by Ezekiel (38:19-20), Joel (3:16), and Zechariah (14:4). This will bring about the destruction of the Gogian host, and thus allow the jubilee trumpet of freedom to be blown for the remaining Israelites, some of whom will remain in Jerusalem (see Zech. 14:2).

The Rainbowed Angel then approaches the city, which will have been to some extent devastated by the earthquake. The Angel demands entry for the Messiah.

> "Lift up your heads, O ye gates; and be ye lift up, ye everlasting doors; and the King of glory shall come in" (Psa. 24:7).

The Hebrew for "lift up" can mean to be "taken or carried away"; in other words to be removed. Thus the demand is for there to be no barrier to the entry of the King of glory. Of course, any human barrier could be swept away in a moment by the Rainbowed Angel. The fact that, instead, a request for access to the city is made, is possibly an act of Divine mercy. Consider the situation in which the surviving inhabitants of Jerusalem will find themselves. They will have been under oppressive Gogian occupation for a period of time (the Scriptures do not reveal how long). They will have experienced a severe earthquake, and will presumably suspect that the occupying forces have been adversely affected, if not completely destroyed. Against this background they will surely be puzzled by another approaching force. The request, or rather the instruction to be let in gives an opportunity for the Rainbowed Angel to explain who it is that is now coming to take possession of the city, rather than merely effecting forced entry.

Although the word is not an unusual one in the Old Testament, it is ironic, and possibly deliberately so, that the form of words used by the Rainbowed Angel employs the word *rosh*, translated "heads". Rosh, or Gog, has been destroyed. Maybe this is a conscious play on the word, and the name of Rosh.

But the remnant of the Jews in Jerusalem are puzzled. Who is it who now wishes to enter the city. So they ask:-

"Who *is* this king of glory?" (verse 8).

The majestic, and almost unbelievable reply comes back;

"Yahweh strong and mighty, Yahweh mighty in battle" (Psa. 24:8).

The Hebrew for "strong" is only used here and once in Isaiah where it is translated "power". The context there relates to the destruction of both the Chaldean and Egyptian armies in Israel's earlier history.

"Thus saith Yahweh, your Redeemer, the Holy One of Israel; For your sake I have sent to Babylon, and have brought down all their nobles, and the Chaldeans, whose cry *is* in the ships. I *am* Yahweh, your Holy One, the creator of Israel, your King. Thus saith Yahweh, Which maketh a way in the sea, and a path in the mighty waters; Which bringeth forth the chariot and horse, the army and the **power**; they shall lie down together, they shall not rise: they are extinct, they are quenched as tow" (Isa. 43:14-17).

There is a contrast here between the power of the God of Israel, who delivered Israel by dividing the Red Sea, and the utter destruction of the

Chapter 13 – Lift up your heads, O ye gates, and the King of glory shall come in

Eqyptian and Chaldean forces; those latter forces are simply extinct. Notice how the Rainbowed Angel, in speaking to this remnant of Jews, will take them back to their Old Testament history, and remind them that in a sense this deliverance is nothing new. But of course there is a new element, and this may be hinted at by the repeated use of the word "mighty" (Heb. *gibbor*). There may well be a deliberate allusion here to another of Isaiah's prophecies, where the word is associated with the Lord Jesus Christ. The one who is to shoulder the government of both Israel and the world is called "The mighty God", or *Ail Gibbor*. Furthermore, that same passage in Isaiah reminds us, as no doubt it will remind that future Jewish remnant in Jerusalem that Yahweh is not only mighty in battle, but when manifest in His Son, He is also the "Prince of Peace" (Isa. 9:6).

So, following this explanation, the request for entry to the city is repeated.

> "Lift up your heads, O ye gates; even lift *them* up, ye everlasting doors; and the King of glory shall come in" (Psa. 24:9).

"Everlasting" translates *olahm*, while the word for "doors" means the "entry, entrance". This presents us with the beautiful idea that this is the entrance to the *olahm*, the future Millennial age! But still the inhabitants of the city are unsure. Again they ask:-

> "Who is this king of glory?" (verse 10).

Still the Rainbowed Angel is patient, but now gives what is surely the definitive answer.

> "Yahweh of hosts, He *is* the King of glory" (verse 10).

Yahweh tsebaah, 'He Who shall be hosts or armies' is the multitudinous manifestation of Almighty God in a host of glorified saints in military array, the King of glory. They have come to establish God's long promised righteous kingdom throughout the earth, by setting Israel's Messiah on the restored throne of David and demanding and requiring that all nations bow at his footstool.

Behold your God

The process, of which we have just considered the culmination in Psalm 24, is summarised by Isaiah. He first declares God's message to Jerusalem that her time of everlasting peace has finally arrived. She is to be delivered once and for all from enemy occupation.

> "Comfort ye, comfort ye my people, saith your God. Speak ye comfortably to Jerusalem, and cry unto her, that her warfare is accomplished, that her iniquity is pardoned: for she hath received of Yahweh's hand double for all her sins" (Isa. 40:1-2).

Next Isaiah speaks of a way prepared through the wilderness. Initially this referred to the coming of John the Baptist who prepared the way for the first appearing of the Messiah. But ultimately it speaks of the way prepared through the wilderness for the Lord Jesus Christ and his redeemed saints to come from Sinai to Jerusalem to deliver Israel. Thus the message of comfort is delivered to the inhabitants of Jerusalem.

> "O thou that tellest good tidings to Zion, get thee up into the high mountain: O thou that tellest good tidings to Jerusalem, lift up thy voice with strength; lift it up, be not afraid; say unto the cities of Judah, Behold, your God (Heb. *elohim*, "mighty ones")! Behold, the Lord GOD (Heb. *Adonai Yahweh*, "He who shall be rulers") will come as a mighty one, and his arm shall rule for him: behold, his reward is with him, and his recompence (KJV = "work") before him" (Isa. 40:9-10, ERV).

We have quoted from the ERV here as it reverses the sense of the opening phrases of verse 9 in a way that better fits the context. Instead of Zion telling good tidings, it speaks of good tidings being brought to Zion, tidings of deliverance. The one who is shown as bringing this deliverance is the multitudinous manifestation of Yahweh, not just as a multitude, but as a multitude of rulers or princes; that is, the Rainbowed Angel. The phrase rendered "will come as a mighty one" in the ERV appears to present difficulty to the translators. The word for "mighty one" is *chazaq*, which is not one of the Divine Names. The KJV has "will come with strong *hand*", interpolating the word "hand". In fact the KJV margin seems to make good sense to the present writer, offering the rendering "will come against the strong". This would refer to Gog,

Chapter 13 – Lift up your heads, O ye gates, and the King of glory shall come in

the occupying power, strong in human terms, but before the Rainbowed Angel a mere "mountain... (to be) made low" (verse 4).

Thus, it would seem that these verses announce the arrival of the Rainbowed Angel at Jerusalem, and thus this passage tallies with Psalm 24. Although he comes to render just recompense to the invader, he comes to deal gently, and in mercy, with the remnant of Israel.

> "He shall feed his flock like a shepherd: he shall gather the lambs with his arm, and carry *them* in his bosom, *and* shall gently lead those that are with young" (Isa. 40:11).

An aside concerning Ezekiel's temple

There are verses in Ezekiel, concerning the Millennial sanctuary which may also appear to be parallel with Psalm 24 and Isaiah 40 as expounded above. The prophet sees, in vision, the glory of God coming from the east and entering into the temple. He explicitly links it with the vision of the cherubim in Ezekiel 1, and the figure likening the voice to the noise of many waters tells us that a multitude is involved in this vision of glory.

> "Behold, the glory of the God of Israel came from the way of the east: and His voice *was* like a noise of many waters: and the earth shined with His glory. And *it was* according to the appearance of the vision which I saw, *even* according to the vision that I saw when I came to destroy the city: and the visions *were* like the vision that I saw by the river Chebar; and I fell upon my face. And the glory of Yahweh came into the house by the way of the gate whose prospect *is* toward the east" (Eze 43:2-4).

This may also be linked with the final phrase of Ezekiel's prophecy (48:35). This reads "The LORD *is* there", in Hebrew, *Yahweh shammah.*

However, we believe that these passages refer to a later development. At the point when the Rainbowed Angel arrives in Jerusalem the temple of Ezekiel's prophecy will not have been built. This is to follow later once the enemy power has been evicted and destroyed. Only once the temple has been built can the glory of God enter "into the house". And

203

only then, once the whole covenanted land is ordered according to the Divine plan for the duration of the Millennium will it be able to be said in the fullest sense "The LORD *is* there".

We now turn to consider another part of Isaiah's prophecy which uses very similar language to Psalm 24, but which we believe relates to the next phase of the work of the Rainbowed Angel.

Chapter 14 – Open ye the gates

Psalm 24 and Isaiah 26

As indicated at the end of the previous chapter we now wish to consider a prophecy in Isaiah which seems to be closely related to Psalm 24, which we looked at in some detail in chapter 13. First of all, there are noticeable parallels in the language used.

Table 16 – Isaiah 26 and Psalm 24 parallels

Isaiah 26	Psalm 24
v 2 – Open ye the gates	**vv 7/9** – Lift up your heads, O ye gates
v 2 – that the righteous nation which keepeth the truth may enter therein	**vv 7/9** – the King of glory shall come in
v 1 – We have a strong city	**v 8** – Yahweh strong and mighty

However, before we consider these verses in Isaiah 26 in detail, it is necessary to link it to the previous chapter. In fact, as we have noted earlier when glancing at the overall structure of Isaiah (see chapter 12), this whole section deals with events surrounding Armageddon, the judgments on the nations and the establishment of the kingdom of God. We will confine ourselves here merely to going back to Isaiah 25. First of all, note verse 2.

> "For Thou hast made of a city an heap; *of* a defenced city a ruin: a palace of strangers to be no city; it shall never be built".

There are two definite references here to the end of the wilderness march of the children of Israel, itself a type of the march of the Rainbowed Angel. The first city in the promised land that Israel had to conquer as they neared the end of their march from Sinai was Jericho. It admirably fits the description of a "defenced city".

> "Now Jericho was straitly shut up because of the children of Israel: none went out, and none came in" (Josh. 6:1).

But when, after seven days, "the wall fell down flat… and (Israel) burnt the city with fire" (verses 20, 24), it did indeed become "a ruin".

205

The second city taken by the children of Israel was Ai. The name "Ai" means "a heap". Thus it is recorded;

> "Joshua burnt Ai, and made it an heap for ever, *even* a desolation unto this day" (Josh. 8:28).

Although the Hebrew for "an heap" in Isaiah 25:2 is different, there is clearly a play on the meaning.[1] So it would seem that Isaiah 25 is taking us back, by allusion, to the conclusion of the wilderness journey of Israel, a type of the march of the Rainbowed Angel.

The gates of Jerusalem are opened

We shall refer to Isaiah 25 again later in this chapter. But as we now turn to chapter 26, it should be no surprise to discover that it has a similar allusion back to the children of Israel in the wilderness.

> "Open ye the gates, that the righteous nation which keepeth the truth may enter in. Thou wilt keep *him* in perfect peace, *whose* mind *is* stayed *on thee*: because he trusteth in thee. Trust ye in Yahweh for ever: for in the LORD JEHOVAH *is* everlasting strength:" (Isa. 26:2-4).

There is a considerable emphasis on the memorial Name of God in these verses. As well as using "Yahweh" at the start of verse 4, the words "LORD JEHOVAH" translate "Yah Yahweh". So the Divine Name occurs three times in these two short phrases, once in its shortened, contracted form. This gives considerable force to the other descriptions of God. He can be trusted "for ever" (Hebrew *ad*). He also possesses "everlasting (Hebrew *olahm*) strength".

This strength is encapsulated in the Hebrew word so translated. It is one of the Hebrew words for "rock"; *tsoor*, and is a word that takes us back to Israel in the wilderness. Moses is the first to use it in Exodus in relation to the "rock" that he smote to bring out water for Israel to drink. But remarkably, he uses it no less than seven times in Deuteronomy 32

1. The Hebrew for "an heap" in Isa. 25:2 is *galgal*, which is the name of the place (i.e. Gilgal), at which Israel had renewed the covenant of circumcision (in Joshua 5) just before conquering Jericho and Ai.

(in verses 4, 13, 15, 18, 30, 31, and 37) towards the close of his final address to Israel before he died.

God is presented as the "rock" of Israel, but yet to be "lightly esteemed" by Israel. Moses predicted that they would prefer to trust in other 'rocks', which in fact were mere idols. But ultimately they would be brought to realise that these 'rocks' were worthless and powerless to deliver.

> "*He* (Yahweh) *is* the Rock, His work *is* perfect: for all His ways *are* judgment: a God of truth and without iniquity, just and right *is* He… Of the Rock *that* begat thee thou art unmindful, and hast forgotten God that formed thee… And He (Yahweh) shall say, Where *are* their gods, *their* rock in whom they trusted" (Deut. 32:4, 18, 37).

This focus on the "Rock" leads up to verses which speak of God's vengeance on Israel's enemies, and the deliverance of His chosen people. These verses are surely describing the work of the Rainbowed Angel, as a manifestation of Christ, for "that Rock was Christ" (1 Cor. 10:4). This work of vengeance and judgment is picked up again later in the same chapter in Deuteronomy.

> "To Me *belongeth* vengeance, and recompense; their foot shall slide in *due* time: for the day of their calamity *is* at hand, and the things that shall come upon them make haste. For Yahweh shall judge His people, and repent Himself for His servants, when He seeth that *their* power is gone, and *there is* none shut up, or left… If I whet My glittering sword, and Mine hand take hold on judgment; I will render vengeance to Mine enemies, and will reward them that hate Me. I will make Mine arrows drunk with blood, and My sword shall devour flesh; *and that* with the blood of the slain and of the captives, from the beginning of revenges upon the enemy. Rejoice, O ye nations, *with* His people: for He will avenge the blood of His servants, and will render vengeance to His adversaries, and will be merciful unto His land, *and* to His people" (Deut. 32:35-36, 41-43).

This expression of God's triumph on behalf of Israel is prophetic of triumph to come when Jerusalem and Israel are finally delivered from the hand of the oppressor. This will happen when "the righteous nation which keepeth the truth" (Isa. 26:2), that is, the redeemed and immortalised saints, enters through gates that have been thrown open, into the city of Jerusalem. The Hebrew word *shamar* is translated "keepeth" here. This word first occurs in Genesis 2:15, where Adam was placed in the garden in Eden "to dress it and to keep (*shamar*) it". The word has the sense of 'having a charge, guard, preserve'. Adam failed in his responsibilities, and so he and Eve were driven from the garden at the entrance to which the cherubims were placed, with "a flaming sword which turned every way, to keep (*shamar*) the way of the tree of life" (Gen. 3:24). The way to the tree of life has indeed been preserved, by the Lord Jesus Christ, who did no sin, and who was "the way, the truth, and the life" (Jno. 14:6). Thus it is that "the righteous nation that keepeth the truth" is the body of saints in their future glory.

Born in Zion

God's vengeance on His and Israel's enemies, which will allow the gates of Jerusalem to be opened to the Rainbowed Angel, is because:-

"His foundation *is* in the holy mountains. Yahweh loveth the gates of Zion more than all the dwellings of Jacob" (Psa. 87:2).

It is worth quoting most of the remaining words of Psalm 87, because they go on to speak of that multitude of people who will make up the Rainbowed Angel, along with their Master, the Lord Jesus Christ.

"Glorious things are spoken of thee, O city of God. Selah. I will make mention of Rahab (i.e. Egypt) and Babylon to them that know Me: behold Philistia, and Tyre, with Ethiopia; this *man* was born there. And of Zion it shall be said, This and that man was born in her: and the Highest himself shall establish her. Yahweh shall count, when He writeth up the people, *that* this *man* was born there. Selah" (Psa. 87:3-6).

The Psalmist is writing of those whose spiritual birthplace is Zion. He will insist that the fact that Zion is the spiritual home of certain people is openly declared to all nations; to Egypt, Babylon, Philistia, Tyre, and Ethiopia. Yahweh has the names of all the saints written in His book of life. When the saints, as the Rainbowed Angel, enter into the gate of Zion they will all be counted in. None will be missing or lost. This is emphasized when we connect the closing words of Psalm 87 with words from Psalm 24.

"As well the singers as the players on instruments *shall be there*: all My springs *are* in thee" (Psa. 87:7).

"This *is* the generation of them that seek Him, that seek Thy face, O (God of (KJV margin)) Jacob" (Psa. 24:6).

What a privilege it will be to be among that glorious number entering through those gates of Jerusalem, so beloved of God; gates that will be thrown wide at the command of the Rainbowed Angel. "Open ye the gates".

Seven shepherds and eight principal men

As a slight digression at this point, there is an interesting passage in Micah that seems to confirm and reassure us of this principle; that God knows the individual names of his saints who will be in the kingdom. Micah prophesied of the birth of Christ at Jerusalem, and states his destiny; "he (shall) come forth unto me *that* is to be ruler in Israel" (5:2). A fascinating verse then follows concerning one aspect of the future work of Christ, and those who will be associated with him.

"This *man* shall be the peace, when the Assyrian shall come into our land: and when he shall tread in our palaces, then shall we raise against him seven shepherds, and eight principal men" (Mic. 5:5).

"This *man*" clearly refers to Christ, as in the previous verse he is described as "stand(ing) and feed(ing) in the strength of Yahweh". The same verse also states that he shall "be great unto the ends of the earth" (verse 4). Bearing in mind earlier exposition in chapter 12, "the Assyrian" can with some certainty be identified as Gog. So this verse in Micah is talking about Christ's victory over Gog, when he is evicted from Jerusalem, and destroyed on the mountains of Israel. As we know from previous exposition, he will be accompanied in this enterprise by the saints; together they form the Rainbowed Angel. Micah describes those accompanying Christ as "seven shepherds, and eight principal men". It would seem that this is speaking of the leaders of the body of saints.

On the one hand are "shepherds". The Hebrew is the usual word for "shepherd" (*raah*) which also means "to feed". This identifies the role of the shepherd; one who ensures that the flock in his care has pasture and food. This is clearly a spiritual role in this context, which was exemplified by Jesus as the "good shepherd", even to the extent of giving his own life to ensure life eternal for his sheep. It is a role required of elders in the ecclesia who are to "feed the flock of God which is among you" (1 Pet. 5:2).

209

On the other hand are "principal men", or "princes of men" as suggested by the KJV margin and the ERV. The word for "principal" is *neciyk*. It comes from a root meaning to "pour out" and is sometimes used of drink offerings. The sense may therefore be of princes or rulers who, like the good shepherd, have shown themselves willing to be poured out as drink offerings in a sacrifice in order that God's people may be ruled acceptably.

It is interesting that there seem to be seven men in Scripture singled out as shepherds or keepers of sheep, and eight men identified as "princes" who ruled God's people in humility and righteousness. We tentatively list them below, along with the Scriptural references to support the suggestions. Four names appear on both lists. This probably indicates how rare such qualities are, and may show that those men will, in a sense have a dual responsibility, both shepherding and ruling God's people, as well of course as playing their part in overcoming Gog. Just possibly then these men will be the leaders in the Rainbowed Angel community.

Table 17 – Seven shepherds and eight principal men

Seven shepherds		Eight principal men	
Abel	Gen. 4:2	Melchisedec	Gen. 14:18
Jacob	Gen. 30:43	Joseph	Gen. 41:39-44
Joseph	Gen. 37:2	Moses	Exo. 2:14
Moses	Exo. 3:1	David	1 Sam. 16:10-13 2 Sam. 5:3
David	Psa. 78:70-72	Hezekiah	2 Kgs. 20:5 ("captain")
Peter	Jno. 21:15-17	Daniel	Dan. 6:1-3
Jesus	Jno. 10:14	Michael	Dan. 12:1
		Jesus	Dan. 9:25-26

One generation of saints

We quoted earlier from Psalm 24:6; "This is the generation of them that seek Him". It seems that the body of redeemed saints who will enter Jerusalem as the Rainbowed Angel will, in Scriptural terms, comprise a single "generation", regardless of which human epoch they lived in. The same idea is repeated elsewhere in the Psalms, and is also picked up in the New Testament.

> "A seed shall serve him; it shall be accounted to the Lord for a generation." (Psa. 22:30).

The multitudinous seed of the Abrahamic promises who are Christ's are a single generation, born again in him. This seed is pleasing to Yahweh, because it arises out of the great sacrifice that He made, in giving His only begotten and sinless Son as a sacrifice for sin.

> "Yet it pleased Yahweh to bruise him; He hath put *him* to grief: when Thou shalt make his soul an offering for sin, He shall see *his* seed, He shall prolong *his* days, and the pleasure of Yahweh shall prosper in his hand" (Isa. 53:10).

So it is that the apostle Peter can address all the saints in Christ Jesus "a chosen generation" (1 Pet. 2:9). Although each of these saints is born again of the incorruptible seed of the Word of God (1 Pet.1:23), the fullness of that new birth takes place when this whole body of saints truly becomes incorruptible in the same moment ("we shall all be changed, in a moment" (1 Cor. 15:51-52)), following approval at the judgment seat. There appears to be a reference to this event in Isaiah 25, in the words "He will swallow up death in victory" (v 8). This we believe is parallel to the words of Psalm 68, discussed earlier. In that prophetic Psalm, dealing with the body of saints gathered to judgment at Sinai, and following the pattern of the children of Israel taken there from Egypt, it is stated that "unto Yahweh Adonai *belong* the issues from death" (Psa. 68:20). The issue of life or death is finally resolved, and those who are approved will be given the gift of immortality there, at Sinai. This however leads us now to consider the relationship of this truly amazing reward for the saints that will be granted to them at Sinai, and the marriage supper of the Lamb.

When and where will the marriage supper of the Lamb take place?

We have earlier alluded to the fact that though it seems that the gift of immortality will be given to the faithful saints at Sinai, thus constituting them, along with Christ, as the Rainbowed Angel, it also appears that the marriage supper of the Lamb will not take place until later, at Jerusalem. We now need to consider whether this view is Scripturally sound.

First, let us go back to the verse from Isaiah 25 quoted in the previous section.

> "He will swallow up death in victory; and Adonai Yahweh ('He Who shall be rulers') will wipe away tears from off all faces; and the rebuke of His people shall He take away from off all the earth: for Yahweh hath spoken *it*." (Isa. 25:8).

It is fascinating to note that this verse is quoted in three places in the New Testament, in contexts which clearly support the view expressed above, that there are distinct phases of development of the redeemed body of Christ. The first phrase of the verse is quoted by Paul in relation to the resurrection.

> "Behold, I shew you a mystery; we shall not all sleep, but we shall all be changed, in a moment, in the twinkling of an eye, at the last trump: for the trumpet shall sound, and the dead shall be raised incorruptible, and we shall be changed. For this corruptible must put on incorruption, and this mortal *must* put on immortality. So when this corruptible shall have put on incorruption, and this mortal shall have put on immortality, then shall be brought to pass the saying that is written, **Death is swallowed up in victory**" (1 Cor. 15:51-54).

It is of course clear from other Scriptures that the saints do not emerge immortal from the grave. The judgment intervenes. Then, for those who are approved, they are all changed in a moment from mortality to immortality. This process is summarised by Paul, through the Spirit, by quoting the opening of Isaiah 25:8; "Death is swallowed up in victory". In passing, it is also interesting to note that the trumpet sounding that is referred to here is probably not the trumpet that calls the sleeping dead to life and judgment. Paul writes to the Thessalonians of that trumpet, saying that "the Lord himself shall descend from heaven with a shout...

and with the trump of God: and the dead in Christ shall rise first" (1 Thess. 4:16).

Rather the trumpet sound referred to in Corinthians is **after** the judgment, and heralds the change in nature for the faithful saints. It may be an allusion back to the "voice of the trumpet" (Exo. 19:16) which sounded when Israel were first gathered at Sinai.

The next phrase in Isaiah 25:8 is quoted twice in Revelation. In both places the setting is Jerusalem, and on the second occasion it is quoted, the context is also that of the marriage supper of the Lamb. The second quotation of this verse from Isaiah 25 is as follows.

> "For the Lamb which is in the midst of the throne shall feed them, and shall lead them unto living fountains of waters: and God shall **wipe away all tears from their eyes**" (Rev. 7:17).

Those who are led by the Lamb are those who are "arrayed in white robes" (verse 13), and who are defined as who have "washed their robes, and made them white in the blood of the Lamb" (verse 14). These are the redeemed saints who are closely associated with the Lamb as he sits on his throne. They cry:-

> "with a loud voice, saying, Salvation to our God which sitteth upon the throne, and unto the Lamb" (Rev. 7:10).

They are "before the throne of God" (verse 15), and are led by the Lamb who is "in the midst of the throne" (verse 17).

The throne of God and of the Lamb is in Jerusalem (cf. 1 Chron. 28:5 and 29:23). So at the point when the Lamb wipes away tears from their eyes the saints are in Jerusalem. So, piecing the evidence together, we deduce that Isaiah 25:8 is referring to two stages of the process of the redemption of the saints; firstly, to the bestowal of Divine nature at Sinai, and secondly, to the consummation and celebration of the reward at Jerusalem, once the Rainbowed Angel has been victorious over his enemies.

Before moving on from Isaiah 25 to consider the sequence of events that leads up to the marriage supper of the Lamb, and the third quotation in Revelation from Isaiah 25:8, we wish to look briefly at the two preceding verses in Isaiah.

"In this mountain shall Yahweh of hosts make unto all people a feast of fat things, a feast of wines on the lees, of fat things full of marrow, of wines on the lees well refined. And He will destroy in this mountain the face of the covering cast over all people, and the vail that is spread over all nations" (Isa. 25:6-7).

Bearing in mind that we have identified this chapter as a lead up to the entry of the Rainbowed Angel into Jerusalem at the start of chapter 26, it is reasonable to ponder whether this "feast of fat things" is also a reference to the marriage supper of the Lamb. In fact, this does not appear to be so. The Hebrew for "feast" here refers to a feast or banquet of drinking. A different word is used to refer to the feasts of the Law. The feast of Isaiah 25 symbolises the destruction of those who are God's enemies. Ezekiel uses a similar metaphor, which seems to indicate that the nations, represented by flesh-eating birds and animals, participate in the destruction and devouring of Gog.

"Son of man, thus saith the Lord Yahweh; Speak unto every feathered fowl, and to every beast of the field, Assemble yourselves, and come; gather yourselves on every side to My sacrifice that I do sacrifice for you, *even* a great sacrifice upon the mountains of Israel, that ye may eat flesh, and drink blood. Ye shall eat the flesh of the mighty, and drink the blood of the princes of the earth, of rams, of lambs... And ye shall eat fat till ye be full, and drink blood till ye be drunken, of My sacrifice which I have sacrificed for you" (Ezek. 39:17-19).

This is not the marriage supper of the Lamb.

From arrival in Jerusalem to marriage supper

We now need to trace the sequence of events from the arrival of the Rainbowed Angel in Jerusalem up to the marriage supper.

In chapter 12 we noted that as the Rainbowed Angel approaches Jerusalem, described there as the "Name of Yahweh (coming) from far", the Angel will "have a song, as in the night *when* a holy solemnity is kept" (Isa. 30:29). There, the Hebrew for "solemnity" (*chag*) is indeed the word used in the Law to describe the feasts of Yahweh. The Angel is described in the same verse as coming with "gladness of heart" to "the mountain of Yahweh, to the mighty One of Israel". The Hebrew for "mighty" here is *tsoor*, one of the Hebrew words for "rock". But it also occurs in Isaiah 26 in the context of the Rainbowed Angel actually entering through the gates of Jerusalem, where it is translated "strength" in verse 4; "for in Yah Yahweh is everlasting strength". This confirms for us that the Rainbowed Angel has a special appointment and joyous feast to keep in Jerusalem; the marriage supper of the Lamb.

But it does not happen immediately. Gog is destroyed on the mountains of Israel. This is represented in Isaiah 25:2 by ruining the defenced city (originally Jericho), and making a city into a heap (originally Ai). The destruction of the bulk of Gog's forces on the mountains of Israel has been discussed previously in chapter 12. But it would seem that some of Gog's forces are destroyed in Egypt, and this would appear to follow the Rainbowed Angel's victory over his main forces on the mountains of Israel. This Egyptian phase of the Rainbowed Angel's works seems to be the subject of Isaiah 19. We know that when the king of the north (Gog) moves south that "the land of Egypt shall not escape" (Dan. 11:42). Presumably, when "tidings out of the east and out of the north… trouble him", and he plants his tabernacles and palace in "the glorious holy mountain" (Dan. 11:44-45), he leaves some forces behind in an attempt to secure Egypt. Isaiah 19 appears to deal with their fate.

The chapter begins with a summary of what follows in the remaining verses.

> "The burden of Egypt. Behold, Yahweh rideth upon a swift cloud, and shall come into Egypt: and the idols of Egypt shall be moved at His presence, and the heart of Egypt shall melt in the midst of it" (Isa. 19:1).

Here is a picture of the Christ and the saints, represented by Yahweh riding on a cloud, arriving in Egypt, to execute judgment. The "cloud" is the "cloud of witnesses" (Heb. 12:1), the saints, in whom Yahweh is now manifest. They arrive in Egypt, not merely to execute judgment on Egypt, but also to complete the destruction of Gog's armies, described by Isaiah as "cruel lord" who has moved beyond Israel in to the land of Egypt further south.

> "The Egyptians will I give over into the hand of a cruel lord; and a fierce king shall rule over them, saith the Lord, Yahweh of hosts" (Isa. 19:4).

This chapter in Isaiah describes final judgment on Egypt and her idolatry, the destruction of their conqueror, and the spiritual healing of the nation of Egypt. Under the heel of Gog, Egypt will…

"…cry unto Yahweh because of the oppressors, and He shall send them a saviour (the Rainbowed Angel of verse 1), and a great one, and he shall deliver them" (Isa. 19:20).

The prophet then goes on to describe the judgment, repentance, education, and healing of Egypt.

"Yahweh shall be known to Egypt, and the Egyptians shall know Yahweh in that day, and shall do sacrifice and oblation; yea, they shall vow a vow unto Yahweh, and perform *it*. And Yahweh shall smite Egypt: He shall smite and heal *it*: and they shall return *even* to Yahweh, and He shall be intreated of them, and shall heal them" (Isa. 19:21-22).

The chapter then concludes with a picture of two archetypal Old Testament enemies of Israel united with the nation of Israel, and blessed by Yahweh.

"In that day shall there be a highway out of Egypt to Assyria, and the Assyrian shall come into Egypt, and the Egyptian into Assyria, and the Egyptians shall serve with the Assyrians. In that day shall Israel be the third with Egypt and with Assyria, *even* a blessing in the midst of the land: whom Yahweh of hosts shall bless, saying, Blessed *be* Egypt My people, and Assyria the work of My hands, and Israel Mine inheritance" (Isa. 19:23-25).

It is also possible that, as well as being literally true, Egypt and Assyria are representative in this passage of all the Gentile nations, who are joined with Israel in acknowledging the kingship and supremacy of Yahweh God of Israel. If this is so, then these final three verses of Isaiah 19 summarise the result of the work of Christ that will follow on from the destruction of the Gogian hosts, which we will now consider.

Once Gog is totally defeated Christ will then establish himself on Yahweh's throne in Zion, and issue an edict to the rest of the nations to submit to his righteous and Divinely appointed rule.

"Yet have I set My king upon my holy hill of Zion. I will declare the decree: Yahweh hath said unto me, Thou *art* my Son; this day have I begotten thee. Ask of Me, and I shall give *thee* the heathen *for* thine inheritance, and the uttermost parts of the earth *for* thy possession... Be wise now therefore, O ye kings: be instructed, ye judges of the earth. Serve Yahweh with fear, and rejoice with trembling. Kiss the Son, lest he be angry, and ye perish *from* the way, when his wrath is kindled but a little" (Psa. 2:6-8, 10-12).

This edict is issued to the remaining nations and religious authorities in the earth following Gog's demise. However, they are not prepared to submit, as the same Psalm makes clear. The rule of the Rainbowed Angel (Jesus Christ and his saints) is beginning to be established, and many do not like the rules and restraints being imposed.

"Why do the heathen rage, and the people imagine a vain thing? The kings of the earth set themselves, and the rulers take counsel together, against Yahweh, and against His anointed, *saying*, Let us break their bands asunder, and cast away their cords from us" (verses 1-3).

But there can be no compromise.

"He that sitteth in the heavens shall laugh: the Lord shall have them in derision. Then shall He speak unto them in his wrath, and vex them in His sore displeasure... Thou shalt break them with a rod of iron; Thou shalt dash them in pieces like a potter's vessel" (verses 4-5, 9)

It would seem that this rebellion is led by the apostate system termed "Babylon the great" in the Apocalypse. The Papacy will see the enthroned Lord Jesus Christ as a direct challenge and threat, and will in effect mount the final 'Christian' crusade, in alliance with a number of sympathetic "horn" powers in Europe.

"The ten horns which thou sawest are ten kings, which have received no kingdom as yet; but receive power as kings one hour with the beast. These have one mind, and shall give their power and strength unto the beast. These shall make war with the Lamb, and the Lamb shall overcome them: for he is Lord of lords, and King of kings: and they that are with him *are* called, and chosen, and faithful" (Rev. 17:12-14).

The "beast" is the political and military system of Europe; a rebirth of the old Holy Roman Empire, in the form of the European Union. The rider of the beast is the apostate woman of Rome, who as its rider, controls its movements. But their challenge is doomed to ignominious failure since their opponent is the Lamb of God, now the Lion of the tribe of Judah, accompanied by the called, chosen, faithful, the immortal saints. In corporate form this is the Rainbowed Angel who is about to cry...

> "with a loud voice, as *when* a lion roareth: and when he had cried, seven thunders uttered their voices" (Rev. 10:3).

The result of the victory of the Lamb and his companions is the complete and final fall of the apostasy.

> "After these things I saw another angel (not one of the angels with the seven vials who has spoken to John in chapter 17) come down from heaven, having great power; and the earth was lightened with his glory. And he cried mightily with a strong voice, saying, Babylon the great is fallen, is fallen, and is become the habitation of devils, and the hold of every foul spirit, and a cage of every unclean and hateful bird... And a mighty angel took up a stone like a great millstone, and cast *it* into the sea, saying, Thus with violence shall that great city Babylon be thrown down, and shall be found no more at all" (Rev. 18:1-2, 21).

The other "angel" who has "great power", and who lightens the earth with his glory, is surely the Rainbowed Angel. The angel does not literally "come down from heaven". This is a symbolic way of saying that the angel appears with heaven-given power, to judge in righteousness. Thus Christ and the saints are the agency of the fall of Babylon the great. In this work they are fulfilling Isaiah's prophecy.

> "He will destroy in this mountain the face of the covering cast over all people, and the vail that is spread over all nations" (Isa. 25:7).

All nations have indeed been duped by the lies of the apostasy, not least with the echo of the serpent's original lie, "Ye shall not surely die", through their doctrine of the immortal soul. Based on the deceit and unrighteousness of this system, God has sent the nations a "strong delusion, that they should believe a lie". This vail or delusion that has been spread over the minds of all peoples of the earth because they

Chapter 14 – Open ye the gates

"believed not the truth, but had pleasure in unrighteousness", will finally be removed in the destruction of the apostasy based in Rome. That "Wicked" system shall be consumed by the Lord "with the spirit of his mouth", and will be destroyed by "the brightness of his coming" (see 2 Thess. 2:3-12).

The way will then be clear to manifest the fullness of the glories of the Millennial age. Thus we move into the next chapter of Revelation.

> "After these things I heard a great voice of much people in heaven, saying, Alleluia; Salvation, and glory, and honour, and power, unto the Lord our God… And I heard as it were the voice of a great multitude, and as the voice of many waters, and as the voice of mighty thunderings, saying, Alleluia: for the Lord God omnipotent reigneth. Let us be glad and rejoice, and give honour to him: for the marriage of the Lamb is come, and his wife hath made herself ready. And to her was granted that she should be arrayed in fine linen, clean and white: for the fine linen is the righteousness of saints. And he saith unto me, Write, Blessed *are* they which are called unto the marriage supper of the Lamb. And he saith unto me, These are the true sayings of God" (Rev. 19:1,6-9).

The body of redeemed saints have completed their work of judgment, and are now to be constituted, formally as it were, as the bride of the Lamb of God. In realisation of these things they repeat "Alleluia" or "Hallelujah", which is basically Hebrew, signifying "Praise to Yah", Whose work of redemption is now complete. His glory and righteousness are manifest throughout the earth. Christ and the saints can now truly and fully celebrate their one-ness of nature; one spirit, in contrast to the "one flesh" of mortal marriage.

The picture is reinforced again in chapter 21.

> "I John saw the holy city, new Jerusalem, coming down from God out of heaven, prepared as a bride adorned for her husband. And I heard a great voice out of heaven saying, Behold, the tabernacle of God *is* with men, and he will dwell with them, and they shall be his people, and God himself shall be with them, *and be* their God" (Rev. 21:2-3).

Although this is not literal Jerusalem, it seems to underpin the thesis that the marriage supper of the Lamb will be in Jerusalem, once the

Rainbowed Angel has occupied the city, and after the apostasy has been destroyed. For it is in Jerusalem that God has always desired to dwell with His people.

What is now remarkable is that the passage continues by quoting again (the third time this verse is quoted, as mentioned earlier) from Isaiah 25:8, with regard to wiping away tears.

> "God shall **wipe away all tears from their eyes**; and there shall be no more death, neither sorrow, nor crying, neither shall there be any more pain: for the former things are passed away" (Rev. 21:4).

This confirms what we have said earlier; that Isaiah 25:8 refers to two separate phases of the redemption and glorification of the saints; first the reward of immortality at Sinai, then their celebration with the bridegroom, some time later, at Jerusalem.

The earth shall be full of the knowledge of Yahweh

This subheading above takes us back to Isaiah 11 and 12, where we have the conclusion of Isaiah's vision from chapter 7 onwards, which concludes with the earth filled with God's glory. This is parallel with the conclusion of Isaiah 19, and the marriage supper of the Lamb, both discussed earlier in this chapter. Chapter 11 opens with a description of the righteous rule of Christ in the Kingdom to come. It opens with the words that establish the credential of the ruler of this future age.

> "There shall come forth a rod out of the stem of Jesse, and a Branch shall grow out of his roots: and the spirit of Yahweh shall rest upon him" (Isa. 11:1-2).

Through his rule the nations will be at peace. In the visions of Daniel and the apostle John the nations are presented as wild, hideous beasts. But under the righteous rule of the Son of God they are all tamed and submissive.

> "The wolf also shall dwell with the lamb, and the leopard shall lie down with the kid; and the calf and the young lion and the fatling together; and a little child shall lead them. And the cow and the bear shall feed; their young ones shall lie down together: and the lion shall eat straw like the ox" (Isa. 11:6-7).

Notice that the lion, bear, and leopard of Daniel 7 are all here present. The wolf may equate to the fourth great and terrible beast of that chapter; the "wolf" description highlighting the links of that fourth beast with the Roman apostasy and the ability to deceive. Christ himself warned his disciples of the danger of such creatures, a warning that is still relevant today.

> "Beware of false prophets, which come to you in sheep's clothing, but inwardly they are ravening wolves" (Matt. 7:15).

Not only will the wild nations be tamed in the kingdom of our Lord and of His Christ, but through their righteous rule the power and influence of sin will be severely curtailed, until it is finally ended at the end of the thousand years. The work of removing the influence of the wild beast nations will be part of the work of the Rainbowed Angel after arrival in Jerusalem, and after the marriage supper of the Lamb. Isaiah describes the result of the Angel's work.

> "The sucking child shall play on the hole of the asp, and the weaned child shall put his hand on the cockatrice' (KJV margin has "adder's) den" (11:8).

The prophet then goes on to show what else will happen "in that day", a phrase which recurs four times in the succeeding verses (11:10-11; and 12:1,4). The first key event will be the complete re-gathering of the Jews out of all nations.

> "It shall come to pass in that day, *that* the Lord shall set His hand again the second time to recover the remnant of his people, which shall be left, from Assyria, and from Egypt, and from Pathros, and from Cush, and from Elam, and from Shinar, and from Hamath, and from the islands of the sea. And He shall set up an ensign for the nations, and shall assemble the outcasts of Israel, and gather together the dispersed of Judah from the four corners of the earth" (Isa. 11:11-12).

Once this re-gathering is complete, and the remnant of Israel is brought into the bonds of the covenant, they will be linked to Egypt and Assyria, as we have previously seen in Isaiah 19.

> "Yahweh shall utterly destroy the tongue of the Egyptian sea; and with His mighty wind shall He shake His hand over the river, and

shall smite it in the seven streams, and make *men* go over dryshod. And there shall be an highway for the remnant of his people, which shall be left, from Assyria; like as it was to Israel in the day that he came up out of the land of Egypt" (Isa. 11:15-16).

This work of re-gathering and educating the scattered remnant of Israel will also be part of the work of the Rainbowed Angel. It is presented in the vision of the cherubim or living creatures of Ezekiel 1, who, symbolically in the person of Ezekiel are sent "to the children of Israel, to a rebellious nation (Ezek. 2:3).

(For further comments on the work of the Rainbowed Angel regarding the destruction of the 4th beast apostasy, and the re-gathering of Israel, the reader is referred back to chapter 3.)

Conclusion

The end result will be unparalleled joy when Christ dwells in, and with his bride in Jerusalem; a perfect manifestation of the glory of Yahweh in His Son and His people. The work of the Rainbowed Angel as a body prepared for war will have been completed. The seven thunders will have uttered their voices, and their work will be complete. The redeemed saints will then begin a new phase in their work, to educate the nations in the ways of Yahweh, and how He must be worshipped.

"Sing unto Yahweh; for He hath done excellent things: this *is* known in all the earth. Cry out and shout, thou inhabitant (KJV margin = "inhabitress"; i.e. the bride of Christ) of Zion: for great *is* the Holy One of Israel in the midst of thee" (Isa. 12:5-6).

"They shall not hurt nor destroy in all My holy mountain: for the earth shall be full of the knowledge of Yahweh, as the waters cover the sea" (Isa. 11:9).

Concluding exhortations

Who shall receive the blessing?

Having reaffirmed that God is the Creator of the heavens and the earth, and that He therefore possesses all things, the Psalmist asks who will be found worthy to receive eternal blessings from the Almighty.

"Who shall ascend into the hill of Yahweh? or who shall stand in His holy place?" (Psa. 24:3).

Before we look at the Scriptural answer, this is a question that we need to ask ourselves. Will we be among that glorious multitude who will constitute the Rainbowed Angel? Or will we be rejected at the judgment seat, and have to go away with unspeakable remorse into a world of chaos, to endure the consequences of our folly until mortality has run its course, and we perish for ever? Having asked the question of ourselves, we will be able to consider whether we meet the criteria that are set out in those very same passages that speak of the Rainbowed Angel.

"He that hath clean hands, and a pure heart; who hath not lifted up his soul unto vanity, nor sworn deceitfully" (Psa. 24:4).

"Open ye the gates, that the righteous nation which keepeth the truth may enter in. Thou wilt keep *him* in perfect peace, *whose* mind *is* stayed *on Thee*: because he trusteth in Thee" (Isa. 26:2-3).

The answer is that we **will** receive the blessing if our manner of life matches these standards, and if, when we fail, we seek forgiveness and the strength to overcome our temptations. We will then be justified by faith, and made white by the shed blood of the Lamb.

It is interesting that these two passages that we have considered earlier in relation to the Rainbowed Angel contain seven criteria or characteristics that the saint must develop in order to be granted the gift of the eternal Divine blessing. Seven is of course the number of Divine completion or perfection, and is thus appropriate in these contexts. The characteristics are set out in the table below.

Table 18 – The seven qualities of the saints who will enter the new Jerusalem

Reference	Quotation	Comment
Psa. 24:7	"He that hath clean hands	Purity in action
	and a pure heart	Purity in mind, thought, and motive
	who hath not lifted up his soul unto vanity	True worship
	nor sworn deceitfully."	Honesty and sincerity
Isa 26:2	"The righteous nation which keepeth the truth"	Holding fast to, and contending for the Truth
Isa 26:3	"Whose mind is stayed"	Steadfast faith
	"Because he trusteth in Thee."	Faith in God, and in His promised reward

Those who match these Divinely appointed characteristics will be accounted righteous for their faith, and will be granted the promised reward.

"He shall receive the blessing from Yahweh, and righteousness from the God of his salvation" (Psa. 24:5).

Notice that the Psalmist is quite specific in this statement. Those who manifest these qualities will be given **"the blessing"**. Elsewhere the Psalms are explicit about what this blessing is.

"As the dew of Hermon, *and as the dew* that descended upon the mountains of Zion: for there Yahweh commanded **the blessing**, *even* **life for evermore**" (Psa. 133:3).

May we all meditate carefully and prayerfully on the blessings promised in God's Word, and then prepare ourselves in faith and practice, so that we may be accounted worthy to be among that cloud of the redeemed, even that "mighty angel… (with) a rainbow… upon his head" (Rev. 10:1).

"Even so, come, Lord Jesus".

Biblography

Barling, W.F. 1952. *Law and grace.* Birmingham: The Christadelphian.

Strong, J. 1939. The exhaustive concordance of the Bible. London: Hodder & Stoughton.

Thomas, J. 1909. *Eureka: an exposition of the Apocalypse, in harmony with the 'The things of the kingdom of the Deity, and the Name of Jesus Anointed'.* Volume II. Birmingham: C.C. Walker.

Thomas, J. 1902. *Eureka: an exposition of the Apocalypse, in harmony with the 'The things of the kingdom of the Deity, and the Name of Jesus Anointed'... .* Volume III. Birmingham: C.C. Walker.

Thomas, J. [no date]. *Phanerosis: an exposition of the doctrine of the Old and New Testaments concerning the manifestation of the invisible eternal God in human nature.* London: Maranatha Press.